Healing Developmental Trauma

How Early Trauma Affects Self-Regulation, Self-Image, And The Capacity For Relationship

Laurence Heller, Ph.D.
Aline LaPierre, PsyD

EasyRead Large

Copyright Page from the Original Book

Copyright © 2012 by Laurence Heller, PhD, and Aline LaPierre, PsyD. All rights reserved. No portion of this book, except for brief review, may be reproduced, stored in a retrieval system, or transmitted in any form or by any means—electronic, mechanical, photocopying, recording, or otherwise—without the written permission of the publisher. For information contact North Atlantic Books.

Published by
North Atlantic Books
Berkeley, California

Cover design by Claudia Smelser
Cover photo © iStockphoto.com/Jasmina007
Printed in the United States of America

Healing Developmental Trauma: How Early Trauma Affects Self-Regulation, Self-Image, and the Capacity for Relationship is sponsored and published by the Society for the Study of Native Arts and Sciences (dba North Atlantic Books), an educational nonprofit based in Berkeley, California, that collaborates with partners to develop cross-cultural perspectives, nurture holistic views of art, science, the humanities, and healing, and seed personal and global transformation by publishing work on the relationship of body, spirit, and nature.

North Atlantic Books' publications are available through most bookstores. For further information, visit our website at www.northatlanticbooks.com or call 800-733-3000.

MEDICAL DISCLAIMER: The following information is intended for general information purposes only. Individuals should always see their health-care provider before administering any suggestions made in this book. Any application of the material set forth in the following pages is at the reader's discretion and is his or her sole responsibility.

Library of Congress Cataloging-in-Publication Data
Heller, Laurence
 Healing developmental trauma : how early trauma affects self-regulation, self-image, and the capacity for relationship / Laurence Heller and Aline LaPierre.
     p. cm.
 Summary: "Written for those working to heal developmental trauma and seeking new tools for self-awareness and growth, this book focuses on conflicts surrounding the capacity for connection and introduces the NeuroAffective Relational Model, a unified approach to developmental, attachment, and shock trauma"—Provided by publisher.
 Includes index.
 ISBN 978-1-58394-489-9
 1. Neuropsychology. 2. Traumatic shock—Treatment. 3. Psychic trauma—Treatment. I. LaPierre, Aline. II. Title.
 QP360.H448 2012
 612.8—dc23   2012004952

6 7 8 9 10 SHERIDAN 20 19 18 17
Printed on recycled paper

North Atlantic Books is committed to the protection of our environment.
We partner with FSC-certified printers using soy-based inks and
print on recycled paper whenever possible.

TABLE OF CONTENTS

ACKNOWLEDGMENTS	i
LIST OF FIGURES	v
LIST OF TABLES	vi
Introduction to the NeuroAffective Relational Model™	viii
PART A: The Five Adaptive Survival Styles	
1: Overview	3
2: Connection	15
3: Attunement	33
4: Trust	53
5: Autonomy	77
6: Love and Sexuality	99
PART B: The Connection Survival Style	
7: Physiology and Trauma	123
8: The Beginning of Our Identity	189
9: Transcript of a NARM™ Therapy Session with Commentary	265
10: Moving Toward Resolution	306
11: Healing the Relational Matrix	424
12: Healing the Distortions of the Life Force	504
FURTHER READING	539
ABOUT THE AUTHORS	544
BACK COVER MATERIAL	547
Index	551

ACKNOWLEDGMENTS

Larry

They say the third time is a charm, and it is certainly true about this book. Although the book had been in process for seven years, it is only in the past three, when Dr. Aline LaPierre joined me on the project, that it finally came together. My first attempt to write the book on my own bogged down. A second try with a professional writer did not work either. It was finally with Aline, who as an experienced somatic psychotherapist herself could understand what I had been attempting to communicate, that this book at last took shape. Aline's clinical experience and structured approach gave her a unique ability to work with me to draw out and formulate NARM and put down in writing what are at times highly complex concepts. This book is the result of a joint process, written together at our home, on planes, trains, hotels, and ships in at least ten foreign countries.

I will forever appreciate the dedication she brought to this project.

To all my students worldwide who saw value in the developing NARM system and helped me fine-tune my understanding and capacity to teach this material.

My acknowledgment to Peter Levine for his groundbreaking work clarifying the role of the nervous system in trauma treatment and for his dedication in bringing trauma healing to an ever-expanding clinical audience.

My appreciation to my dear friend Jim Jonell for the hundreds of hours we spent together developing a detailed understanding of the role of the body in psychotherapy.

My thanks to my son Kevin Jon Heller who, early on, helped us find the voice for this book.

Aline

Writing this book with Larry was a remarkable journey into creative collaboration. As the book evolved, it was with growing respect and admiration that I experienced the breadth of his knowledge, the depth of his clinical experience, and the artistry of his finely tuned understanding of human nature.

I am indebted to many pioneering women, and I am particularly grateful for the work of Emily Conrad and Bonnie Bainbridge Cohen. Their exploration of the evolutionary principles and essential movements of life initiated me into the mysteries of the body and informs my work as a psychotherapist.

My gratitude goes to my clients whose feedback and appreciation continue to highlight the value of NeuroAffective Touch in healing developmental trauma.

***

We both thank Victor Osaka for the valuable technological skills he brought to our project and for his collaboration in developing the graphics for this book and Margaret O. Ryan who brought the wisdom of her thirty years as editor of psychological books to our project, making sure that our voice rang true and clear.

Our gratitude goes to North Atlantic Books for their enthusiastic reception of our work and to Emily Boyd for her expert guidance in the production of the book.

LIST OF FIGURES

I.1:	Exercise to Help Identify Experiences of Expansion and Aliveness
I.2:	Distortions of the Life Force
I.3:	Top-Down and Bottom-Up Information Flow
I.4:	The Distress Cycle
I.5:	The NARM Healing Cycle
6.1:	Distortions of the Life Force in Each of the Five Adaptive Survival Styles
7.1:	Schema of the Nervous System
10.1:	Exercise to Help Identify Positive Resources
10.2:	Exercise to Explore Early Gaze Dynamics
12.1:	Distortions of the Life Force (Same As Figure 1.2)
12.2:	Exercise to Support the Exploration of One's Relationship to Anger

LIST OF TABLES

I.1:	NARM's Five Core Needs and Their Associated Core Capacities
I.2:	The Five Adaptive Survival Styles and Their Core Difficulties
I.3:	Development of Core Capacities and the Formation of Adaptive Survival Styles
I.4:	Shame-Based Identifications and Pride-Based Counter-Identifications for Each Adaptive Survival Style
1.1:	Foreclosure of the Self to Maintain the Attachment Relationship
2.1:	Key Features of the Connection Survival Style
2.2:	Therapeutic Strategies for the Connection Survival Style
3.1:	Comparison of the Two Attunement Survival Style Subtypes
3.2:	Key Features of the Attunement Survival Style
3.3:	Therapeutic Strategies for the Attunement Survival Style
4.1:	Key Features of the Trust Survival Style
4.2:	Therapeutic Strategies for the Trust Survival Style
5.1:	Key Features of the Autonomy Survival Style
5.2:	Therapeutic Strategies for the Autonomy Survival Style

6.1:	Key Features of the Love-Sexuality Survival Style
6.2:	Therapeutic Strategies for the Love-Sexuality Survival Style
7.1:	Sympathetically and Parasympathetically Driven Changes that Occur in the Body in Response to Stress or Threat
7.2:	Some Physiological Markers of the Differences between Coherence and Activation
8.1:	Recognizing the Symptoms of Early Trauma
8.2:	Early Sources of Trauma
8.3:	Distortions of Healthy Aggression
8.4:	Effects of Early Trauma on Health
8.5:	Characteristics of Healthy and Compromised Energetic Boundaries
10.1:	Primary Principles, Tools, and Techniques Used in the NARM Approach
10.2:	Overview of the Basic Steps to Reconnection
10.3:	Impact of Trauma on the Eyes
10.4:	Techniques Useful in Managing the Therapeutic Process of Connection
10.5:	Therapeutic Themes to Keep in Mind When Working with the Connection Survival Style
10.6:	Shame-Based Identifications and Pride-Based Counter-Identifications (partial list)
10.7:	Summary of Principles and Techniques that Inform the NARM Therapeutic Process with the Connection Survival Style

Introduction to the NeuroAffective Relational Model™

The price of freedom is eternal mindfulness.

This is a book about restoring connection. It is the experience of being in connection that fulfills the longing we have to feel fully alive. An impaired capacity for connection to self and others, and the ensuing diminished aliveness, are the hidden dimensions that underlie most psychological and many physiological problems. Unfortunately, we are often unaware of the internal roadblocks that keep us from experiencing the connection and aliveness we yearn for. These roadblocks develop in reaction to developmental and shock trauma and the related nervous system dysregulation, disruptions in attachment, and distortions of identity. The goal of the Neuro Affective Relational Model (NARM) is to work with these dysregulations, disruptions, and distortions while never losing sight of supporting the development of a healthy capacity for connection and aliveness. In this book we address conflicts around the capacity for connection and explore how deeper connection and aliveness can be supported in the process of healing developmental trauma.

Although the original intention was to write a book for clinicians, it soon became clear that NARM's understanding of the profound ambivalence human beings have about connection could be helpful to anyone on a path of self-discovery seeking new tools for self-awareness, growth, and healing. This book will be useful to clinicians who are looking to add a new dimension to their clinical practice, but it also stands alone as a guide for those interested in developing a greater capacity for connection and well-being.

Many systems of psychotherapy are based on the medical model of disease, and as a result they focus on psychopathology; commonly, psychotherapy investigates a person's past and seeks to identify the dysfunctional cognitive and emotional patterns that underlie psychological problems. However, as new information emerges on how the brain and nervous system function, traditional psychological methods have come into question and the need for new clinical approaches has become increasingly clear. It now appears that it is a misguided assumption to think that if we know what has gone wrong in a person's life, we will also know how to help that person resolve their difficulties. For example, we now know that when we focus on dysfunction, we risk reinforcing that dysfunction: if we focus on deficiency and pain, we are likely to get better at feeling deficiency and pain. Similarly, when we focus primarily on an individual's past, we build skills at reflecting on the past, sometimes making personal history seem more important than present experience.

Healing Developmental Trauma introduces the NeuroAffective Relational Model, a somatically based psychotherapy that focuses on supporting an individual's capacity for increasing connection and aliveness. It is a model for human growth, therapy, and healing that, while not ignoring a person's past, more strongly emphasizes a person's strengths, capacities, resources, and resiliency. NARM explores personal history to the degree that coping patterns learned early in life interfere with our capacity to feel connected and alive in the present moment. NARM helps build and expand upon our current capacity for connection to our body and emotions as well as to our capacity for interpersonal connection—capacities that are, as we will see, intimately related.

Five Biologically Based Core Needs

NARM recognizes five biologically based core needs that are essential to our physical and emotional well-being: the need for connection, attunement, trust, autonomy, and love-sexuality. When a biologically based core need is not met, predictable psychological and physiological symptoms result: self-regulation, sense of self, and self-esteem become compromised. To the degree that our biologically based core needs are met early in life, we develop core capacities that allow us to recognize and meet these needs as adults (Table i.1). Being attuned to these five basic needs and capacities means that we are connected to our deepest resources and vitality.

Although it may seem that humans suffer from an endless number of emotional problems and challenges, most of these can be traced to early developmental and shock trauma that compromise the development of one or more of the five core capacities. For example, when children do not get the connection they need, they grow up both seeking and fearing connection. When children do not get their needs met, they do not learn to recognize what they need, are unable to express their needs, and often feel undeserving of having their needs met.

To the degree that the internal capacity to attend to our own core needs develops, we experience self-regulation, internal organization, expansion, connection, and aliveness, all attributes of physiological and psychological well-being. Supporting the healthy development of the core capacities is central to the NARM approach.

CORE NEED	CORE CAPACITIES ESSENTIAL TO WELL-BEING
Connection	Capacity to be in touch with our body and our emotions
	Capacity to be in connection with others
Attunement	Capacity to attune to our needs and emotions
	Capacity to recognize, reach out for, and take in physical and emotional nourishment
Trust	Capacity for healthy dependence and interdependence
Autonomy	Capacity to set appropriate boundaries
	Capacity to say no and set limits
	Capacity to speak our mind without guilt or fear
Love-Sexuality	Capacity to live with an open heart
	Capacity to integrate a loving relationship with a vital sexuality

TABLE I.1: NARM's Five Core Needs and Their Associated Core Capacities

Five Adaptive Survival Styles

Five adaptive survival styles are set in motion depending on how well the five biologically based core needs are met—or not met—in early life. These adaptive strategies, or survival styles, are ways of coping with the disconnection, dysregulation, disorganization, and isolation that a child experiences when core needs are not met. Each of the five adaptive survival styles is named for the core need and missing or compromised core capacity: the Connection Survival Style, the Attunement Survival Style, the Trust Survival Style, the Autonomy Survival Style, and the Love-Sexuality Survival Style (Table i.2).

As adults, the more the five adaptive survival styles dominate our lives, the more disconnected we are from our bodies, the more distorted our sense of identity becomes, and the less we are able to regulate ourselves. Though we may feel constrained by a survival style and the physiological patterns that are part of it, we are often afraid to move beyond it. When we identify with a survival style, we stay within the confines of learned and subsequently self-imposed limitations, foreclosing our capacity for connection and aliveness.

All of us, clinicians included, are often overwhelmed by the wide range and seeming complexity of psychological and physiological problems that human beings experience. Understanding adaptive survival styles provides five basic organizing principles that offer a clear focus for therapy and personal development. NARM works with each core capacity to support the process of personal development (Table i.3).

Part A of this book introduces the five adaptive survival styles. Part B presents an in-depth understanding of how the earliest survival style—what in NARM is called the Connection Survival Style—develops as an adaptation to early shock and developmental/relational trauma. This first stage of development is presented in depth because from a psychobiological perspective, difficulties in this stage are not well understood yet have a foundational impact on our vitality, the resiliency of our nervous system, the formation of our sense of self, and our capacity for relationship.

ADAPTIVE SURVIVAL STYLE	CORE DIFFICULTIES
The Connection Survival Style	Disconnected from physical and emotional self
	Difficulty relating to others
The Attunement Survival Style	Difficulty knowing what we need
	Feeling our needs do not deserve to be met
The Trust Survival Style	Feeling we cannot depend on anyone but ourselves
	Feeling we have to always be in control
The Autonomy Survival Style	Feeling burdened and pressured
	Difficulty setting limits and saying no directly
The Love-Sexuality Survival Style	Difficulty integrating heart and sexuality
	Self-esteem based on looks and performance

TABLE I.2: The Five Adaptive Survival Styles and Their Core Difficulties

> **DEVELOPMENT OF CORE CAPACITIES**
> Core Needs → Attuned Caregivers → Core Capacities for Connection, Aliveness, and Creativity
>
> **FORMATION OF ADAPTIVE SURVIVAL STYLES**
> Core Needs → Caregiver Failures → Disconnection → Compromised Core Capacity → Adaptive Survival Style

TABLE I.3: Development of Core Capacities and the Formation of Adaptive Survival Styles

CORE NARM PRINCIPLES

The NeuroAffective Relational Model focuses on the interconnection of biological and psychological development. The NARM model:

- Clarifies the role of connection difficulties as they affect a person on all levels of experience: physiological, psychological, and relational.
- Develops the use of somatic mindfulness and an orientation toward personal strengths to increase the capacity for self-regulation and the freedom from the limitations of the fixed identities of the adaptive survival styles.

Self and Affect Regulation

In recent years, the importance of self-regulation has been extensively researched in the field of neuroscience and has become a prominent construct in psychological thinking. It is now understood that one of the most significant consequences of early relational and shock trauma is the resulting lack of capacity for emotional and autonomic self-regulation. Shock and developmental trauma compromise our ability to regulate our emotions and disrupt autonomic functions such as breathing, heart rate, blood pressure, digestion, and sleep.

Stated simply, *self-regulation* means that when we are tired we can sleep, and when we are stressed we have healthy ways to release that stress. *Affect regulation* involves how we manage our emotions: how we handle sadness, joy, anger, excitement, challenge, fear—the gamut of human emotions. Symptoms of emotional dysregulation develop when we are unable to feel our emotions, when they overwhelm us, or when they remain unresolved. It is essential to our well-being to be able to manage the intensity of both our positive and negative emotions. When we are unable to manage powerful or difficult emotions, or when we are anxious or depressed, we are in a state of dysregulation. Disrupted sleep or eating patterns, anxiety, panic attacks, compulsive behaviors, depression, and addiction are some of the more common symptoms of dysregulation.

In the beginning of life, connection with the mother or primary caregiver functions as the regulator of the baby's nervous system; the capacity for self-regulation is first learned by the infant through the relationship with the mother or a close caregiver. In Attachment Theory, it is well documented that a healthy connection between caregiver and infant is of essential importance in shaping the development of the infant's capacity for regulation. Each time a mother successfully soothes her baby, she is effectively regulating her baby's nervous system—although, of course, she does not usually think of the mothering process in these terms. Attachment Theory documents how chronically depressed, anxious, angry, or dissociated mothers impact their developing infant; the disruption of the connection between infant and mother is traumatic. If, for whatever reason, the regulation process between mother and infant is disrupted, the infant does not develop the core capacity for regulation. If a mother's capacity for self-regulation is compromised, she cannot soothe herself and therefore cannot adequately regulate her baby's nervous system. The stability of this early connection is particularly important in shaping an individual's patterns of relationship to body, self, and others. A compromised capacity for self-regulation can negatively impact a person for a lifetime. If a healthy capacity for self-regulation does not become an integral part of our development, we become destabilized, and without this essential foundational element, life is a struggle. Affect dysregulation is believed to be at the core of an individual's increased vulnerability to stress and trauma and is seen to be a foundational element of psychological and physical problems.

The need to feel regulated, at ease in our body and in our life, is so important that when we are in a state of dysregulation, we attempt to find the regulation we need, often at any cost. For example, the need to feel regulated is so strong that people smoke despite the fact that they know it is damaging to their health. Smoking seemingly functions as an emotional regulator because nicotine reduces anxiety and, for a short while, can relieve depression. Dysregulated individuals smoke to gain a sense of relief even though they know smoking can kill them. Attempts to stop smoking or give up any sort of self-destructive addictive substance or behavior, such as drugs, alcohol, hypersexuality, overeating, or overworking, often fail because it is very difficult to give up a means of self-regulation even when it is unhealthy until it can be replaced with a better form of self-regulation.

Bringing Self-Regulation into Clinical Practice

NARM brings the current understanding of nervous system regulation into clinical practice. It is a key NARM concept to support healthy ways of regulating the nervous system by emphasizing connection to the parts of self that are organized, coherent, and functional. Analyzing problems and focusing primarily on what has gone wrong in a person's life does not necessarily support self-regulation, and in some cases, increases dysregulation. As we will see, NARM promotes an individual's potential for health by using specific techniques that support the autonomic and emotional self-regulation that underpin the capacity for connection and aliveness.

> ***Experiencing Expansion and Aliveness***
>
> Take a moment to think about a time in your life when you felt particularly alive. Choose an event that ended well (or at least did not end badly). It could be an event when you were with someone, in a group, or by yourself. It could be anything from a time in nature to the birth of your child to making love.
>
> Let yourself remember as many of the sensory details of that experience as you can: colors, sounds,

temperature, smells, etc. As you bring up these sensory details, notice how you are affected. Notice your physical experience if possible. For those who have difficulty sensing in the body, let yourself notice the overall impact of the memory.

Take your time with this exercise, and pay attention to any thoughts, judgments, or emotions that get in the way of sensing your aliveness and expansion. Even if you are successful in feeling increased well-being, don't be surprised if some sadness surfaces with the expansion, because the happy time you are remembering may be over. If you feel any sadness, notice it, but do not make it the primary focus of your attention.

***

There is no correct reaction to this exercise, but one response that many people have is that simply remembering such a time may activate a sense of flow, warmth, and pleasure, a sense of aliveness and expansion.

***

FIGURE I.1: Exercise to Help Identify Experiences of Expansion and Aliveness

Supporting an Increasing Capacity for Aliveness

Our greatest desire is to feel alive. Meaninglessness, depression, and many other symptoms are reflections of our disconnection from our core vitality. When we feel alive, we feel connected, and when we feel connected, we feel alive. Although it brings mental clarity, aliveness is not primarily a mental state; nor is it only sensory pleasure. It is a state of energetic flow and coherency in all systems of the body, brain, and mind. Human beings respond to shock and developmental/relational trauma by dissociating and disconnecting. The result is a dimming down of the life force that leaves a person, to varying degrees, exiled from life. In NARM, working with the roadblocks that are in the way of reconnecting with aliveness is a key organizing principle.

In our many years as a clinicians, teachers, and supervisors, we have noticed a need for a more comprehensive and unified understanding of emotional regulation. NARM presents a clear understanding of how to work with emotions; learning how to be in touch with our emotions and appropriately express them is a fundamental part of this approach. By tracking the physical, sensate, and energetic experience of emotion in the body, NARM emphasizes somatic mindfulness—the containment, deepening, and support for the biological completion of affective states. Tracking and containing emotions in this way puts us progressively more in touch with our core aliveness.

The Life Force, Aliveness, and Emotions

We have created two charts to understand and work with emotions in the context of increasing the capacity for aliveness. Figure i.2 tracks how the life force becomes diminished and distorted in reaction to the adaptations a child makes to environmental failure. It also shows the similarities and differences between developmental and shock trauma. Figure 6.1 specifically tracks the distortions of the life force in each adaptive survival style. Both figures clarify emotional and autonomic regulation as they relate to the sympathetic and parasympathetic functions of the nervous system and integrate an understanding of how the distortions of the life force impact our psychology and physiology.

Distortions of the Life Force

The following section explains how to use the chart in Figure i.2 from the bottom up to track distortions of the life force as a person experiences and then adapts to developmental and shock trauma.
- *Core Energy/Life Force:* The first level of the chart represents undifferentiated core energy or life force. It is what the French call élan vital and what other cultures call

prana, reiki, chi, and essence, to mention but a few of its more commonly known names.

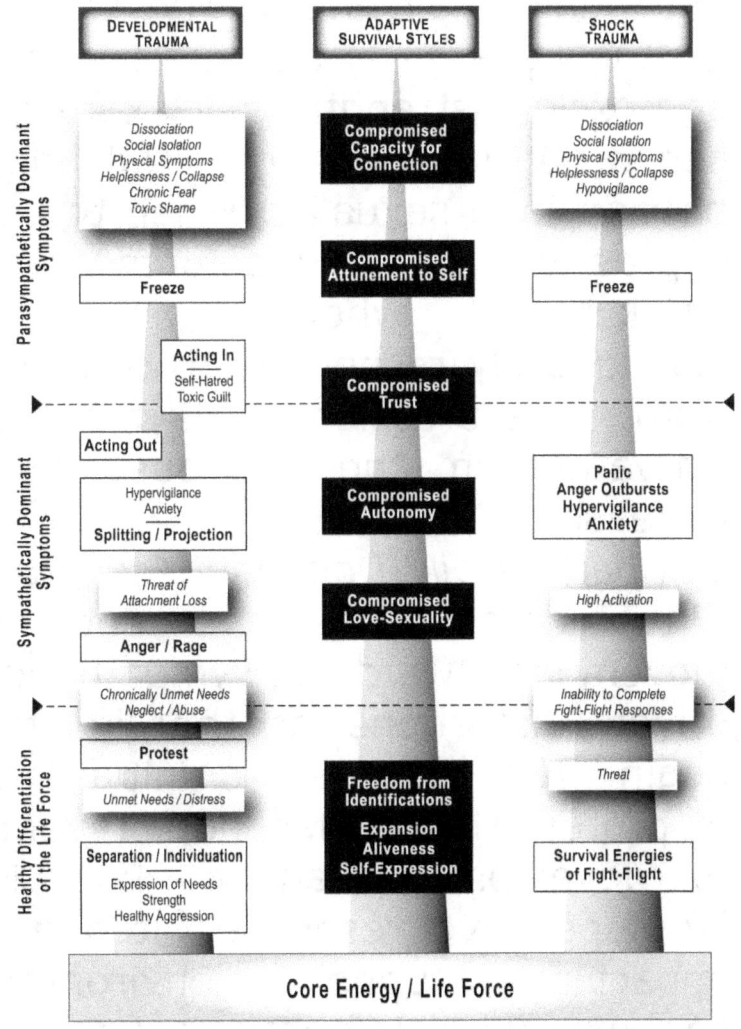

FIGURE I.2: Distortions of the Life Force. To understand how the life force becomes distorted, read the chart from the bottom up. To understand the therapeutic or growth process, read the chart from the top down.

- *Healthy Differentiation of the Life Force:* The second level maps the various expressions of core needs and healthy aliveness. The life force is the energy that fuels healthy aggression, strength, self-expression, separation/individuation, fight-flight, passion, and sexuality. When the core expressions of the life force are not supported, when they are inadequately responded to or blocked from expression, sympathetic activation in the nervous system increases.
- *Sympathetically Dominant Symptoms:* When core needs are not met, movement toward the sympathetically driven distortions of the life force begin. The response is initially one of protest that, when not responded to, develops into anger. Anger is a life-supportive response intended to impact an unsupportive environment. For example, infants express their need for touch, nourishment, love, and connection at first by fussing and crying, which is simply an expression of healthy aggression. Attuned mothers recognize their child's need

and respond appropriately. If the infant's need is not appropriately responded to, the infant escalates the demand, ramping up the sympathetic branch of the autonomic nervous system, protesting the lack of response, and finally erupting into anger. In neglectful and abusive environments, when lack of adequate response is chronic, anger and aggression cannot be resolved. When infants feel chronic anger toward their caregiver, it is instinctively experienced as a threat to the attachment relationship and therefore as dangerous to survival. Symptoms of undischarged sympathetic activation develop, leaving children, and later adults in states of high arousal, anxiety, and irritability, prone to temper outbursts, fearfulness, and even panic attacks. We will see that all of the survival styles develop as an attempt to protect the attachment relationship by foreclosing core expression, anger, aggression, and, ultimately, authenticity.

- *Parasympathetically Dominant Symptoms:* When aggression, anger, and other forms of protest are ineffective, not possible, or dangerous, children adapt. At a certain point, if the lack of attunement persists, the chronic sympathetic arousal overloads the nervous system; children adapt through resignation, shutting down the angry protest as well as the need itself, and move into the parasympathetically dominant freeze response. This shut-down does not resolve the basic problem but effectively numbs children to their needs and emotions. The unfulfilled needs and unresolved feelings are bound in the body and nervous system in the form of undischarged arousal, which is held as physical tension or as collapsed and frozen states.

Working Therapeutically with Distortions of the Life Force

It is central to the NARM approach to keep in mind the underlying theme of supporting aliveness and connection when working with symptoms, remembering that symptoms reflect disconnection—a diminishment of the connection to the life force. Working from the top of Figure i.2 (most symptomatic) to the bottom (most alive), we present in Chapter 12 therapeutic strategies for working with the acting in and acting out of unintegrated aggression. As rage, anger, and then healthy aggression are progressively integrated, anxiety, depression, and other symptoms recede. As the developmentally unmet core needs are recognized, connection to the life force is progressively strengthened.

The work of integrating all emotions plays a significant role in supporting reconnection to the life force. When working with emotions, NARM therapists keep the following question in mind: *what is the implicit intention of the emotion?* Helping clients understand and integrate the core intention of their emotions leads to greater biological and emotional completion, which in turn leads to more connection to the life force. By supporting a process of containment and deepening of affects, greater emotional range and increasing self-regulation become possible.

Somatic Mindfulness

The practice of mindfulness comes to us from Eastern traditions and is becoming an increasingly popular psychotherapeutic tool. Mindfulness, in the most general of terms, means paying attention to our experience: listening to ourselves, to our thoughts, to our emotions, and to our bodily sensations. Ultimately, we learn to listen in such a way that we don't push elements of our experience away but come to see that thoughts, emotions, and sensations come and go. The appeal of mindfulness is the freedom that we experience and the sense of flow and fluidity that comes *when we are present to but not identified with* our thoughts, feelings, and sensations.

The NARM process adds two new refinements to the traditional practice of mindfulness:
- Somatic mindfulness

- Mindful awareness of the organizing principles of our adaptive survival styles

In traditional mindfulness practice, an individual is generally taught to hold an open awareness to all experience. Traditional mindfulness is most effective when a person has experienced little trauma. When there has been major trauma, maintaining an open awareness is extremely difficult and may even lead to overwhelming emotional reactions. The more trauma a person has experienced, the more difficult the practice of open awareness.

Trauma, because of the associated nervous system hyperarousal and the resulting systemic dysregulation, keeps us from being present in our bodies. The tendency for traumatized individuals is to disconnect from the body by becoming overly cognitive or by numbing bodily experience, or both. When there is high arousal and dysregulation, it is painful to be in our bodies. This is why the NARM approach has added somatic mindfulness to the practice of traditional mindfulness. The purpose of somatic mindfulness is to progressively support nervous system re-regulation by adapting techniques from Somatic Experiencing® such as grounding, orienting, titration, pendulation, and discharge that are designed to address the high arousal, collapse, and shock states that traumatized individuals experience. In NARM the practice of somatic mindfulness integrates the established ancient understanding of mindfulness with twenty-first-century knowledge of nervous system regulation.

Mindfulness of the Adaptive Survival Styles

The second aspect of mindfulness used in NARM involves bringing our adaptive survival styles and the organizing principle of each style into mindful awareness. Awareness of survival styles usually begins after a certain capacity for self-regulation has been established. As a person becomes more regulated and embodied and as internal distress states diminish, the capacity for self-awareness becomes stronger. Integrating somatic mindfulness with the mindful awareness of survival styles allows us to work with a person's life story from a perspective that is deeper and broader than the narrative itself. The two processes of somatic mindfulness and mindful awareness of our survival styles reinforce each other and enhance the effectiveness of psychological and physiological healing work.

Shame-Based Identifications and Pride-Based Counter-Identifications

Each adaptive survival style has underlying shame-based identifications that develop to make sense of early environmental failure. In addition, in reaction to underlying shame, most people also develop pride-based counter-identifications, an ego ideal that reflects how they would like to see themselves or want others to see them. The pride-based counter-identifications, traditionally thought of as defenses, are an attempt to turn shame into virtue, but paradoxically, the more energy a person invests in the pride-based counter-identifications, the stronger the shame-based identifications become. These are briefly presented in Table i.4.

NARM holds that both the shame-based identifications and the pride-based counter-identifications, while often feeling quite real, are illusions. The pride-based counter-identifications, sometimes dismissed as defensiveness, resistance, and denial, function to protect against the painful shame-based identifications that result from developmental trauma and represent their own kind of illusion. There is a danger in challenging only the protective pride-based counter-identifications, the so-called defenses, without simultaneously working through the shame-based deeper identifications, which otherwise might be reinforced. Without this understanding of the nature of these two levels of identifications, the therapeutic process can become needlessly painful and sometimes even harmful.

SURVIVAL STYLE	SHAME-BASED IDENTIFICATIONS	PRIDE-BASED COUNTER-IDENTIFICATIONS
Connection	Shame at existing	Pride in being a loner
	Feeling like a burden	Pride in not needing others
	Feeling of not belonging	Pride in not being emotional
Attunement	Needy	Caretaker
	Unfulfilled	Pride in being the shoulder everyone cries on
	Empty	Make themselves indispensable and needed
	Undeserving	Pride in not having needs
Trust	Small	Strong and in control
	Powerless	Successful
	Used	Larger than life
	Betrayed	User, betrayer
Autonomy	Angry	Nice
	Resentful of authority	Sweet
	Rebellious	Compliant
	Enjoys disappointing others	Good boy/girl
		Fear of disappointing others

Love-Sex-uality	Hurt	Rejects first
	Rejected	Perfect
	Physically flawed	Does not allow for mistakes
	Unloved and unlovable	"Seamless," having everything together

TABLE I.4: Shame-Based Identifications and Pride-Based Counter-Identifications for Each Adaptive Survival Style

The Distress Cycle

NARM supports the development of the capacity for connection, aliveness, and creativity. Disrupted attachment, as well as early developmental and shock trauma, interfere with healthy self-regulation, cause disconnection from self and others, distort identity, and undermine self-esteem. Indeed, developmental trauma is a major contributor to the dysregulation and associated disturbances that lead to countless psychological and physiological problems, as well as to compulsive, addictive, and self-destructive behaviors. Survival styles begin as adaptive, life-saving strategies that help us in early life to manage and survive painful traumatic experiences. Paradoxically, as we become adults, these same survival strategies become the cause of ongoing nervous system dysregulation, dissociation, and self-esteem difficulties. The once-adaptive survival styles, when continued beyond their usefulness, create a distress cycle (Figure i.4).

To understand how a distress cycle is set in motion, it is important first to comprehend how information flows both *top-down* and *bottom-up* in the nervous system. The term top-down refers to how cognitive structures of the brain impact the emotional and instinctive systems of the body. The term bottom-up refers to how regulation in the nervous system impacts cognitions. Top-down, our thoughts, judgments, and identifications affect how we feel and impact the nervous system's capacity for regulation. Bottom-up, regulation/dysregulation in our nervous system affects our emotions and thoughts.

Bottom-up mechanisms are involuntary, most often unconscious, and related to the physical effects of environmental stimuli upon the body.

In contrast, top-down mechanisms can be voluntary, conscious, and pertain to how memory, motivational relevance, emotion, attention, and imagery shape perception. Top-down therapeutic approaches focus on the cortical functions of cognition. Bottom-up therapeutic approaches focus on the body, the felt-sense, and the instinctive responses as they are mediated through the brain stem and move upward to impact the limbic and cortical areas of the brain. Continuous loops of information travel from the body to the brain and from the brain to the body. Similar loops of information move among cognitive, emotional, and instinctive structures within the brain (Figure i.3).

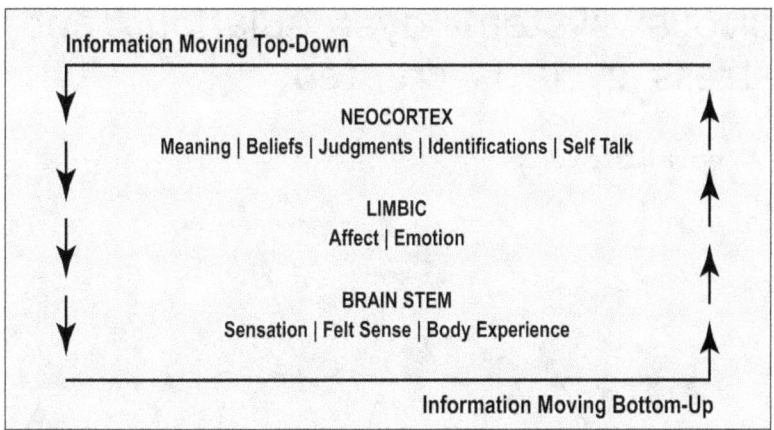

FIGURE I.3: Top-Down and Bottom-Up Information Flow

It can be argued that babies mostly rely on bottom-up perceptual mechanisms. When a child experiences early trauma, a distress cycle is set in motion that initially moves bottom-up *and* later top-down in continuous self-reinforcing loops. Bottom-up, trauma creates nervous system dysregulation. When people experience trauma, they *feel* bad; children, in particular think they *are* bad when they feel bad. Chronic bottom-up dysregulation and distress lead to negative identifications, beliefs, and judgments about ourselves. These negative identifications, beliefs, and judgments in turn trigger more nervous system dysregulation, and a distress cycle is created.

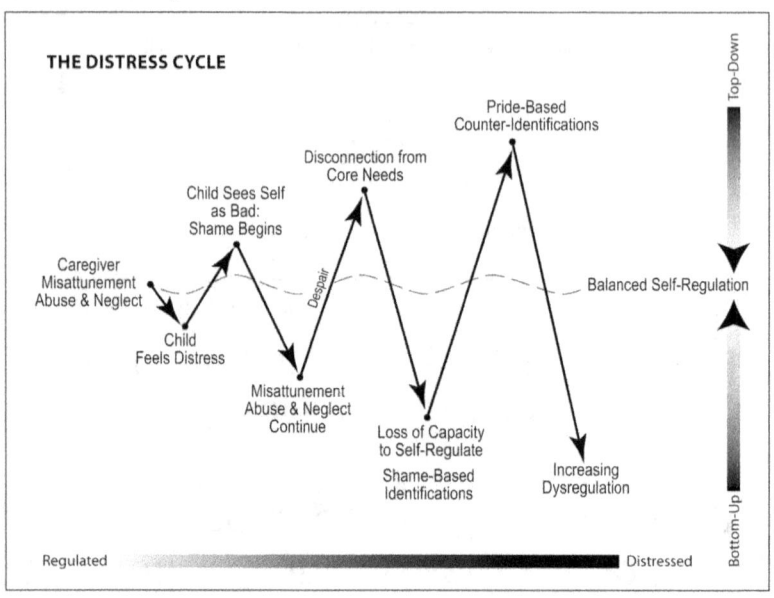

FIGURE I.4: The Distress Cycle

The NARM Healing Cycle

Most therapeutic and personal growth traditions tend to focus on either top-down or bottom-up aspects of the circular flow of information, working either from the body to the brain or from the brain to the body; as a result, they do not address the self-perpetuating aspects of the information loop and, by not doing so, often miss the pernicious links that keep the distress cycle in operation. NARM integrates both top-down and bottom-up orientations, explicitly working with the information flow in both directions. This disrupts the self-perpetuating closed loops of distress and supports the shift to *a healing cycle.*

NARM views the mindful bottom-up experience of the body as the foundation of the healing process. The body is our connection to reality, the platform from which NARM works. By paying attention to the body, we are more easily able to recognize the truths and fictions of our personal narrative. As shock states held in the nervous system are discharged, we come into more contact with our body. A positive cycle is established in which the more self-regulated we become, the more we are in touch with our body, and the more in touch with our body we are, the greater our capacity for self-regulation.

At the same time that NARM is grounded, bottom-up, in somatic mindfulness, it uses the mindful awareness of survival styles to bring a process of top-down inquiry to our sense of self which includes our fixed beliefs (identifications and counter-identifications), our self-hatred, self-rejection, and judgments. NARM also uses inquiry to help dissolve the fixed, narrow ideas about others and the world that limit our life. Since many of our identifications develop in the first five years of life, distortions in identity keep us seeing ourselves and the world from a child's perspective.

As the NARM process unfolds, a healing cycle (Figure i.5) is set in motion in which nervous system regulation increases and distorted identifications and beliefs diminish and eventually resolve. In a positive healing cycle, the increasing nervous system regulation helps dissolve painful identifications, and as painful identifications and judgments dissolve, increasing capacity for self-regulation becomes possible.

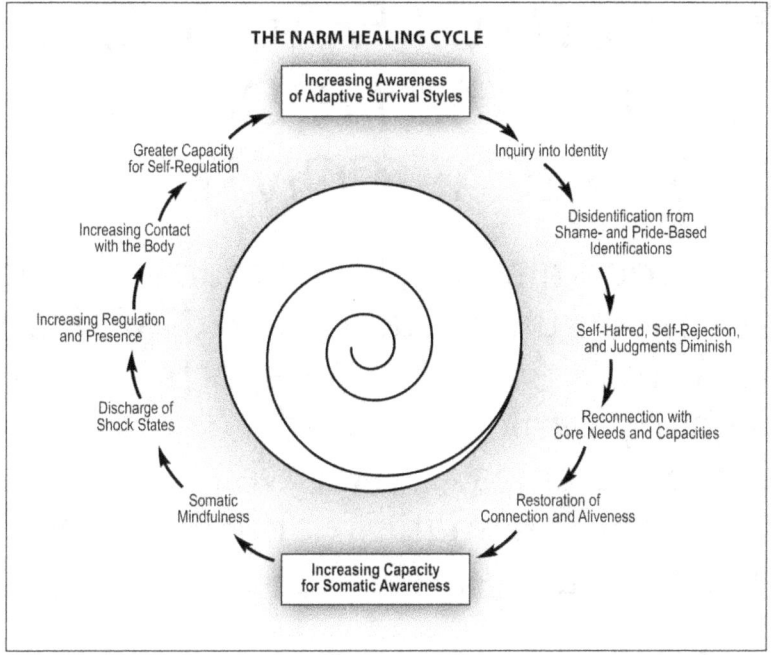

FIGURE I.5: The NARM Healing Cycle

This figure should be read clockwise from the bottom-up. In this self-reinforcing cycle each step builds upon the previous and makes the next possible. The cycle repeats as clients continue to move toward reintegrating their core capacities and life force. Initially, it may not be possible for traumatized individuals to access their somatic awareness; in such cases any experience of self-reference can serve as a starting point.

THE NEUROAFFECTIVE RELATIONAL MODEL IN HISTORICAL CONTEXT

A brief historical summary will help the reader understand how NARM both integrates and departs from psychodynamic and cognitive psychotherapies, as well as from traditional somatic and expressive psychotherapies.

Psychodynamic Psychotherapies

Psychoanalysis and psychodynamic psychotherapies have established the significant influence of attachment dynamics, early family life, and personal history on the developing personality. The NARM approach integrates elements of various psychodynamic clinical orientations: ego psychology, object relations, self psychology, and the important recent developments of attachment and relational theories.

NARM departs from psychodynamic approaches, however, in how it clinically applies the understanding of these approaches. Whereas psychodynamic therapies focus on attachment and developmental themes with the perspective that the past determines who we are in the present, NARM explores personal history to clarify patterns from the past that interfere with being present and in contact with self and others in the here and now. It brings an active process of inquiry to clients' relational and adaptive survival styles, building on clients' strengths and helping them to experience agency in the difficulties of their current life. While it is true that a psychotherapist must be able to traverse difficult affects with the client, in order to avoid regression the NARM therapist always supports a mindful *dual awareness* of past and present—staying anchored in the bodily experience of the present moment, NARM supports the awareness of the distinction between what was then and what is now. The focus is less on *why* people are the way they are and more on how their survival style distorts their experience and their life in the present. Avoiding the trap of making the past more important than the present, NARM uses a dual awareness that is anchored in the present moment while exploring cognitive, emotional, and physiological patterns that began in the past. The NARM approach of emphasizing the here-and-now expression of survival styles, rather than focusing on a person's history, is a complex and intricate process that is detailed in Chapter 10.

Working with the NARM approach progressively reinforces the connection to self in the present moment. Using resource-oriented techniques that work to recognize subtle shifts in the nervous system adds significant effectiveness. Tracking here-and-now experience in the nervous system is fundamental to disrupting the predictive tendencies of the brain. Paying close attention to the process of connection/disconnection, of regulation/dysregulation, in present time, helps us strengthen our sense of agency, feel less at the mercy of our childhood experiences, and most importantly, it supports the re-regulation of our nervous system. It is in the connection to our body and in relationship with other people that healing is possible.

Transference Dynamics

Psychodynamic psychotherapies often advocate the use of the transference relationship to facilitate the repair of attachment wounds. Psychodynamic psychotherapists implicitly encourage their clients to re-experience their original relational dynamics within the transference relationship, believing that it is intrinsic to the therapeutic process.

Recognizing transference dynamics is an important aspect of the NARM approach as well. However, NARM's nervous system perspective adds significant clinical interventions to working with transference. In early attachment dynamics, the baby's nervous system is first organized in an implicit way, responding to and being regulated by the healthy nervous system of the mother. Because the process of attachment follows a nervous system–based developmental sequence, it is premature to focus on transference dynamics when self-regulation has been strongly impaired or disrupted by early trauma. The underlying deficits in nervous system organization must first be addressed. It is our sense that many of the problematic transference reactions that analysts and psychotherapists describe may be needlessly difficult, or even terrifying, because the therapist has not taken into account that the foundation of nervous system organization and regulation is not yet in place. A nervous system–based approach can avoid the re-traumatizing abreactions and regressions that are created when the transference is used as the primary vehicle for the therapy before clients have developed sufficient neural organization. Prematurely focusing on the transference relationship can quickly plunge a person into disorganization and distress. Tending to the basic organization of the nervous system is a fundamental element of working with transference processes that needs to be integrated into mainstream clinical interventions.

NARM works with the vulnerable preverbal and nonverbal elements of an individual who has suffered early shock or developmental/relational trauma. Individuals manage this kind of early trauma by developing the Connection Survival Style. These clients come to therapy struggling with the regressed elements of their personality and with ideas about themselves developed in response to early environmental failures. They need help to learn to self-regulate. Therapy for the Connection Survival Style can become re-traumatizing when it is not sufficiently titrated or resource oriented. On an identity level, using the transference relationship as the primary organizing principle may reinforce identifications with regressed aspects of self rather than release them. To regulate the nervous system, it is more effective to work consistently with the organized "adult" aspects of the self in order to integrate the disorganized, regressed "child" aspects. By supporting a dual awareness that is firmly anchored in the organizing here-and-now felt sense experience, we can explore adaptive survival styles that began in childhood while avoiding painful regression and abreaction and the trap of making the past more important than the present.

Somatic Psychotherapies

For the last seventy years, a cornerstone of somatic psychotherapy has been that our aliveness, vitality, and authenticity are accessed in connection to the body. The Western somatic psychotherapy tradition began with Wilhelm Reich, a medical doctor and psychoanalyst, as well as Freud's pupil and later colleague. Reich was the first psychoanalyst to emphasize the importance of including the body in psychotherapy; his goal was to anchor in the body Freud's belief in the biological foundation of the psyche. Reich believed that our biologically based emotions govern our psychological processes. He is best known for his insights on what he called character structures, which, he contended, are kept in place by defensive armoring, the muscular rigidity that is the protective response to living in emotionally repressive environments that are hostile to aliveness and the life force.

Building on Reich's breakthrough understanding of the functional unity of body and mind, Alexander Lowen, MD, developed Bioenergetics, a somatic approach that included his own psychodynamically based character structure system. Lowen identified five basic developmental character structures, which, consistent with the thinking of his time, were given names that emphasized their pathology: schizoid, oral, psychopathic, masochistic, and rigid. Lowen's five character structures clearly tapped into a fundamental understanding of human nature and have influenced many subsequent body-based psychotherapies, including NARM.

Similar to Reich, Lowen believed that character structures were the outcome of thwarted drives. Wilhelm Reich and Alexander Lowen retained the pathologizing orientation consistent with the psychoanalytic principles of their time in that they emphasized the importance of working with defenses, repression, and resistance. Reich's and

Lowen's therapies encouraged regression, abreaction, and catharsis. They both believed that the therapist's job was to break through a patient's character armor—the psychological and somatic defenses—in order to release the painful emotions held in the body.

Bioenergetics, for example, recognizes that deep emotion, conscious or unconscious, is held physically. It encourages clients to express their emotions through kicking, hitting, biting, and yelling, with the goal of discharging these powerful affects and in the hope that doing so will lead to greater emotional freedom and health. Reich's and Lowen's unique contribution was to recognize that defenses were held not only in the mind but also in the body's nervous system, musculature, and organs. This significant breakthrough was ahead of its time and anticipated many current developments in the neurological and biological sciences.

The Reichian/Bioenergetic tenet of the functional unity of mind and body is consistent with NARM. NARM's nervous system work, however, is much subtler, consistent with the advances in neuroscience research of the past two decades. We will see how using the two organizing principles of somatic mindfulness and mindfulness of adaptive survival styles can guide a gentle return to nervous system coherency with far less possibility of re-traumatization.

From a NARM perspective, intensely cathartic affective interventions can have the unintended effect of causing increased fragmentation and re-traumatization. Focusing on the pain, emptiness, or rage caused by early loss, neglect, or trauma does not in itself lead to healing. The orientation in the NARM approach is to use mindful awareness to help the client tolerate strong emotion, neither acting it out against the environment nor directing it against the self. Rather than being discharged through catharsis, powerful emotional and energetic states are contained so that they can be integrated and transformed into an increased capacity for connection. Mindfully staying present to and containing intense affect increases nervous system resiliency and supports the development of emotional depth.

Somatic Experiencing®

Somatic Experiencing® (SE) was originally developed by Peter Levine, PhD, and elaborated upon by the senior faculty of the Somatic Experiencing Trauma Institute, which includes co-author Laurence Heller. It is an effective short-term, bottom-up approach to therapy that supports nervous system re-regulation in the aftermath of shock trauma. SE is a step-by-step approach designed to treat shock trauma and the resulting nervous system dysregulation. It is a progressive and gentle approach that supports the biological completion and discharge of the intense survival energies of the body's fight-flight responses.

Traditionally, SE does not focus on attachment, emotional, or relational issues as part of its therapeutic scope. NARM adds to SE by providing additional tools to address developmental, attachment, relational, affective, and transferential issues.

Gestalt Therapy

Gestalt therapy is an existential, phenomenological approach developed by Fritz Perls, MD, who early in his career was a psychoanalyst but later strongly rejected psychoanalysis. Gestalt's phenomenological orientation involves paying attention to what the client is experiencing in the moment. From the NARM perspective, this shift represents a significant therapeutic step forward, because it addresses the client's direct experience and moves the emphasis away from the endless exploration of personal history. Incorporating the role of the body and the importance of emotions, as Gestalt did, was a movement forward from psychodynamic therapies that ignore the present moment and the body. Both Bioenergetics and Gestalt encourage catharsis and emotional release. It is our experience that, for many clients, catharsis is not helpful and can even impair the capacity to self-regulate. The more traumatized and disorganized a person's nervous system, the more likely catharsis can be re-traumatizing.

Cognitive Therapy

Cognitive therapy focuses on identifying cognitive distortions and their negative impact in our lives. This is an important contribution and brings the focus of the therapy into the here and now, emphasizing a person's agency in his or her life difficulties. However, when dealing with developmental trauma, attachment difficulties, and early shock, the new understanding from the neurosciences supports the importance of working with affect regulation over cognition. Working with affect regulation and the nervous system is an essential element of the NARM approach.

Cognitive therapy introduced an important version of mindfulness to clinical psychological practice by helping clients examine their thinking and teaching them to interrupt and be mindful of their negative thought patterns. However, cognitive therapy does not address the nervous system imbalances that drive cognitive distortions; particularly when working with early trauma cognitive therapy is only minimally effective. In the case of the earliest Connection Survival Style, for example, focusing on changing distorted cognitions is particularly difficult because with early trauma, the cortex is not yet fully developed, and it is mostly the underlying bottom-up nervous system and affective imbalances that drive the cognitive distortions.

NARM presents a broader clinical application of mindfulness than is found in cognitive therapy by separating the story related to the distress states from the physiological distress itself. As the nervous system becomes more regulated, many cognitive distortions drop away. Elements of cognitive therapy are useful in working with the top-down aspects of the distress cycle, but particularly when working with someone who has experienced early trauma, it is essential to work with the distress cycle both top-down and bottom-up.

Affective Neuroscience

Significant developments in the field of neuroscience in the last twenty years have established and documented the biological foundation and psychological importance of affect regulation and interpersonal and social connection. Important developments in affective neuroscience include Stephen Porges, PhD's research on the polyvagal system and his focus on the role of the Social Engagement System (SES); Daniel Siegel, MD's interpersonal neurobiology, which clarifies the role of the neural substrate of relationship; and Allan Schore, PhD's regulation theory, which documents the critical function of the right orbitofrontal cortex in supporting resonant contact and the repair of attachment wounds. These findings, as well as the research of other major neuroscientists, provide a scientific basis for the clinical approach that has been developing in NARM since the 1970s.

Esoteric Approaches

The limitation of what we take to be our personal identity is addressed in many esoteric traditions and has been popularized by well-known authors such as Eckhart Tolle and Ken Wilber.

Psychodynamic orientations work to solidify the sense of identity and strengthen the ego, whereas esoteric orientations hold that Ego is an illusion that separates us from Being and keeps us from experiencing the spaciousness, fluidity, and fullness of our essential nature. Both perspectives are important. Esoteric approaches address the limitations of what they call Ego but generally do not incorporate the clinical awareness of the importance of attachment and developmental trauma in the creation of our sense of self. In addition, esoteric approaches do not address the primary role of nervous system dysregulation in the formation of the fixed identifications that come to be confused with identity.

NARM integrates both psychological and esoteric traditions and adds a biologically based approach that at times helps to solidify a person's sense of identity and at other times supports the exploration of the fluid nature of identity. The NARM approach holds that the most immediate access to spiritual dimensions is through a regulated physiology. Whereas for hundreds of years, the body, particularly in Western traditions, was seen as an impediment to spirituality, it is a NARM premise that a coherent biological/psychological self is a springboard to the higher Self. It is only when individuals have a solid sense of who they are that they can open to the fluid nature of Self.

The meditation technique of Vipassana is one important tool in the mindfulness process that can lead to the awareness and direct experience of the fluid nature of the Self. Because it is a powerful tool, however, it can potentially opens meditators to painful or overwhelming affective states that they are not equipped to process. We have worked with many individuals who during meditation retreats became anxious and overwhelmed by their emotions. Any system of self-exploration that does not take into consideration trauma and attachment issues and the resulting disrupted functioning of the nervous system creates the danger of dysregulating and re-traumatizing its practitioners.

One of Eckhart Tolle's core principles is that nothing that happened in the past can keep us from being fully in the present moment. Although theoretically true, this orientation can be hurtful to those who have experienced trauma and suffer from significant nervous system disorganization. Traumatized individuals, which includes most of us to differing degrees, need both top-down and bottom-up approaches that address nervous system imbalances as well as issues of identity. Many people recognize the "power of now," as Tolle calls it, but because of their nervous system dysregulation they are unable to remain in the present moment. Falling short of this ideal becomes another reason for individuals with trauma to feel bad about themselves.

A FUNDAMENTAL SHIFT

NARM utilizes elements of all the approaches mentioned above in a system that introduces a significant and fundamental shift in how these theoretical elements are applied. NARM holds psychodynamic, nervous system–based, and Eastern healing traditions as equally important and complementary. Building on and moving beyond the approaches mentioned above, NARM is a unified systemic approach that works with both developmental and shock trauma.

A Unified Systemic Model

Building on and adding to psychotherapeutic, meditative, and personal growth traditions, NARM offers an understanding and techniques that use connection to the parts of self that are organized, coherent, and functional to support new patterns in the nervous system. NARM is resource oriented, non-regressive, and non-cathartic. It works in the present moment with the felt sense using somatic mindfulness to help regulate the nervous system in order to support the increasing capacity for connection and aliveness. In this approach we see that it is in the connection to ourselves, to our body, and in relationship that we find healing regulation.

The NARM approach to growth and therapy is an antidote to deterministic approaches and maintains that the past does not determine the present. It is the persistence of adaptive survival styles along with the related nervous system disorganization and distortions of identity that negatively affect our present experience. Understanding adaptive survival styles provides practical tools and techniques to address these distortions of identity and nervous system dysregulation. Being present and regulated in our bodies helps us become aware of and disidentify from the many inaccurate ideas and judgments that we have about ourselves, other people, and the world.

Working with the Life Force

The spontaneous movement in all of us is toward connection, health, and aliveness. No matter how withdrawn and isolated we have become or how serious the trauma we have experienced, on the deepest level, just as a plant spontaneously moves toward sunlight, there is in each of us an impulse moving toward connection and healing.

This organismic impulse is the fuel of the NARM approach.

PART A
The Five Adaptive Survival Styles

1
Overview

Paradoxically, the more we try to change ourselves, the more we prevent change from occurring. On the other hand, the more we allow ourselves to fully experience who we are, the greater the possibility of change.

A core NARM principle is that the capacity for connection, with both self and others, defines emotional health. In the Introduction, we saw that all children need to feel connected to themselves and to their caregivers: they require loving attunement to their needs and emotions, and they need to be supported enough to feel safe in their dependence as well as in their independence. Finally, they need attuned acceptance of their developing sexuality and heart-centered relationships in order to integrate their capacity to love. The fulfillment of these needs is essential to the success of our formative years and continues to be of primary importance throughout our adult lives. To the degree that children's core needs are attuned to and reasonably satisfied, they feel safe, trusting of the world, and connected to their bodily and emotional selves. They grow up experiencing a sense of well-being, regulation, and expansion.

The Need-Satisfaction Cycle

A primary need emerges and is satisfied. It recedes into the background and another need emerges; and so the cycle continues. When, for a child, this need-satisfaction cycle is significantly interrupted, healthy development is disturbed, and the environmental failure triggers both tension and bracing in the musculature and activation and imbalances in the nervous system and biochemistry—all of which sets the stage for symptoms and disease. When basic needs are not met and the protest to get those needs met is unsuccessful, children come to feel that something is wrong with their needs; they cannot know that it is *their environment* that is not responding adequately. Therefore, they internalize caregiver failures, experiencing them as their own personal failures. Reacting to their caregivers' failure to meet their needs, children come to feel various degrees of anger, shame, guilt, and physiological collapse. Tragically, to the degree that there is chronic lack of attunement to their core needs, children do not learn to attune to the needs within themselves. When basic needs are consistently left unsatisfied, the need-satisfaction cycle is interrupted, and nervous system dysregulation and identity distortions are set in motion that often have a lifelong negative impact.

Adaptive Survival Styles

Human beings are born with an essential adaptive ability: the capacity to disconnect from painful internal and external experience. We are able to disconnect from experiences of pain and anxiety that accompany the lack of fulfillment of our primary needs. To the degree that any core need is chronically unfulfilled, children are faced with a crucial choice: adapt or perish. Any core need that remains consistently unsatisfied threatens children's physiological and psychological integrity and prevents them from fully moving to the next developmental stage. Developmental progression is disturbed or interrupted. In order to survive, children adapt to their compromised situation by developing what in NARM we call an *adaptive survival style.* Survival styles are the result of children's adaptations to the chronic lack of fulfillment of one or more of their biologically based needs: connection, attunement, trust, autonomy, and love-sexuality (see Table 1.1).

Protecting the Attachment Relationship

Survival styles are adaptive strategies children use to protect the attachment relationships with their parents. Children sense the parts of themselves that their parents accept and value as well as the parts of themselves their parents reject. They adapt to their parents' acceptance or rejection in order to maintain and maximize the attachment and love relationship. As shown in Table 1.1, each adaptive survival style reflects the foreclosure of some aspect of the core self in order to maintain parental love.

CORE NEED	SURVIVAL ADAPTATION	STRATEGY USED TO PROTECT THE ATTACHMENT RELATIONSHIP
Connection	Foreclosing connection	Children give up their very sense of existence, disconnect, and attempt to become invisible
	Disconnect from body and social engagement	
Attunement	Foreclosing the awareness and expression of personal needs	Children give up their own needs in order to focus on the needs of others, particularly the needs of the parents
Trust	Foreclosing trust and healthy interdependence	Children give up their authenticity in order to be who the parents want them to be: best friend, sport star, confidante, etc.
Autonomy	Foreclosing authentic expression, responding with what they think is expected of them	Children give up direct expressions of independence in order not to feel abandoned or crushed

Love–Sex-uality	Foreclosing love and heart connection	Children try to avoid rejection by perfecting themselves, hoping that they can win love through looks or performance
	Foreclosing sexuality	
	Foreclosing integration of love with sexuality	

TABLE 1.1: Foreclosure of the Self to Maintain the Attachment Relationship

Identity and Identifications

We survive by adapting to our environment. Initially, our survival strategies are life-saving responses and represent successful adaptations, not pathology. However, the adaptations and accommodations we make, although once protective, limit us as adults. Living life based on adaptations learned in childhood restricts our capacity to respond appropriately and creatively to the many challenges of adult life. The coping strategies that initially helped us survive as children over the years become rigid beliefs about who we are and what the world is like. Our beliefs about ourselves and the world, together with the physiological patterns associated with these beliefs, crystallize into a familiar sense of who we are. This is what we come to view as our identity.

What we take to be our identity is better described as the shame- and pride-based identifications of our survival styles. As children, we learn to live within the limitations imposed by our environment. However, as adults *these initially adaptive limitations become self-imposed prisons.* What in children was adaptive in adults becomes maladaptive. It is the *persistence of survival styles appropriate to the past,* continuing beyond when they are needed, that distorts present experience and creates symptoms. Survival styles, after having outlived their usefulness, function to maintain ongoing disconnection.

Every identification we hold about ourselves disconnects us from the fluidity of our core nature. Our identifications—that is, all the fixed beliefs we take to be our true self—along with the associated patterns of nervous systems dysregulation separate us from ourselves and the experience of being present and engaged. As much as we may feel constrained by our survival styles, we are afraid to, or do not know how to, move beyond them.

Survival Styles and the Body

Our survival styles are reflected in our bodies in two ways: as areas of tension (hypertonicity) and as areas of weakness or disconnection (hypotonicity). Patterns of tension and weakness reveal the ways we have learned to compensate for the disconnection from our needs, core self, and life force. Muscular constriction, bracing, and collapse are the physical mechanisms of adaptive survival styles. Tracking in the body and paying attention to the felt sense gives us an important roadmap for working with the internal conflicts of each survival style.

Looking Through the Lens of Developmental and Relational Trauma

There are many ways that connection can be compromised in human development, including through inadequate parenting or misattunement, shock trauma, and developmental/relational trauma such as abuse, neglect, or early loss. Understanding the process by which each adaptive survival style internalizes and perpetuates the environmental failure distinguishes the NARM approach from other psychodynamic therapies. NARM helps individuals become aware of how they organize their experience using survival styles that have outlived their usefulness.

All of us are somewhere on the continuum of connection to disconnection from our core selves and our bodies. In NARM the focus is less on why individuals are the way they are and more on how their survival style distorts what they are experiencing in the moment. It is not to say that the why of a client's personal history is not part of the therapeutic process. Understanding why patterns begun in childhood can be helpful is useful to the degree that this understanding impacts present experience. Health is restored not simply by exploring personal history but by supporting the ability to reconnect to the basic life force, as seen in Chapter 12.

Looking at human development through the lens of developmental and relational trauma gives us an understanding of the five basic patterns of physiological dysregulation and their accompanying identity distortions. It is helpful to recognize these five basic physiological and identity patterns in order to make sense of what otherwise can seem to be a confusing broad spectrum of symptoms:

- *Connection:* A survival style develops around the need for contact and the fear of it.
- *Attunement:* A survival style develops around the conflict between having personal needs and the rejection of them.

- *Trust:* A survival style develops around both the longing for and the fear of healthy trust and interdependence.
- *Autonomy:* A survival style develops around both the desire for and the fear of setting limits and expressing independence.
- *Love-Sexuality:* A survival style develops around wanting to love and be loved and the fear of vulnerability. It also develops around the splitting of love and sexuality.

The symptoms and emotional suffering particular to each survival style indicate specific patterns of disconnection that are reflected in our bodies, our behavior, our personalities, our relationships, our work life, and even in the illnesses to which we are prone. At the onset, survival styles are lifesaving adaptive strategies that we have all used. It is important never to lose touch with the suffering inherent in each survival style and to approach this suffering with compassion.

Each of the five adaptive survival styles is complex and multifaceted, and the following chapters can provide only

a general orientation. Each description follows a similar organization:
- An introduction to the adaptive survival style
- A description of the early developmental and relational traumas that set the survival style in motion
- How the adaptive survival style continues to impact the adult nervous system and identity
- Growth strategies to help individuals move toward resolution of the core dilemmas of each adaptive survival style

2

Connection

The First Organizing Principle

The Connection Survival Style is introduced in this chapter and is presented in depth in Part B of this book.

As a result of the earliest trauma, individuals with the Connection Survival Style have disconnected from their bodies, from themselves, and from relationship. Connection types have two seemingly different coping styles or subtypes: the thinking and the spiritualizing subtypes. To manage the pain of early trauma, some individuals disconnect from their bodies and live in their minds. They value thinking and logic over feelings and emotions. Other individuals, having never embodied, manage their disconnection by spiritualizing their experience. These individuals tend to live in the energetic field, in more ethereal realms. Individuals of both subtypes are disconnected from their bodies and when asked what they are feeling in their body, find the question challenging, anxiety producing, and often impossible to answer.

DEVELOPMENT OF THE CONNECTION SURVIVAL STYLE

The Connection Survival Style is developmentally the first of the five adaptive survival styles. This style develops as a result of early shock and attachment trauma. When early life experience has been traumatic, the trauma lives on in the form of ongoing systemic high-arousal states. Unresolved high arousal becomes the source of a relentless, nameless dread, a continuous sense of impending doom that never resolves. Adults who develop the Connection Survival Style experience the lifelong difficulty of managing the physiological dysregulation of these high levels of arousal as well as the resulting psychological distortions of identity. They function by using dissociation to disconnect from the distress in their body. As a result, the child and later the adult are left with systemic dysregulation and a narrowed range of resiliency that leaves them vulnerable to later traumas.

THE CONNECTION SURVIVAL STYLE IN THE ADULT

The identity and physiology of adults with early trauma are impacted by the distress and dysregulation they experienced in early life. Early shock and attachment trauma create a distorted template for lifelong psychological, physiological, and relational functioning. Because of their early trauma, both the thinking and the spiritualizing subtypes disconnect from bodily experience and personal relationships. Although initially protective, sustained disconnection from the body and other people creates increasing dysregulation that leads to psychological and physiological symptoms.

The Thinking Subtype

As a result of early trauma thinking subtypes have retreated to the life of the mind and choose theoretical and technical professions that do not require significant human interaction. These individuals tend to be more comfortable behind a computer, in their laboratory, or in their garage workshops where they can putter undisturbed. They can be brilliant thinkers but tend to use their intelligence to maintain significant emotional distance.

The Spiritualizing Subtype

These subtypes are prone to spiritualizing their experience. As a result of either early shock or relational trauma, they did not feel welcomed into the world and grew up believing that the world is a cold, loveless place. Because other humans are often experienced as threats, many individuals with this subtype search for spiritual connection, are more comfortable in nature and with animals, and feel more connected to God than to other human beings. To make sense of the pain of their lives, they often become spiritual seekers trying to convince themselves that someone loves them; if people do not, then God must.

These individuals are often extremely sensitive in both positive and negative ways. Having never embodied, they have access to energetic levels of information to which less traumatized people are not as sensitive; they can be quite psychic and energetically attuned to people, animals, and the environment and can feel confluent and invaded by other people's emotions. They are also unable to filter environmental stimuli—they are sensitive to light, sound, pollution, electromagnetic waves, touch, etc.; therefore they often struggle with environmental sensitivities.

Identity

Regardless of age, Connection types, at some level, often feel like frightened children in an adult world. Because of their inadequate sense of self, they often try to anchor themselves in their roles as scientist, judge, doctor, father, mother, etc. When functioning in a role, they feel comfortable and they know what the rules are; being outside a specific role can feel frightening.

Isolation

Many Connection types feel alone and isolated without realizing how they avoid human contact and isolate themselves; some are aware of their fear of people but believe that it is other people who are the source of the threat they feel. Ambivalence is characteristic of individuals with this survival style, particularly in personal relationships. They simultaneously have an intense need for, and an extreme fear of, contact. They tend to withdraw or break contact in emotionally disturbing or stressful situations.

GROWTH STRATEGIES FOR THE CONNECTION SURVIVAL STYLE

This survival style's deepest longing for connection is also its deepest fear. The therapeutic key is to explore this profound internal conflict as it expresses in the moment-by-moment process of therapy and how it plays out in these clients' symptoms and lives. There is a functional unity between the difficulty of feeling body and emotions and the impaired capacity to make interpersonal connection. Clients with a Connection Survival Style know that at a deep level their survival strategy is not really serving them, but it is frightening to live without it.

> ***Core Fear***
> - "I will die or fall apart if I feel."
>
> ***Compromised Core Expression***
> - "I am ... I have a right to be."
>
> ***Shame-Based Identifications***
> - Terrified and inadequate
> - Shame at existing
> - Feeling like they never fit in
> - Feeling like they are always on the outside looking in
> - Burden on others
>
> ***Pride-Based Counter-Identifications***
> - Based on roles: "I am a mother ... a doctor ... a husband..."
> - Thinking type: Pride in rationality and non-emotionality; contemptuous

and disdainful of others they see as driven by emotion
• Spiritualizing type: Pride in otherworldly orientation

Reality
• "I survived."

Behavioral Characteristics
• Lack of affect
• Feel shame about needing anything from anyone
• Communicate intellectual or spiritual superiority: "I know and you don't."
• Relate to other Connection types who don't challenge their need for personal space
• Use interpersonal distancing as a substitute for adequate boundaries
• Withdraw in emotionally disturbing situations
• Tend to relate in an intellectual rather than a feeling manner
• Seldom aware that they are out of touch with their bodies
• Fear both being alone and overwhelmed by others
• Feel like a frightened child in an adult world; do not know how to deal

with or appropriately manipulate their environment
- Exaggerated fear of death and disease
- Fear their own impulses, particularly anger
- Fear groups and crowds
- Intense ambivalence: deepest desire for contact is also the deepest fear
- Yearn to fill emptiness and fear fulfillment at the same time
- Strong need to control self, environment, and other people
- Difficulty tolerating intimacy
- Want to know reason why; transcendentally or intellectually oriented
- Because of their failure to embody, often have access to esoteric spiritual states
- Drawn to therapies, meditation, and spiritual movements that reinforce dissociation

Energy
- Global high-intensity nervous system activation

- Appearance of low energy; sensation and coherency are compromised
- Dorsal vagal dominance binding high-sympathetic arousal

Breathing Pattern
- Shallow: frozen thorax, particularly diaphragm and abdomen

Symptoms and Disease Tendencies
- Because of the early and profound systemic dysregulation, Connection types experience many different syndromes. The following is a partial list of their many health issues:

Migraines
ADD/ADHD
Colic
Dissociation
Digestive problems
Irritable bowel syndrome
Environmental sensitivities
Asthma
Depression
Fibromyalgia
Chronic fatigue
Scoliosis

Allergies Anxiety Panic attacks ***

TABLE 2.1: Key Features of the Connection Survival Style

Moving Toward Resolution

Connection is the developmental challenge for this survival style. Bringing clients' awareness to how they relate to the organizing principle of connection is essential. Therapies that address the symptoms related to the state of disconnection focus on the pain, the emptiness, and the anxiety that are reflections of the real problem. Instead of focusing on the symptoms of disconnection and disorganization, the organizing principle in NARM is to find and work with areas of organization in order to support increasing connection. For example:

- The therapist tracks moment-to-moment contact and contact ruptures as they unfold in the session.

- Long-term, helping clients develop access to the felt sense is essential. Short-term, however, prematurely inviting the client to track in the body can be re-traumatizing.
- Initially, invite clients to go into the body only when they are in touch with a resource or are in the process of discharging shock energy.
- Explore the attachment dynamics and the various ways these clients turn away from connection both with the therapist and in their lives.

It is necessary to help clients slowly shift their attention from what is not working in their lives and encourage them to focus on any area of experience, external or internal, where there is better functioning. Focusing on the experience of connection, either current or past, when appropriately titrated, is organizing. Shifting clients' attention to positive resources as opposed to having their consciousness trapped in distress states teaches self-soothing and brings more organization to the nervous system.

To stay in empathic resonance, the therapist of course must be available to listen to the client's narrative even when it is distressful. With attuned tact and timing, it is also important to pose questions that evoke positive resources and organization so that clients do not talk endlessly about their emotional pain and other symptoms. Any positive resource is useful in that it supports self-soothing, regulation, and increased organization.

Focusing on positive resources and the associated experience of safety establishes and reinforces oases of organization in the nervous system. As the work with these oases of organization continues, areas of disorganization, including painful affects and other symptoms, will inevitably surface. Clients need the therapist's help to learn how to manage these difficult affects. It is important not to push these painful affects away but at the same time not to identify with them or get submerged in them. This mindful process supports increasing organization, which in turn supports a greater connectedness and regulation.

As this positive cycle of organization increases, clients have an increased capacity to experience other human beings as sources of support rather than as threats. Being present to the process of contact and contact rupture is extremely important when working with the Connection type because the therapist is the representative of social engagement and attachment. Gently explore contact first through verbalizations, the possibility of eye contact, grounding, and orienting. Convey to clients your awareness of what a tremendous charge they are holding inside without pushing for too much contact or feeling.

In successful therapy with these clients, suspicions, anger, and resentments will inevitably surface. This is an important part of the reconnection process. Clients will inevitably be disappointed because the therapist cannot live up to all of their expectations, and it is important to let them know that they have a right to express their needs even if these needs cannot be met.

Connection types fear that if they let out their aggression, they will be destructive. Because of early trauma, neglect, and/or abuse, individuals with this survival style have used splitting to manage frightening levels of anger and rage. How profound shame and low self-esteem result from this dynamic of splitting will be explored in detail in Chapter 8.

Because the original caregiver was rejecting or unavailable, Connection types now have to discover how to ground in their own biological being and that other people are sources of connection. In order for connection to take place without creating further splitting, a trusting therapeutic alliance must develop with the therapist as representative of the "ground" and social connection. This process is sometimes slow and difficult in that becoming grounded and beginning to feel often create a greater threat than the anguish of the non-feeling states. That which constitutes help is exactly that which, in the past, these individuals experienced with fear, terror, and loss of self. It is frightening to come out of dissociation and begin to feel.

- Move slowly. Don't underestimate the need for careful titration. Despite the shut-down appearance, the Connection type is highly activated, filled with terror, and easily overwhelmed.
- Build trust and connection.
- Provide empathic resonance; you may be the first kind person in their lives.
- Mirror all increases in organization during the therapeutic process or in the client's life.
- Help clients learn to listen to and trust their internal experience.
- Hold the overall organization of the therapeutic process, containing the client's fragmentation as it inevitably surfaces.
- Help clients become reacquainted with their own existence by recognizing and feeling their emotions.
- Work with self-hatred and profound shame.
- Learn to integrate their anger, neither acting it out nor acting it in.
- Gradually support feeling, identification with the body, and the

> capacity to track sensation. Establish and progressively deepen and broaden contact with their body, emotions, and other people.
> - Stay available to address the client's suspicions, anger, and resentments.
> - Help clients manage their inevitable disappointment in the therapist.
>
> ***
>
> TABLE 2.2: Therapeutic Strategies for the Connection Survival Style

Connection types have gone into freeze in order to survive. They are sensitive organisms whose capacity for intimacy and independence are greatly limited. Small oscillations in feelings, positive or negative, represent a major risk. Therefore, careful titration and working with the rhythm of connection and withdrawal are crucial factors in the therapeutic process. It is not possible for Connection types to come back to their own aliveness, to reach out to feel again, to come back in connection with self and others, without facing what in their minds is a threat to their survival. When Connection types begin to commit to life and to relationship, they feel anxiety because it is counter to their impulse to withdraw. The therapist needs to remain attuned to the ongoing contact and contact-interruption cycle.

Human contact and warmth bring expansion and aliveness to the body. Making contact and allowing expansion to take place at its own rate begins to melt the frozenness. As shock energy is released, the frozenness progressively melts and more aliveness is possible.

Individuals with the Connection Survival Style began life experiencing rejection and isolation; in turn they have become self-isolating, rejecting of self and of others. It is an important development in their growth process when they become aware of the disparity between what they tell themselves—that they are lonely and want contact—and their emotional reality—that they avoid contact because contact feels threatening.

3

Attunement

The Second Organizing Principle

Individuals with the Attunement Survival Style have difficulty attuning to their own needs; knowing, allowing, and expressing their needs is associated with humiliation, loss, and fear of rejection.

Many individuals with the Attunement Survival Style become caretakers. They have learned to cope by attuning to other people's needs and neglecting their own. They are the givers of the world, the shoulder on which everyone cries, the ones who adopt stray animals and take care of lost people. They can be highly attuned to, and able to identify with and address, the needs of others. The problem is that they are not attentive to their own needs. Because their own needs are not obvious to them, they often develop codependent relationships in which, on the surface, they are the rescuer, the need provider, and the caretaker. This is an indirect way for them to get their own dependency needs met. Given their propensity to take care of others, they are disproportionately represented in service professions such as psychotherapy, nursing, and social work. Identifying as givers, yet having difficulty attuning to their own needs, over time they can become burned out and bitter.

DEVELOPMENT OF THE ATTUNEMENT SURVIVAL STYLE

This survival style has its roots in the first two years of life. At this stage, the baby's brain and nervous system are developing at a rapid rate. During these first two years, a baby's fragile organism is completely dependent on the mother's care, and the infant is learning self-regulation in the attachment relationship with the mother. The baby receives nourishment and learns regulation through attuned gaze, breastfeeding, skin contact, touch, and secure holding during which, ideally, the needs for attachment, nourishment, nurturing, and regulation are lovingly met.

Inadequate Attunement, Broken Attachment, and Deprivation

In the first eighteen months of life, a number of factors, all relating to the themes of misattunement and loss, can compromise a baby's development. The early developmental dynamic for this survival style is as follows:
- The baby cries out for mother. If she does not come or is unable to provide adequate, attuned nurturing, the baby protests.
- When adequate nurturing remains unavailable, the baby experiences frustration and distress, and the protest escalates.
- If the lack of fulfillment becomes chronic, the baby gives up, resigning psychologically and physiologically. Giving up is a parasympathetically dominant collapse state expressed as

profound resignation. This resignation develops into a psychobiological depression that is experienced as the sense that one's needs can never be met.

The Attunement Survival Style develops as an adaptation to experiences of attachment difficulties, inadequate nurturing, scarcity, and deprivation. Infants who experience deprivation give up their demand for caring and love, and this giving up becomes structural in the body and in the identity. Lack of fulfillment is familiar to most individuals with this survival style who have learned to want no more from the environment than what is available and who are used to living with unmet needs. One client succinctly expressed her adaptation to scarcity: "I'm an expert at making do with the minimum."

The Inability to Express Need and Want

Deprivation and attachment difficulties signal the baby's brain and nervous system to implement life-protecting strategies. Depending on the severity and the duration of the nurturing disruptions, there is a progressive loss of the ability to attune to and express one's needs. Along with the loss of attunement comes increasing autonomic dysregulation:

- Babies learn to limit their needs to match the amount of nurturing available. There is intelligence to this strategy because it is the only way dependent babies can cope with a deficit over which they have no control. At the onset, this response reflects a healthy capacity to adapt. However, if the nurturing and attunement deficits continue for too long, the psychophysiology of the developing infant is negatively affected.
- Babies begin to ignore their own needs. Again, there is intelligence to this response because it is too painful for babies to continue feeling their needs when satisfaction is not forthcoming.
- Babies disconnect from—"depress"—their needs and eventually lose touch with them. The

reaction not to need leads to a numbness to sensations and feelings. The bodily signals related to attachment needs, along with the needs for physical and emotional nurturing and nourishment, are foreclosed.
- Some dysregulated mothers use their infant for their own self-regulation. Many infants of mothers in distress learn to attune to their mothers' needs rather than to their own. To the baby, it feels imperative to alleviate the mother's distress which becomes more important than taking care of his or her own distress.
- The relationship with food becomes distorted. Children can become over-focused or under-focused around issues of eating.

Factors that Contribute to the Development of the Attunement Survival Style

- Family trauma, a mother's death, or serious illness during the first two years of a baby's life.

- Mothers with significant developmental difficulties themselves. If a mother has never developed a capacity for secure attachment, she will not be able to provide secure attachment for the infant. When a mother has experienced lack of care and nourishment during her own development, she will lack the resources to care for and nourish her baby. Called upon to give her baby what she never received herself, this mother may be conflicted about giving, unconsciously wanting her baby to give her the love and nurturing she never received.
- Any prolonged separation from the mother. In these early years such a separation can have a profound effect on babies and can interfere with their ability to develop a strong attachment bond.
- A mother's emotional unavailability to her baby. The mother may be physically present and provide adequate nourishment, but if she is chronically depressed, angry, or dissociated, her ability to provide

emotional attunement and nurturing will be compromised.
- Strife in the family. Divorce, unemployment, and a father's extended absence, to name a few, can have a profound effect on the mother's availability to her infant.
- A baby sent to a foster home or given up for adoption.
- The infant's own health problems, especially when there has been early surgery, prolonged hospital stays, or chronic illnesses. Even chronic severe colic can disrupt the nurturing attachment bond.

How Nurturing Deficits Are Managed Through Disconnection

Babies manage prolonged attachment and nurturing disruptions through a process of disconnection, which in turn compromises several aspects of development.
- Expressing need and want becomes too painful.

- The ability to know what they need and want is impaired.
- The ability to express what they need and want does not develop.
- The capacity to take in and integrate experiences of caring and love is significantly compromised.
- The ability to bond and feel connected to a trusted other becomes limited.
- The ability to manage intense affect becomes dysregulated. The younger the baby is at the time of the attachment and nurturing disruptions, the more pervasive the impact and the resulting dysregulation. In particular, the capacity for pleasure becomes compromised.
- Cognitions become distorted by attachment loss and deprivation. On a cognitive level, children try to make sense of their painful experience. Children who are deprived of having their basic needs met come to believe that there is something wrong with their needs. As adults they hold the belief that they are not deserving or entitled to express their

needs or to experience the fulfillment of their needs.
- In attempts to self-regulate, they become susceptible to eating disorders and addictions.

THE ATTUNEMENT SURVIVAL STYLE IN THE ADULT

Because of the lack of environmental attunement, individuals with this survival style do not learn to attune to their own needs, emotions, and body and become so adapted to scarcity that later in life, they are unable to recognize and express their own needs or allow fulfillment. For people with this survival style, there is a conflict between, on one hand, the expression of the need for physical or emotional nourishment, and the expectation of disappointment on the other.

Depending on the timing and severity of the attachment and nurturing difficulties, two different subtypes develop with two different strategies for managing the experience of deprivation:

the inhibited subtype and the unsatisfied subtype. Both subtypes live with a feeling of emptiness and deprivation, but they have different strategies for coping with that experience.

The Inhibited Subtype

When attachment and nurturing losses are early and/or more severe, the tendency is to foreclose the awareness of one's needs. The shame-based identification of these individuals is that needs are bad and wrong and that they are not entitled to have their needs fulfilled. These individuals often develop a counter-identification that is based on being proud of how little they need and how much they can do without. The extreme example of this strategy is anorexia.

The Unsatisfied Subtype

When the attachment and nurturing disruption is later or less severe, the unsatisfied type develops a tendency to be left with a chronic sense of feeling unfulfilled. In contrast to the inhibited type who will not express needs, the unsatisfied type can be very demanding of people in their lives while living with the continual feeling that there is never enough.

A good example to illustrate the difference between the inhibited and unsatisfied types is the state of their cupboards: the cupboards of the inhibited subtype tend to be nearly empty, and these individuals become anxious if their cupboards are too full while the cupboards of the unsatisfied subtype are overflowing, and they become anxious when supplies start to diminish.

THE INHIBITED SUBTYPE	THE UNSATISFIED SUBTYPE
Stops or forgets to eat when stressed	Overeats when stressed
Pride about not needing	Has the feeling of "never enough" in all areas of life
Often thin and unable to gain weight	Tendency toward overweight
Anorexia	Bulimia
Lack of entitlement	Unrealistic entitlement

TABLE 3.1: Comparison of the Two Attunement Survival Style Subtypes

Identity

Individuals with this survival style identify so strongly with the early experience of deprivation that they come to see the world through the prism of scarcity. Their resignation to deprivation and the depression of their needs, which is an adaptation to scarcity, impacts both their psychology and their physiology. Remembering that depression and resignation were originally life-saving, the identity of individuals with this adaptive survival style develops around making sense of, and coping with, their underlying resignation and depression. An identity develops around longing for fulfillment while at the same time, not being able to allow fulfillment.

Giving to Get

Becoming caretakers is the coping mechanism both subtypes have in common. Caretaking is a pride-based strategy that allows them to see themselves as being without needs: "I don't have needs; everyone needs me."

By developing relationships and work situations in which other people depend on them, they do not have to confront the shame they feel about needing or the rejection they fear will happen if they express their needs.

Clients with this survival style have learned to be very perceptive of the needs of others. This becomes the basis for a lifetime of attuning to others' needs instead of their own. They give to others what they want for themselves. Since they believe they cannot express their own needs, they eventually become frustrated and angry that others do not attune to their needs in the way that they attune to the needs of others. Being ashamed of their own needs or finding it difficult to know what their real needs are, they can often express them only with anger after frustration and disappointment have become unbearable. This strategy alienates people around them and ensures that their needs will not be met, thus reinforcing their belief that expressing needs is futile.

Since individuals with the Attunement Survival Style do not want to recognize neediness in themselves, that neediness becomes covert. Looking for recognition for their caretaking or attempting to be the center of attention, they can be draining for the people around them.

Core Fear
- "If I express my needs, I will be rejected and abandoned."

Compromised Core Expression
- "I need."

Shame-Based Identifications
- Needy
- Unfulfilled and empty
- Longing: "When I get [the relationship, the recognition, the money, the fame, etc.] I need, then I will be happy."

Pride-Based Counter-Identifications
- "I don't have needs. I am the giver. Others need me ... I don't need them."

Reality
- The rejection, abandonment, and deprivation they fear have already happened

Behavioral Characteristics

- Difficulty in sustaining energetic charge; they get excited about new projects but have difficulty finishing them
- Longing for their needs to be met without expressing them
- Clinging in a covert way
- Like to talk; getting attention is equated with getting love
- Often describe an emptiness in the belly
- Periods of elation at the beginning of a relationship or new, exciting project without the ability to follow through
- Do not reach out for what they want because of low energy and fear of disappointment
- Expression of anger is weak; tendency to be more irritable than angry
- Resignation
- Relationship to love object is self-oriented: "I love you ... I take care of you ... You have to love me."
- Encourage others to depend on them
- Pick up strays: animals or people

> **Energy**
> • Generally low; they can sustain short-term charge when there is hope of fulfillment
>
> **Breathing Pattern**
> • Depression in the chest
> • Shallow
> • Difficulty taking breath in
>
> ***
>
> **TABLE 3.2:** Key Features of the Attunement Survival Style

GROWTH STRATEGIES FOR THE ATTUNEMENT SUVIVAL STYLE

Traditional therapeutic work often involves a focus on revisiting early experiences of inadequate attunement and nurturing as well as the abandonment that Attunement types have experienced. This regressive orientation can be re-traumatizing because it does not offer resources and can reinforce the identification of being a needy, helpless child.

Moving Toward Resolution

NARM has developed a new orientation to help individuals with this survival style move toward resolution. The challenge for Attunement individuals is to learn how to attune to their own needs, to express them appropriately, and to tolerate more charge, fulfillment, expansion, and aliveness. The overall arc of therapy shifts from reliving experiences of abandonment and scarcity to learning how to tolerate fulfillment and expansion. We explore with these clients how there has been an adaptation to scarcity, to lack of attunement, and to abandonment that has affected both their sense of self and their physiology.

Working therapeutically with these individuals involves confronting the tendency to collapse in the face of strong feelings. Over time, growth takes place as their ability to tolerate more depth and expansion develops. Sadness and depression tend to be default emotions for these individuals, whereas expansive and positive emotions tend to be more challenging. Realizing that it is normal that grief about early broken connections will surface in the reconnection process, this grief needs to be acknowledged and integrated. The challenge for the Attunement type is to acknowledge old grief and loss as part of the growth process. Attunement types need help to work with their tendency to default to the familiar emotion of grief so that the identification with their early losses is not reinforced.

- Build the capacity to experience charge in all of its forms (strong sensations, emotions, attachment connections).
- Work with the cognitive distortion of not deserving.
- Work with the reality that their worst fear, abandonment, has already happened.
- Realize that by always being the giver, they abandon themselves.
- Acknowledge and help them integrate their split-off aggression.
- Work with their identification with longing but not having, with the fantasy "If [or when] I have ... then I will be happy."

- Help them to be realistic about their needs.
- Help them learn how to express their needs directly.
- Build the capacity for fulfillment and consistent connection.

***

TABLE 3.3: Therapeutic Strategies for the Attunement Survival Style

As clients with the Attunement Survival Style work through the shame of needing, they become more able to sustain connection with other people as well as develop an increasing capacity for positive emotion and aliveness. They are able to let go of their compulsive caretaking and find more fulfilling ways of meeting their own needs. Because they are more attuned to their needs does not mean they are any less attuned to the needs of others. A healthy balance is restored.

4

Trust

The Third Organizing Principle

Individuals with the Trust Survival Style seek power and control. They tend to be competitive and believe that "getting to the top" will satisfy their needs. They can be empire builders in both a positive and a negative sense. On the healthier end of the spectrum, Trust types can be visionaries and dynamic leaders; on the more pathological end of the spectrum they can be manipulative and ruthless in achieving their ends. Learning to trust is the missing or compromised core resource for this adaptive survival style.

Trust types compensate for feelings of powerlessness and lack of control by attempting to control others to enhance their own power. They like to dominate and to this end, they can be evasive, slippery, lying, or deceitful. They will do whatever is needed to maintain a sense of control and regain a feeling of domination. To avoid experiences of vulnerability and helplessness, Trust types use anger, drugs, alcohol, and, in worst cases, violence to reinforce their control. For this survival type, anger tends to be the default emotion; it is easily accessible and used to intimidate others.

DEVELOPMENT OF THE TRUST SURVIVAL STYLE

This survival style develops in family situations in which children's dependency and attachment needs are attacked, manipulated, or used against them. Having being manipulated by self-serving parents, individuals with this survival style associate dependency with being used. Dependency, which is basic to being a child, is a painful experience that becomes dangerous to the survival of the self. For these children, the dangers of dependency can take many forms:
- Their dependency needs are used to manipulate them.

- They are rewarded for becoming who the parents want them to be and punished for failing them.
- The family often rewards competitiveness and encourages one-upmanship.
- They are rewarded for taking on responsibility before they are ready and punished when they do not. They are forced to grow up too quickly and are denied a childhood.
- They are given parental scripts to fulfill and are forced to play a role.
- They are given power at an early age. They become mom's confidante or the instrument of dad's frustrated dreams. These children realize that the love they are given is conditional upon fulfilling their parents' needs and not related to who they really are. They feel unloved for their true selves.
- Trusting and depending on others becomes associated with being used and betrayed. As adults, they expect betrayal and will often betray first.

Rewarded for Selling Out

The Trust Survival Style begins when children receive ego gratification for fulfilling their parents' ambitions. The parents of the Trust type may be giving, but they are controlling and undermining at the same time. They do for the child, acting "as if" they are supportive. They act as if they care, but in reality they use the child for their own gratification. One example is the "stage mom" who, out of her own frustrated desire to be famous, drives her daughter to fulfill her failed ambitions. Another is the "football father" who pushes his son to fulfill his dreams of athletic glory. Children will protect the attachment relationship with their parents by adopting the false self that their parents require. Having to choose between their own authenticity and the parents' demands puts these children in an impossible bind. In the process, children of such parents fail to develop an authentic self.

Children develop a false sense of self as the result of a number of family situations.

- Children feel pressured to fulfill their parents' desires. Chaotic, narcissistic, or dependent parents' often-hidden dependency on their children gives the children a false sense of power. These parents view their children as monuments to themselves, using the children to prop up their own shaky sense of self. Carrying their parents' hopes and dreams gives these children the belief that they are the center of the universe while at the same time putting a considerable amount of pressure on them not to disappoint.
- Children learn to act as if they are getting what they need. Parents act as if they are loving, and in turn the children act as if they are loved and feel loving toward the parents. Children who are developing this survival style have an underlying sense of the lie they are living, but they continue the pretense to avoid the painful reality that their parents do not care about who they really are. Instead, the children incorporate the pretense and continue the "as if" behavior into adulthood.

- Children parent their parents. When a parent is chronically depressive, anxious, or chaotic, the roles are reversed and the child ends up parenting the inadequate parent. Parentification also takes place when a child becomes the parent's confidante or best friend: a Hollywood actress, who is a single mother, referring to her ten-year-old daughter in an interview said, "I share everything with my daughter ... she is my best friend." This kind of parentification of children is so common that its destructiveness is not recognized.
- Children become triangulated with warring parents. Within the family system the children are used as pawns in the struggle between the mother and father, and in divorce the children are often forced to take sides. By having to choose between one parent or the other, they are forced into a situation where they are asked to betray one part of their heart or the other.
- Children are pushed to give up their dependency needs and assume

responsibility too early. This is particularly common in alcoholic and dysfunctional families.

Parents of children who develop the Trust Survival Style are often very demanding, with high expectations and high hopes for their children. They make demands of them, "pushing" them for their own good, but the children experience the underlying reality: the parents want them to be successful for their own narcissistic gratification, to prove to themselves and others what good people and what good parents they are.

Such parents use their children to shore up their own feelings of inadequacy. The parents use their children to prop up their own deficient sense of self. Each child is forced into a role that fulfills the parents' needs, whether confidante, sports star, or perfect showpiece. Parents simultaneously "build up" their children's egos while undermining their authentic needs. Children are rewarded for assuming the role desired by the parents; in the process the children are praised for their developing a false self.

In this way they are rewarded for selling themselves out.

These children learn early to live life on their parents' terms. They become who their parents want them to be. They take on their parents' script and in the process lose touch with their own authenticity. They do have an awareness, either consciously or unconsciously, of the lack of support available for who they really are, but they are forced to incorporate the pretense of their family. They become shrewd at determining what their parents (and other people) want of them and give it to them. Later in life, these children may turn against their parents, but early on have no choice but to sell out.

Abuse and Horror

At its extreme, the Trust Survival Style develops when a person grows up in an atmosphere of abuse and horror. Children who witness or experience abuse are helpless and powerless. The horror they witness may involve family violence, such as observing father beating up mother, or witnessing violence in the community, as in ghetto situations. The abuse can involve subtler forms of destruction that the child discerns. Trust types spend their lives seeking personal power in reaction to the overwhelming early life experiences of powerlessness. The more extreme the violence they witness and the greater their feelings of powerlessness, the more likely it is that they will develop symptoms that are on the more pathological end of the Trust Survival Style spectrum.

THE TRUST SURVIVAL STYLE IN THE ADULT

There are two basic strategies that individuals with the Trust Survival Style use in their struggle to exercise their power: they become seductive and manipulative, or they become overpowering.

The Seductive Subtype

Individuals with the Trust seductive subtype use an "as if" strategy. They act as if they care, as if they are present to others, as if they love. They are experts at reading what people need. The "as if" quality is reflected in their chameleon-like ability to be all things to all people. Many people are taken in and believe the "as if" presentation of individuals with this survival subtype, but at some point realize they are being used and betrayed by them.

Seductive subtypes know what people want to hear and say it convincingly. They have an uncanny knack for knowing people's vulnerabilities and can make them feel as if they are the center of the universe. They can skillfully:
- Manipulate or maneuver others to do their bidding.
- Seduce and charm: "I know what you need. I'll take care of you."
- Exert a charismatic attraction.
- Manipulate by presenting the image that will best meet their goals.

The Overpowering Subtype

The overpowering subtype develops as a result of the extreme helplessness these individuals have experienced in situations of abuse and horror. As children, their smallness, vulnerability, and dependency were used against them, and their vulnerability became intolerable. At some point, as they grow older, they make the decision to "turn the tables." They react to their parents' abuse by saying, "Never again! From now on, I'm the one in control." They take control and become the abusers.

Overpowering subtypes live with an underlying feeling of impotence and powerlessness. In reaction, they attempt to gain power over others by:
- Developing physical strength.
- Building empires, becoming rich and powerful.
- Developing their martial arts skills or owning guns.
- Being "one up."
- Gaining power over others then using it for their own purposes.
- Inspiring confidence in others and using it to control them.

- Being power hungry and competitive—always trying to be at the top.
- Having lived with intolerable fear as children, they present an image designed to evoke fear in others.

Identity

Individuals with the Trust Survival Style are very concerned with their image. They tell themselves that as long as they maintain a good front, as long as no one knows what is really going on inside, they are safe. The more negatively seductive subtypes feel about themselves, the harder they work at maintaining a good image. The more fearful overpowering subtypes feel about themselves, the harder they work at inciting fear in others. Sadly, both subtypes become experts at presenting a false image because they have lost touch with their core, with their sense of self.

Control

Trust individuals respond to having been controlled and manipulated as children by attempting to manipulate those around them. Their primary fear is loss of control. They compensate for feeling like losers by always needing to win and counteract feeling "one down" by constantly working to be "one up."

Individuals with the seductive subtype are good at making the proper impression, selling themselves, and influencing and motivating people. They have learned to control people by promising them what they want, pledging to serve them and take care of them. Many religious leaders and politicians fall into this category. They give the appearance of commitment to others and/or to a cause, but their commitment is not genuine. While they claim that their concerns are selfless, their goal is self-aggrandizement.

When their control is threatened, individuals of both subtypes resort to extreme behaviors to bolster themselves. They may use drugs, alcohol, food, or sex, or they may resort to aggressive behaviors and even violence. When the compensations of their survival style fail them they are in danger of collapse, and rather than face their internal emptiness and despair they may become self-destructive.

Power

Having been made to feel unrealistically special by their parents, individuals with this survival style develop a grandiose self-image. They believe they are special and feel they have a mission in life that sets them apart from other people.

Overpowering subtypes exercise their power openly. This is seen in two ways: some individuals are powerful because of their strong physique and/or expertise with weapons or martial arts, whereas others use money, political connections, and influence to amass power and build empires.

Fear of Failure

Trust types are terrified of failure. Although they try to convince themselves that they are winners, and in conventional terms they often are, inside they feel like losers. Working so hard to maintain the image of being winners, it is difficult for them to admit any weakness unless somehow they can use that admission to gain power over others.

Trust individuals can work tirelessly to meet their goals of success and power, fearing that if they are not successful they will end up, as one client put it, "in the gutter." Working to succeed compensates for the powerlessness and lack of control of their early life. The fear of ending up destitute and alone is a projection into the future of the helplessness they experienced as children. Underneath the image of power, they feel powerless, and since they cannot depend on others, they also feel totally alone.

Relationship and Sex

Individuals with this survival style will not allow themselves to be emotionally close to anyone because closeness stirs up feelings of dependency and triggers the fear of being controlled, as they were in early life. They will stay in a relationship as long as they feel that they are in control and can successfully dominate their partner. To this end they often choose Attunement types as partners: Attunement types are caretakers who are happy to serve while Trust types are more than happy to be served.

Both men and women with this survival style use their sexuality as a weapon and sex as an arena for conquest. Women view men in terms of status, power, and money; they use sexual conquest to seduce high-status males in order to gain personal power. Men rank women according to their physical beauty and enhance their power with the sexual conquest of the most beautiful women.

People with this survival style strive to dominate the partner they are with. They find it difficult to sustain a relationship with a truly warm and loving partner; when they are with a loving partner, they can become sadistic, impotent, or break off the relationship. If two individuals with the Trust Survival Style come together, their lives become a power struggle full of ploys, subtle or direct, to dominate the other. Trust types are also attracted to needy partners, whose dependency they encourage. Their strategy is different from that of the Attunement type, who rescues needy partners in order to take care of them. Unlike Attunement types, whose identity revolves around being caregivers, Trust types want power over the needy partner.

Projective Identification

Projective identification takes place when individuals project their unwanted internal states and emotions on another, causing that person to resonate with those negative states as if they were their own. The person who receives the projection does not realize that he or she is internalizing split-off negative states that "belong" to another. Trust types use projective identification masterfully: they maintain their larger-than-life image by making others feel small, their need to be in control by making others feel out of control, their need to feel smart by making others feel dumb, and their need to feel powerful by making others feel powerless.

Denial and Rationalization

Individuals with the Trust Survival Style use denial to negate the reality of their life experience. They maintain their denial by disconnecting from their bodily experience. Since being in touch with their body puts them in touch with the pretense and falsehood of their life, they displace their energy upward into the mind and substitute reason and rationalization for body awareness. They believe that thinking makes it so. They gravitate to self-help systems that reinforce mind over matter and the power of positive thinking. They avoid feeling their anxiety with evasiveness, deceitfulness, and slipperiness. When confronted, they use rage and bombast to "turn the tables," and when this ploy is unsuccessful, become panicky.

GROWTH STRATEGIES FOR THE TRUST SURVIVAL STYLE

For individuals with the Trust Survival Style, coming to therapy is an admission that they need help. The more strongly an individual uses the strategies of this survival style, the more unlikely it is that they will seek therapy—which, for them, evokes their core fear of vulnerability and betrayal.

When Trust types do come to therapy, they will probe for the therapist's weaknesses and work to stay in a one-up position. Individuals with this survival style are difficult to work with because they tend to stop therapy the moment they feel threatened. Because they feel threatened by the therapeutic situation, they will often try to assert their dominance by finding an issue (for example, money, time, or payment policies) to do battle over and get special treatment. When working with individuals with this survival style, therapists must be careful not to get hooked into their seemingly endless attempts at one-upmanship. Individuals with the Trust Survival Style need therapists who are clear and direct, who have strong boundaries, and who will not get pulled into their power games. At the same time, it is essential that the therapist express understanding and empathy for the real suffering that these clients experience.

Core Fear
- Helplessness
- Weakness
- Dependency
- Failure

Difficulty Communicating Directly
- "I need your help"

Shame-Based Identifications
- Small and helpless
- Used
- Betrayed
- Powerless
- Weak

Pride-Based Counter-Identifications
- Strong and in control
- Successful
- Larger than life
- Betrayer
- User

Reality
- Neither as small or helpless as they secretly believe, nor as powerful as they try to appear

Energy

- Ungrounded
- Displaced upward in the body

Behavioral Characteristics

- Underlying feelings of impotence and powerlessness
- Fear of failure
- Feelings of emptiness for always playing a role
- Displacing of blame: always make it someone else's fault
- Not being able to depend on others, they feel alone
- Projective identification making others feel small, weak, stupid, or helpless
- Inflated self-image
- Always needing to be "one up"
- Always wanting to be the best, the winner
- Empire builders; when healthy they can be visionaries
- Deny the reality of their bodily experience
- Act "as if"
- Appearance of commitment to others, but in reality self-serving
- Good at reading other people, particularly their weaknesses

- Become anxious when they cannot avoid or deny
- When the idealized self-image fails, they may become self-destructive, prone to alcohol, drug abuse, and other high-risk behaviors
- Paranoia: life is a jungle—survival of the fittest
- Turn the tables:

"I have lived with fear, now I'll make you afraid."

"I don't get ulcers, I give ulcers."

"I'll never be betrayed again—I'm the betrayer."

Breathing Pattern

- In contrast to the collapse seen in the chest of the Attunement type, the chest of the Trust type is inflated to cover up their feelings of smallness and helplessness
- The highly armored chest is hard and functions to encase the heart, protecting the person from feelings of tenderness and vulnerability

***

TABLE 4.1: Key Features of the Trust Survival Style

Moving Toward Resolution

Because these individuals were truly betrayed as children, addressing the theme of betrayal is essential. The final resolution for individuals with the Trust Survival Style takes place when they become aware of how they have kept the betrayal of their early life alive by creating a false self at the expense of their connection to what is most real in them. It is important for them to understand how they have translated the lack of support they experienced as children into their failure to support their own authenticity. As they acknowledge the reality of having been truly betrayed and deal with the hurt, they can come home to their bodies and to themselves. As their heart opens, their capacity for interdependence continues to increase, and they can reach out for help without losing their sense of self. Having always believed that strength has to do with power over others, they discover that true power is the strength to be vulnerable.

- Help them develop connection to, and compassion for, their underlying hurt and powerlessness.
- Help them develop the courage and strength to allow healthy dependency on others.
- Help them remove the mask of the idealized self-image and move toward increasing authenticity.
- Help them develop the strength to be vulnerable.

***

TABLE 4.2: Therapeutic Strategies for the Trust Survival Style

5

Autonomy

The Fourth Organizing Principle

Autonomy and a sense of independence are the core capacities that have failed to develop fully in those who exhibit this survival style. Autonomy individuals are often kind and openhearted, but they have difficulty setting limits and establishing boundaries. As a result, they easily feel put upon and secretly resentful, particularly in intimate relationships, where they often feel trapped. They prize loyalty and are good friends, but they are so focused on avoiding conflict and pleasing others that they are not forthcoming about negative feelings they may have. As such, it is hard to know where one stands with them.

DEVELOPMENT OF THE AUTONOMY SURVIVAL STYLE

Individuals with the Autonomy Survival Style may have been welcomed into the world and had their dependency needs adequately met. The challenge for them begins between the ages of eighteen months to two years when their capacities for independence and autonomy are in development. It is in this period of the "terrible twos" that toddlers want to learn how to do things for themselves. Parents of children this age have heard many times the age-appropriate "No!" or "Me do it!"

Attuned parents support increasing age-appropriate independence and autonomy. Highly anxious parents undermine their children's developing need for independence because of their own unresolved fears. They prevent their age-appropriate movement toward autonomy in order to "protect" their children. Threats to the child's healthy autonomy also occur when parents see their child as an extension of themselves. These narcissistic parents can be emotionally invasive, enmeshed, or over-controlling. In an attempt to protect their fragile, developing autonomy, children withdraw by superficially going along with their parents' "program" for them while internally reacting to the control by secretly holding out to maintain their sense of autonomy and integrity.

Individuals with this survival style sometimes grow up in rigid, authoritarian homes with parents who believe that they always know what is "best" for them. Obviously, children need limits, but over-controlling parents believe that their rigid rules, beginning with eating habits and toilet training, are necessary for their children's own good. When children resist, these parents withdraw their "love" and use shame, guilt, and sometimes power to force obedience. To avoid humiliation and abandonment, the children develop a superficial niceness that communicates "yes," but at the same time, they also develop a secret self that holds a hidden resentment containing an unspoken "no." On the surface, these children seem to accept the parents' demands, but internally they hold out to avoid feeling controlled. Their hidden self-assertion is, "You have my body, but you'll never have my soul."

Some mothers, and occasionally fathers, feel abandoned by their child's developing independence and use guilt or the threat of abandonment to undermine it. Their discouragement or obstruction may be overt or covert, but either way, it takes the form of disapproval, derision, or implied threats. When parents align themselves against the child's appropriate expressions of autonomy and independence, the child comes to experience these impulses as dangerous. As the child grows older, obtaining love from the parents becomes linked to pleasing them, so that love is associated with duty, burden, and bondage. For many with this survival style, obtaining love becomes inextricably tied with the necessity to please, often at the expense of their own integrity and autonomy.

Individuals with the Autonomy Survival Style have had to face the dilemma of choosing between themselves or their parents. To submit to their parents leaves them feeling invaded, controlled, and crushed. On the other hand, their loving feelings and the need to maintain the attachment relationship keep them from overtly challenging parents. Faced with the impossible choice of trying to maintain the integrity of the self while keeping the love of the parents leaves them in a no-win situation. These children adapt to this dilemma by overtly submitting to parental power while secretly holding out. To do this, these children develop a powerful, though often covert, will.

THE AUTONOMY SURVIVAL STYLE IN THE ADULT

In adults who have developed this adaptive survival style, self-assertion and overt expressions of independence and autonomy are experienced as dangerous and to be avoided. The major fears that fuel this survival adaptation are the fears of being criticized, rejected, and abandoned.

Paralyzed by Internal Conflict

What was once a struggle with their parents is now internalized so that individuals with the Autonomy Survival Style spend their lives playing out the conflict between the internalized demanding parent and the withholding child. As a result, they feel paralyzed and bound by the internal contradictions inherent in the interplay of these two roles. Extreme ambivalence and a resulting immobilization are characteristics of this survival style.

Fear of Intimacy

Given their childhood experience, it is easy to understand how love and intimacy are associated with fears of invasion, of being controlled, smothered, crushed, or overwhelmed. These individuals long for closeness but associate it with losing their independence and autonomy.

Individuals with the Autonomy Survival Style are placaters and are afraid to expose their true feelings.

Instead, they play the role of the "good boy" or the "nice girl" because they feel that since playing this role won their parents' "love," it will win other people's love as well. A key statement for this adaptive survival style is, "If I show you how I really feel, you won't love me—you'll leave me." Because they are afraid to stand up for themselves, they blame others for taking advantage of "their good nature." Unfortunately, playing the role of the "good boy" or "nice girl" puts them in a no-win situation. Playing a role brings constant disappointment, resentment, and anger because, given that they are not authentic, they cannot feel loved for who they really are even when people respond favorably to the persona they have created. They develop a distrust of the world, a cynical belief that no one can really accept them as they are.

In personal relationships, these individuals allow frustrations to build without addressing them until they reach a point where they can no longer tolerate the accumulated resentments. They usually have escape strategies that allow them to leave relationships without confrontation: they withdraw without explanation, or they make their partner miserable so that the partner rejects them. This rejection by the other allows them to achieve "freedom" without the guilt of saying no, while at the same time reaping the secondary benefit of being the "innocent" injured party.

Living with Pressure

Living with pressure is an ongoing experience for these individuals. They are in fact so used to pressure that they do not recognize it as such. Having grown up feeling under pressure to live up to their parents' expectations and demands, they have internalized this pressure and as adults, put tremendous pressure on themselves to be agreeable, responsible, trustworthy, and to do what is expected of them. Externally oriented, they are extremely sensitive to what they perceive as others' expectations of them and experience these expectations, in intimate relationships and work situations, as pressures to perform.

Parental pressures are internalized as high expectations of themselves. Individuals with the Autonomy Survival Style are extremely judgmental of themselves. They are ruled by "shoulds" and strive endlessly to become who they think they "should" be. They perceive the continual pressure they feel as coming from outside themselves and not from the internal demands they put on themselves. Well-meaning friends and family, when trying to help Autonomy types with their dilemmas, feel frustrated about their complaints and their unwillingness to do anything to resolve their issues.

Rumination

The tendency to brood and ruminate is typical of this survival style. These individuals ruminate after personal encounters, berating themselves about whether they did or said the right thing, chastising themselves for any "mistakes" they feel they made in the interaction, wondering if they said the right thing or hurt the person's feelings.

Ambivalence Toward Authority

A key aspect of the Autonomy Survival Style identity is a deep-seated ambivalence toward authority. Overtly, Autonomy types are deferential to authority, but covertly they harbor resentments and rebellious impulses. When dealing with authority, they feel that the only options they have are to submit to it or rebel against it. This "submit or rebel" dilemma leaves them in a no-win situation that has profound implications for the therapeutic relationship.

GROWTH STRATEGIES FOR THE AUTONOMY SURVIVAL STYLE

In the therapeutic process with individuals with the Autonomy Survival Style, it is important to keep in mind how paralyzed they feel as a result of their own internal contradictions. Not realizing how much pressure they put on themselves or how they constantly judge themselves, they experience their internal struggle as resulting from external circumstances. Growth takes place when they become aware that the pressures they experience are primarily the result of their own internal demands.

Not recognizing that their struggle is internal, they look to the therapist to align with one side or the other of their internal conflict. For example, they may come to therapy complaining about a project they are unable to finish. They identify their "procrastination" as the problem and ask the therapist for behavioral strategies to help them overcome their procrastination. For individuals who struggle with the Autonomy Survival Style, the request to help them find a solution to their procrastination is an invitation to frustration for both therapist and client. What is needed is a therapist who can remain neutral and bring to awareness these clients' internal ambivalence around finishing the project without offering solutions. As soon as a therapist sides with one aspect of their internal struggle, these clients will take the opposite side: "Yes—but..." Or they may give the appearance of trying hard to follow the therapist's suggestions while secretly resenting them. Ultimately, their resentment surfaces as sabotage, because successfully meeting the stated goal becomes associated for these clients with trying to please the therapist. Winning—that is, achieving the stated goal—feels like losing because it is associated with giving up their integrity to the authority of the therapist.

Core Fear
- "If people really knew me, they wouldn't like me."
- "If I show you how I really feel, you won't love me."

Compromised Core Expression
- "No."
- "I won't."
- Any expression that might evoke conflict

Shame-Based Identifications
- Angry
- Rebellious
- Resentful of authority

- Enjoy disappointing expectations others have of them
- Burdened

Pride-Based Counter-Identifications
- Nice, sweet, compliant
- Good boy/good girl
- Fear of disappointing others
- Pride at how much they can take on their shoulders: "I can take it."

Reality
- Autonomy comes from knowing what is right for them and the ability to express it to others so that their "Yes" is a real yes, and their "No" is a real no

Coping Mechanisms
- Indirectness: Not laying cards on the table
- Will: efforting, trying
- Passive aggression
- Guilt
- Rumination
- In relationship, rather than communicate their real feelings, they strategize
- Projects authority onto others
- Procrastination

Behavioral Characteristics

- Ambivalent, paralyzed by their internal contradictions
- Often complain of feeling stuck or in a morass
- Fear of losing their independence when they become intimate
- Choose to please others over themselves and then feel resentful
- Will-based, stubborn identity based on efforting
- Fear of their own spontaneous expression
- Fear of being rejected or attacked if they are openly oppositional
- Global feeling of guilt, inappropriately apologetic
- Superficially eager to please
- Covertly feeling spite, negativity, and anger
- Passive-aggressive; self-assertion and access to healthy aggression is limited
- Secretive about their pleasures for fear that they will be taken away
- Feel their only choices are to submit to authority or rebel against it

- Strong fear of humiliation
- Often complain of feeling "stuck"
- Forceful in defending others but not themselves
- Will avoid or distance themselves from a situation rather than confront it
- Projection of authority on others
- Believe that others have an agenda for them; imagine it even when not true
- Want to know what is expected of them so they can do the opposite
- Pressure themselves constantly while imagining the pressure as coming from the outside
- Continual self-judgment and self-criticism
- Confuse their unwillingness to stand up for themselves with flexibility
- Use the pressure of waiting until the last minute before a deadline as a motivating force to break through their paralysis in order to complete tasks about which they are ambivalent

Energy
- High energy, contained as if in a vice

- Compressed and dense
- Because of their pressured existence, they are prone to psychosomatic problems such as neck and back problems, ulcers, colitis, high blood pressure, pinched nerves

Breathing Pattern
- Contained
- Heavily armored chest

***

TABLE 5.1: Key Features of the Autonomy Survival Style

Moving Toward Resolution

Working with individuals with the Autonomy Survival Style is complex; there are many traps into which therapists and clients can fall. The dilemmas of this survival style cannot be resolved by efforting—by the use of will—by taking sides in the client's conflict, or by presenting a goal-oriented approach. These clients focus on what they think they should do and lose connection with what they really want to do. They don't know how to work out the conflicts that arise from their competing needs.

The following are some of the will-based efforting traps that Autonomy clients create for themselves:
- How can I change this?
- What can I do about it?
- Do you have any homework for me?
- So what should I do?

Non-Goal Orientation

Being goal-oriented avoids or overlooks the client's conflicted internal world. Paradoxically, the less these individuals and their therapists try to force change, the more they are apt to change. Clients may complain about feeling put upon at work or in a personal relationship. The therapist, wanting to be helpful, offers suggestions about how they can stand up for themselves. What seems like a simple interaction to the therapist evokes complex emotions in the client. By focusing on a behavioral strategy, the therapist misses the childhood fear that self-assertion—in this case standing up for themselves—will bring abandonment.

Feeling unconsciously that their internal world is being missed yet again, they experience the therapist as one more parent figure that is trying to impose their personal agenda on them.

Autonomy types will try to figure out the therapist's program and will attempt to be the best possible client. For example, if the therapist believes in getting anger out by beating on a pillow, they will go at it enthusiastically. If the therapist believes in the importance of feeling the body, they will pressure themselves to feel their bodies. This kind of "winning" by being the good client feels like "losing" or selling out to the therapist's agenda, and these clients will ultimately sabotage the process.

It is important for the therapist to communicate to these clients that they are accepted as they are, and that the therapist has no personal stake in getting them to change. This can be difficult to get across to these individuals. Autonomy types want the therapist to have expectations of them so that their internal struggle can become externalized. Autonomy types are very sensitive to a therapist's subtlest expectation. Even when therapists have no expectations, these clients will imagine/project them. The greatest gift a therapist can offer these clients is unconditional acceptance. Paradoxically, this acceptance also creates the most powerful frustration because now these clients have no one upon whom to externalize their struggle.

It is therapeutically helpful to support their self-awareness through mindfulness and to help them increase their capacity to accept all parts of themselves. When these clients effort toward a goal, the opposite side of their internal conflict will surface and sabotage their efforts. Until clients can learn to listen to all sides of their internal struggle—until all sides are allowed a voice and taken seriously—Autonomy types will not experience internal peace.

These individuals need to see that as long as they continue to choose to please others at their own expense, they will be trapped. They need to discover how they try to control other people's responses by being the "good boy" or "nice girl" for them. They need to find the courage to give up that control by being frank and honest with people and allowing them to respond as they will. Resolution of the dilemma for the Autonomy Survival Style is achieved when these clients let themselves be honest and forthright in close relationships and allow intimacy while remaining in touch with their independence.

- Encourage them to be curious about their internal conflicts rather than judging themselves and "efforting" to resolve them.
- Explore internal conflicts without taking sides.
- Support non-efforting and a non-goal orientation.
- Have a clear contract about what clients want from therapy: Make sure they set the intention.
- Be careful not to have an agenda for them.
- Do not let them externalize their conflict into the therapeutic process.

- Watch out for their "good client" behavior that can lead to sabotaging the therapy.
- Explore the difference between counter-dependency, rebellion, and true autonomy.
- Help them learn that they can have intimacy without giving up their autonomy.
- Know that any authority, including the therapist's, will evoke resentment.
- Help them see their hidden contrariness and rebelliousness.
- Support their developing capacity to self-reference.
- Support the possibility of self-expression.
- Help them see how they get others to reject them so they can be "free."
- Reflect to them, but do not get caught in their internal struggles, their self-created pressures and the unrealistic expectations they hold for themselves.
- Help them develop a sense of personal authority.

- Help them learn to say no and to set realistic limits with people without feeling guilty.
- The antidote to the will and efforting is the development of trust and self-confidence.

***

TABLE 5.2: Therapeutic Strategies for the Autonomy Survival Style

6

Love and Sexuality

The Fifth Organizing Principle

Individuals with the Love-Sexuality Survival Style are highly energetic, attractive, and successful. They are the doers and the winners of the world, the sports heroes, cheerleaders, top actors and actresses, the people who often become the icons of our collective consciousness. However, regardless of how attractive or accomplished they appear, they rarely live up to their own high expectations: on one hand, they seem full of confidence but on the other, they feel they are only as good as their last performance. Since they base their self-worth on looks and performance, their self-esteem is conditional; underneath their beautiful exterior they feel highly flawed.

This high-energy survival style develops around the issue of heartbreak, the result of unacknowledged or rejected loving feelings, particularly from the opposite-sex parent. Because of their early heartbreak around loving, maintaining a consistent love relationship as adults is challenging for them. Their developmental challenge is to integrate an open and loving heart with a vital sexuality.

DEVELOPMENT OF THE LOVE-SEXUALITY SURVIVAL STYLE

Though all human beings are hardwired to be loving and sexual, individuals who have significant developmental trauma in earlier stages of development do not move fully into this fifth stage of development. For example:

- *Connection types,* who have difficulty with close contact with other human beings, continue to struggle with this basic conflict and therefore cannot truly engage the more mature demands of an adult love relationship. They tend to be impersonal and disconnected, and

their sexuality in particular can be depersonalized.
- *Attunement types,* who are fixated on getting nurturing and nourishment, view love and sexuality through the prism of that "younger" need fulfillment.
- *Trust types,* with their need to dominate and control, are incapable of a mutual, healthy love relationship.
- *Autonomy types,* whose concern is to avoid domination and control by others, and who have difficulty being authentic and setting boundaries, see love relationships as traps wherein they lose their freedom and independence.

There are two important time periods in the development of the Love-Sexuality Survival Style: four to six years of age and the onset of puberty at roughly twelve to fifteen. In young children love and sexuality are integrated, and love for the parent is a whole-body experience. Difficulties surface between four and six years of age when parents reject, shame, or punish the child's emerging sexual expression and curiosity. These parents may encourage heart expressions but recoil at nascent expressions of sexuality. This reaction forces children to split off their sexuality from their expressions of love.

Essentially, individuals with the Love-Sexuality Survival Style experience rejection or wounding during the periods of sexual awakening. At puberty, the parents' attitude toward sexuality and how they handle their adolescents' changing bodies contributes significantly to the development of this survival style. The adolescent's sexual awakening may be completely ignored or met with open rejection, disdain, or disapproval. Fathers of pubescent girls often have difficulty handling their daughter's changing body and transition into womanhood, and some even become jealous of their increasing interest in boys. How a father handles this transitional time can determine a young girl's sense of herself as a woman: if the father withdraws his love and attention, the adolescent girl may feel deeply hurt, which leads to a sense of shame about her developing body and sexuality. Similarly, how mothers respond to their adolescent sons' nocturnal emissions, masturbation, and increasing interest in girls can also cause deep shame in young boys. There are many possible and damaging scenarios, but overall, when the expression of their sexual selves is handled in a shaming way, adolescents' sense of identity is wounded and their budding sexuality is negatively affected.

Love-Sexuality types often grow up in families with a rigid atmosphere where sexual awakening is judged or condemned: expressions of love, tenderness, and emotions are not openly communicated and are even frowned upon. In certain families, love is conditional, predicated on looks and performance. As a result, adolescents' experience of what they are told is love and their relationship to their own bodies become distorted. Experiencing love as conditional and sexuality as shameful creates a lack of integration between loving and sexual feelings that has lifelong repercussions for how they relate to their own bodies and to an intimate partner. They relate either from the heart or from their sexuality but find integrating both difficult and anxiety-producing.

THE LOVE-SEXUALITY SURVIVAL STYLE IN THE ADULT

Individuals who have navigated the first four developmental stages with relative success and whose life force has not been distorted by earlier trauma tend to be high-functioning adults. They have energy to meet their life goals and tend to be well integrated physically, which makes them attractive to other people.

When individuals experience misattunement to their love and sexuality needs at this stage, one of two subtypes develop—the romantic subtype or the sexual subtype—each favoring one aspect of the love-sexuality split.

The Romantic Subtype

These individuals romanticize love and marriage. They are openhearted but often disconnected from their sexuality and may even be terrified of it; they have difficulty integrating a vital sexuality into their love relationships. In the early stages of a relationship, they can feel more sexual, but as the relationship deepens, their sexual feelings diminish. Less integrated romantic subtypes, having disconnected from their sexual impulses, can become the moral crusaders, the self-appointed guardians of public morality who attempt to enforce their moral code on others. In the repressed romantic subtype who professes a strong and often judgmental position about the sexuality of others, the sexual impulses have been driven underground and are sometimes expressed in covert and secret acting out.

The Sexual Subtype

Individuals with the sexual subtype have a tendency toward seductive behavior as a way to make themselves desirable. They seek out and use attractive partners to bolster their own self-esteem and measure sexual satisfaction by the frequency, rather than by the depth, of their experience.

Their seductiveness is not used for control, as with the Trust type, but as a way to prevent real intimacy. Because of their fear and avoidance of intimacy, they often have the feeling that they are incapable of loving. Sexual subtypes consider themselves sexually sophisticated, and sexual potency and performance are important to them. Frequently, however, their sexuality is mechanical and disconnected, centered more on conquest and performance than on heart connection.

For this subtype, the love-sexuality split results in both alienation from deep sexual pleasure and obsession with genitally focused sexuality. Individuals in this sexual subtype may be obsessed with sex and pornography; they may be highly promiscuous, constantly seeking the sexual satisfaction that their rigid, defended bodies will not allow them to fully experience.

In relationship, they experience an initial period of intense sexuality, but as the possibility of a heart connection develops, they often lose sexual interest or break off the relationship. They are able to be sexual with relative strangers but not with the person they love. This split is reflected in their inability to maintain a strong sexual connection beyond the early courting period. As a relationship progresses and the partner becomes less of a stranger and more like family, sexual subtype individuals cannot maintain a sexual charge. They cope by changing relationships relatively frequently to maintain their sexual interest or by staying in one relationship and feeling sexually frustrated. Sometimes, they will stay in one relationship to fulfill their need for love but have affairs to fulfill their sexual needs.

Identity

The identity of Love-Sexuality types is based on looks and performance; their highest priority is to look good and perform well. Individuals with this survival style spend their lives compensating for their early heartbreak and rejection by trying to perfect themselves. Having experienced rejection, their mantra becomes, "I will be so perfect, so attractive, that everyone will be drawn to me, and I will never have to face rejection again." They are often driven and demanding and hold high standards of perfection for themselves and others. Their pride-based identifications involve the relentless pursuit of perfection, whereas their shame-based identifications, often unconscious, reflect a sense of hurt, rejection, and feeling flawed.

Doers

A general characteristic of individuals with this survival style is a tendency to do rather than to feel; they distrust emotions. The constant focus on doing helps them stay out of touch with their feelings. They distrust emotions because emotions put them in touch with a level of vulnerability they prefer to avoid. They often consider emotions to be a sign of weakness and can be insensitive to both their own and others' tender feelings.

Relationships

Love-Sexuality types, focusing more on surface image than on the core of the relationship, choose partners who reflect well on them. They like to bathe in the narcissistic glow of their partner's good looks and accomplishments.

Individuals with the Love-Sexuality Survival Style have a tremendous fear of vulnerability. They may be aware of strong feelings of affection for their partner but will show marked restraint in revealing them. When feeling wounded, their rigid pride reveals itself; they wait for their partner to initiate reconciliation. Having invested energy in creating an image of perfection, they fear that nobody could possibly love them if their flaws were revealed. They also fear that they are not capable of loving anyone, and they constantly question whether love is even possible.

Core Fear
- "There is something fundamentally flawed in me."

Compromised Core Expression
- "I love you."

Shame-Based Identifications
- Hurt
- Rejected
- Flawed
- Feeling unloved and unlovable

Pride-Based Counter-Identifications

- "I'll never let anyone hurt me again."
- Reject first
- Self-esteem based on appearance and image
- Perfect, seamless, flawless

Reality

- Love that is conditional upon looks and performance is not love at all

Behavioral Characteristics

- Perfectionistic and critical; impossibly high standards for self and others
- Hard on themselves when they fail to live up to their high standards
- Continually oriented toward self-improvement
- Drawn to working out, plastic surgery, wanting to make their hard bodies even harder
- Mistake admiration for love
- Difficulty feeling heart and sexual connection together; tendency to shut down sexually when heart opens

- Difficulty maintaining relationships
- Sexually acting out—or moralistic, prim, and prudish
- Self-righteous, judgmental, stiff with pride
- Driven, compulsive, rigid, black-and-white thinking
- Orientation toward doing rather than feeling and being
- Sex as their primary way of being in touch with the body
- Seductive, then rejecting; will always reject first
- Base sense of sexual desirability on sexual conquests
- Afraid to open heart: "I'm not sure I even know what love is."
- Competitive
- Fear of surrender; difficulty allowing vulnerability in love relations

Energy
- High energy focused on discharge through motor activity: doers
- Sympathetically dominant

Breathing Pattern
- Armored around the heart

> ***
> **TABLE 6.1:** Key Features of the Love-Sexuality Survival Style

It is important to remember that individuals with the Love-Sexuality Survival Style have experienced intense hurt and rejection. To avoid rejection, they hold back on their impulses to open up and reach out. The unconscious decision they made as children—"I'll never let anyone hurt me like this again"—leads them to reject others before they can be rejected.

GROWTH STRATEGIES FOR THE LOVE-SEXUALITY SURVIVAL STYLE

Individuals with the Love-Sexuality Survival Style come to therapy with concerns about relationships. Either they are unhappy in a current relationship, or they have had a series of less-than-satisfying relationships and feel anxious about whether or not they are capable of having a good relationship.

The following vignette illustrates a classic relationship pattern for individuals with the Love-Sexuality Survival Style.

Robert and Jessica met in their late teens and immediately felt a strong physical attraction and intense sexuality. After dating for nine months, they married, and shortly afterward Robert noticed that he started feeling less sexually attracted to Jessica. Sexual intensity diminished for both of them. The original sexual attraction between Robert and Jessica had been intense and initially involved little heart connection from either of them. As their relationship progressed and heart feelings emerged, the love-sexuality split became more evident.

Jessica became pregnant. After she gave birth, the sexual interest on both their parts diminished even more. Robert related that he continued to love his wife but that she started to feel more like a sister than a lover, and for the first time in his life, he experienced difficulties with potency. Complicating the situation was the fact that as Jessica bonded with her baby, she lost interest in being sexual with her husband. The baby required a lot of her attention, and Robert began feeling left out and resentful. Rather than sharing his feelings with his wife, he had a brief affair. He experienced potency in the affair, which convinced him that his lack of interest in sex was really his wife's "fault." When Jessica found out about the affair, she divorced him.

After the divorce, Robert decided to continue in individual therapy. Over time he came to realize how difficult it was for him to feel both sexual and loving toward the same woman. Robert began to understand his experience of impotency with Jessica from a different perspective. Previously, he had been looking for a mechanical fix. Now he could see that he was not the victim of a random symptom but that his impotence was a message; as soon as he felt emotionally close to a woman, anxiety would emerge and his sexual feelings would diminish. At first he could relate only to his lack of sexual feeling as boredom. He then came to see that his inability to maintain a sexual and loving relationship had to do with a lifelong love-sexuality split that had remained unresolved.

Moving Toward Resolution

The therapeutic task involves helping individuals with the Love-Sexuality Survival Style become aware of their relationship patterns. Projecting their early childhood experience, Love-Sexuality types feel in jeopardy of getting their heart broken if they love deeply. The rejection they fear is both a memory of their early rejection and a reflection of how rejecting they are of themselves. On an emotional level, working through love-sexuality issues involves learning to allow more vulnerability, to open the heart, and ultimately, to surrender.

> - Struggling with a love relationship that has failed provides an opportunity for therapy and growth.
> - Support these clients to move from blaming their partner for the relationship difficulties to seeing their own contribution in the dynamic.

- The emotional work of learning to recognize and allow tender and vulnerable feelings is a central theme.
- Work slowly to support and allow tenderness and vulnerability toward self and others to emerge in these clients.
- Help them deepen their bodily awareness, not just beautify or objectify their body.
- Support mindful awareness of how doing helps them avoid their vulnerability and underlying hurt.
- Help them understand that their constant striving for the idealized self-image actually reinforces the shame-based image of feeling flawed and unlovable.
- Help them understand that love based on looks and performance is not love at all.
- Work with their tendency toward a rigid, black-and-white belief system.
- Work on their ability to feel and open themselves to their heart responses.
- Work on the hidden shame related to sexuality.

- Work toward resolving the split between love and sexuality.

***

TABLE 6.2: Therapeutic Strategies for the Love-Sexuality Survival Style

Growth for Love-Sexuality types involves learning that surrendering to love is not about surrendering to another person but about surrendering to their own feelings. When asked to get in touch with a time in their life when they gave in to their heart feelings, they often remember their newborn child or a pet they deeply loved. When asked to remember the feeling in their body, they describe a melting feeling and a fullness of the heart—which helps them begin to understand "opening the heart" from a different perspective. This can be the first step in a process whereby they come to experience love as its own reward.

Shame about sexuality is present even in the apparently most sexually sophisticated individuals with the Love-Sexuality Survival Style. These clients have to work through the shame about their sexuality to be able to make the final integration. For Love-Sexuality types, integrating love and sexuality in a committed relationship brings the most profound level of vulnerability. The final healing of the love-sexuality split comes as individuals work through the many conscious and unconscious layers of shame that are associated with their sexual feelings and as they learn to integrate their vital sexuality with an open heart.

IN CONCLUSION: THE FIVE SURVIVAL STYLES

The goal of the NARM approach is to help clients experience and live their original core expression and recover their right to life and pleasure. Growth and change happen as connection to the core resources are reestablished and strengthened. In the process of therapy, clients learn how they have incorporated and perpetuated their original environmental failures into their sense of self, body, and behavior in order to survive. Overall:

- *Connection types* learn to see how isolating and life-denying they have become. They learn to acknowledge their own needs and their own aggressive feelings and begin to live more fully in their body.
- *Attunement types* learn how they deny and reject their own needs, giving to others what they want for themselves and, in the process, abandoning themselves. They learn to attune to, express, and allow the fulfillment of their needs.
- *Trust types* experience how they betray not only others but also themselves. They give up their need for control, learn to ask for help and support, and allow healthy interdependency with others.
- *Autonomy types* learn to see how they pressure and judge themselves. Through an increasing capacity to self-reference, they learn to develop their own personal sense of authority and set appropriate limits.
- *Love-Sexuality types* experience how conditional on looks and performance their self-acceptance has been. They

learn to open their hearts and integrate love with a vital sexuality.

The Diminishment of Aliveness in the Five Adaptive Survival Styles

Figure 6.1 presents an outline of the diminishment and distortion of aliveness through each of the five adaptive survival styles. This outline should be read from the bottom up.

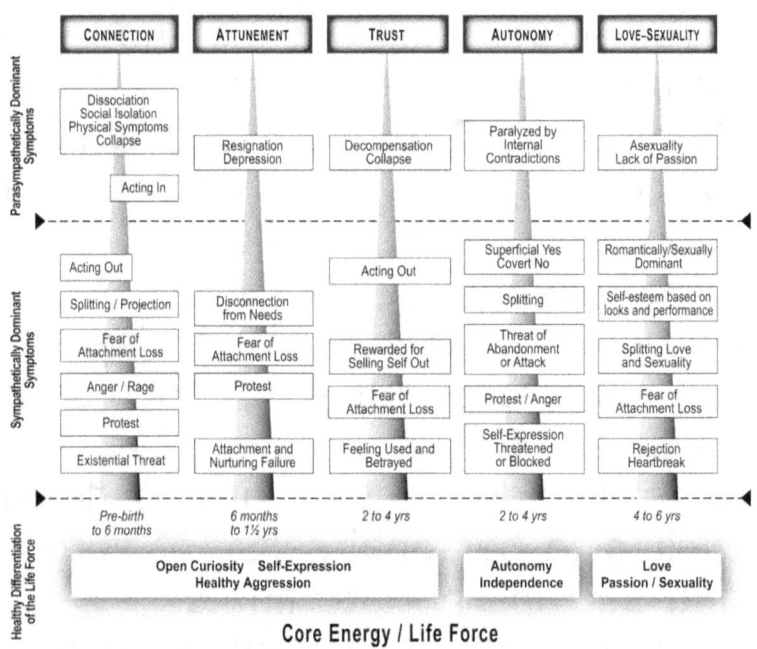

FIGURE 6.1: Distortions of the Life Force in Each of the Five Adaptive Survival Styles

PART B
The Connection Survival Style

7

Physiology and Trauma

Understanding the Impact of Trauma on Development

In the presence of danger, pain, extreme distress, or injury, a number of profound physiological changes ready the body for survival. To understand the core dilemmas of a child experiencing trauma, it is useful to have knowledge of the body's communication and memory systems and of its survival and adaptive mechanisms. For readers who may not be familiar with the basic ways the body organizes, regulates, and remembers its experiences, Section I of this chapter provides a summary of the structure and function of the nervous and endocrine systems and of the memory system. Much of what we present is a simplification of complex functions, but it nevertheless offers an overall template from which to orient our understanding of the physiological organization upon which psychological experience is built. Section II presents an overview of the responses that occur in the face of threat, and Section III discusses the impact of trauma on early life.

There is no doubt that scientific expansion of our knowledge about the brain and body has opened new options for developing more effective clinical treatments. However, it is important to keep a balanced view that takes into account what we know against what we do not yet know. The body is extremely complex and research, as impressive as it is, is limited by available technology. For example, much is known about certain areas of the brain, not necessarily because they are more important but because they are more readily accessible given current research technology.

Even as NARM builds upon physiological and psychological knowledge already gained, it also makes room, through mindfulness, for the body's innate intelligence and its surprising adaptive creativity, which can seemingly miraculously take us beyond what we can consciously and intellectually understand. It is an important NARM value to remain respectful of the body's wisdom, knowing that it goes far beyond what is currently known. It is with this caution in mind that we look into the physiological basis of the foundations of self.

SECTION I: THE BODY'S COMMUNICATION AND INFORMATION NETWORKS

The billions of cells in our human body communicate with each other primarily through two systems: the nervous system and the endocrine system. These two systems are closely allied and cooperate to monitor and regulate the body's many functions. For example, in digestion the nervous system manages the muscular aspects of the process while the endocrine system directly organizes the absorption of nutrients, establishes the secretion and assimilation activities of the cells, and influences the exchanges that take place between the various tissues. The nervous and endocrine systems are the great communicators and regulators of the body and are responsible for maintaining the body's physiological stability or homeostasis.

There is a growing medical realization that most illnesses and diseases are the result of dysregulation and disorganization within the neuroendocrine communication network. NARM's primary principles of tracking connection/disconnection, organization/disorganization, and somatic mindfulness work directly with the dysregulated physiology and the disorganizing repercussions a dysregulated nervous system has on the emotional and psychological self.

The Nervous System

Although there is actually only one nervous system, it can be separated into several divisions based on structure and function. Structurally, the nervous system is seen as having two divisions: the central and peripheral nervous systems. Functionally, it has three roles: to detect information received by our senses and internal organs, to organize that information, and to activate appropriate responses.

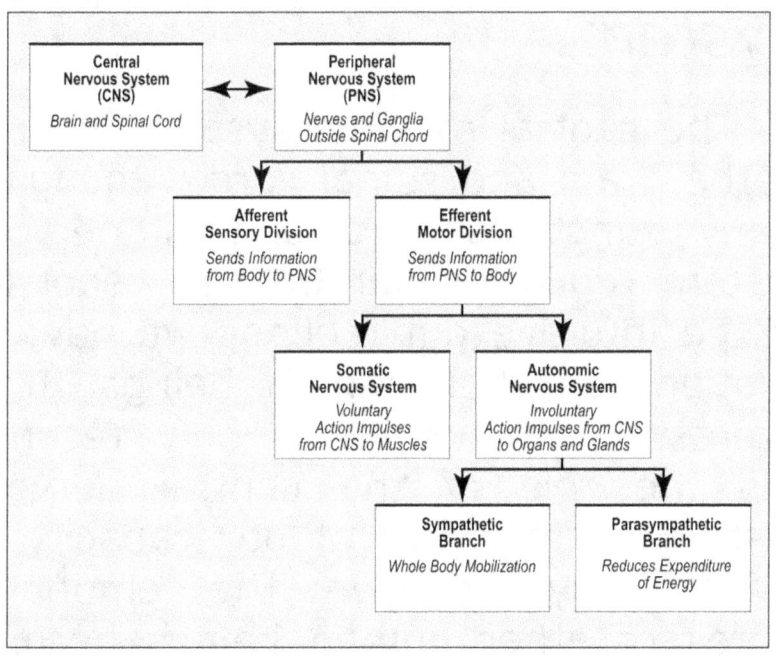

FIGURE 7.1: Schema of the Nervous System

In this section, we first present a short overview of the divisions of the nervous system in order to orient the reader to its complex organization. We then specifically focus on the role of the sympathetic and parasympathetic branches of the autonomic nervous system because of the important role they play in maintaining a regulated physiology and because of the devastating dysregulation that trauma has on their balanced interaction.

The Central Nervous System

The central nervous system consists of the brain and spinal cord. Among its many functions, the central nervous system regulates our body's responses to the intuitive gut feelings we have in relation to other human beings. It is interesting to note that only recently has the role of the central nervous system as mediator of our capacity to empathically perceive the emotional states of other human beings become clear.

The Peripheral Nervous System

The peripheral nervous system consists of the nerves and ganglia outside the brain and spinal cord. Its main function is to connect the limbs and organs to the brain and spinal cord in the central nervous system.

Functionally, the peripheral nervous system comprises two divisions:
- *The afferent sensory division* is responsible for the detection of information in our external environment and internal organs. This division relays the detected information to the central nervous system. The brain then integrates and organizes that information in preparation for appropriate action.
- *The efferent motor division* sends motor information from the central nervous system to various areas of the body so that we can take action. This motor division has two subdivisions:
    - *The somatic nervous system,* whose *voluntary* motor functions are under conscious control. This system relays impulses for action from the central nervous system to the skeletal muscles and skin.
    - *The autonomic nervous system,* whose involuntary motor functions cannot be consciously controlled. It oversees largely unconscious bodily functions, such as heart rate and respiration, and

it mediates, through the vagus system, our capacity for social engagement, trust, and intimacy. This system also relays impulses from the central nervous system to the smooth muscles, cardiac muscle, and glands. Its two divisions, the sympathetic and parasympathetic branches, respond extremely rapidly to the signals they receive from the central nervous system.

The Autonomic Nervous System

Is it good or bad? Is it familiar or unfamiliar? Is it safe or dangerous? The autonomic nervous system evaluates events and people for their survival significance and prepares the body to take appropriate action. Under ideal conditions, the sympathetic branch of the autonomic nervous system initiates whole-body mobilization to get us ready for action. When individuals are under stress, the sympathetic branch of the nervous system prepares them to manage stressful or threatening situations: it initiates the reactions required for aggressive or defensive behavior known as fight-flight responses. It rapidly mobilizes the physiological resources needed to move into action, stimulating involuntary muscular activity and increasing glandular secretions. It elevates blood sugar to increase energy and quickens the heart rate to increase blood supply to the muscles. It dilates the bronchii to increase the breathing rate; dilates the pupils; increases sweating; speeds up mental activity; all actions that ready us to respond to threat.

The parasympathetic branch of the autonomic nervous system modulates sympathetic arousal by reducing the body's expenditure of energy in order to conserve it. It help us rest and regenerate by maintaining the various organs at levels of activity that are most efficient to preserve the body's internal homeostasis. For example, it slows down the heart rate; lowers blood pressure; allows for breathing to return to normal; increases digestion, bowel, and bladder activities; and re-establishes immune functions.

With few exceptions, the organs of the body are innervated by both the sympathetic and parasympathetic branches of the autonomic nervous system. When the sympathetic and parasympathetic branches move in a flowing, reciprocal manner, the body's internal state is said to be regulated. In the relaxed state of autonomic balance, we experience ourselves as steady, strong, present, and at ease. Table 7.1 summarizes the functions of the sympathetic and parasympathetic branches of the autonomic nervous system.

The Polyvagal Theory

There is more complexity to the autonomic nervous system than simply the paired opposition of its sympathetic and parasympathetic branches. The Polyvagal Theory, developed by Stephen Porges, PhD, expands our understanding of the autonomic nervous system by showing how the evolutionary, layered development of our brain and nervous system contributes to our capacity to switch between defensive strategies and a socially engaged sense of safety and connection.

Area of the Body	Sympathetic Stimulation	Parasympathetic Stimulation
Heart	Increased rate and force of contraction	Decreased rate
Smooth Muscles		
Arrector pili muscles	Contraction	No innervation
Digestive tract	Decreased peristalsis	Increased peristalsis
Lungs	Dilation of bronchioles	Constriction of bronchioles
Urinary bladder	Relaxation	Contraction
Eye:		
Iris	Dilation of pupil	Contraction of pupil
Ciliary muscle	No innervation	Contraction to assist near vision
Blood Vessels of		
Salivary glands	Constriction	Dilation
Skin	Constriction	No innervation
Skeletal muscles	Dilation	No innervation
Viscera	Constriction	Dilation
External genitalia	Constriction	Dilation
Glands		
Salivary	Viscous secretion / low enzyme content	Thin secretion / high enzyme content
Digestive tract	Inhibition	Stimulation of secretion
Pancreas	Inhibition	Stimulation of secretion
Adrenal medulla	Secretion	No innervation
Sweat glands	Secretion	No innervation
Liver	Increased release of glucose	No innervation

TABLE 7.1: Sympathetically and Parasympathetically Driven Changes that Occur in the Body in Response to Stress or Threat

Our Bottom-Up Evolution

To grasp the evolutionary dimension of the Polyvagal Theory, as well as the importance of working therapeutically bottom-up and top-down, it is useful to remember that the human brain evolved from the *bottom up,* with the higher centers developing as elaborations of lower, more ancient parts.

Newer brain structures that perform more adaptive functions were built on older structures, keeping those areas that had proved useful and slowly *adding complexity* and sophistication. The human brain and nervous system thus retain features of our reptile, mammal, and primate ancestors. In spite of its layered evolutionary architecture, the healthy brain and nervous system largely operate as an integrated whole.

- First came the *brainstem,* which surrounds the top of the spinal cord and is preprogrammed to regulate bodily processes and vital functions such as the sleep-wake cycle, heartbeat, respiration, and body temperature. The capacity for self-regulation and self-soothing starts at the level of the brainstem, in the dorsal branch of the vagal system.
- Next, our reptilian ancestors developed the *basal ganglia,* responsible for behavioral-motor routines learned from repeated behaviors, which then become automatic. This portion of the brain

makes it possible for us to ride a bicycle or play the piano.
- With the emergence of mammals came a ringlike section surrounding the brainstem called the *limbic* (Latin for ring) *system.* Also called the emotional brain, it is from the limbic system that emotion and the mammalian behaviors of nursing, parental care, and play evolved. The limbic system added powerful tools to upgrade the organism's capacity to adapt to the changing demands of the environment: learning, memory, and the beginning of socialization. In the simplest terms, the emotional limbic system uses pleasurable and unpleasurable stimuli to organize and guide how we respond to the events of our lives. The limbic system impacts the encoding of memory in that personally relevant and emotionally arousing events are more likely to be remembered.
- Finally, the *cortex,* considered the most highly evolved part of the brain, brings in rational thought and the ability to strategize and plan long

term in order to fine-tune the subcortical functions of the limbic system and brainstem. With its capacity to plan for the future, direct attention to a task, regulate affect, and control voluntary movement, the executive *prefrontal cortex* is the most developed area of the cortex. From a cortical perspective, putting our emotional and sensory experiences into words—creating a narrative for the nonverbal subcortical signals as they arise, bottom-up, into awareness—teaches the cortex new ways to relate and respond to sensations and emotions.

Workers, Managers, and Executives

A useful metaphor to illustrate the hierarchy of the brain and nervous system is the organization of a company. In the highly organized "company" that is our body, the working sensory neurons gather information and bring it to the managers in the brainstem and limbic systems, who sort it, store it, and send it on to the appropriate executives in the cortical offices. The executives interpret the incoming information and formulate a plan of action. Once the plan of action is made, the executives send it back to management, who discusses how the plan will be carried out and assigns specific tasks to the working action neurons. This is perhaps an oversimplification, but it serves to illustrate the importance of using both a bottom-up and top-down perspective when working to repair a breakdown in neural communication.

The Polyvagal System

In his groundbreaking work on the autonomic nervous system, Porges emphasizes the phylogenetic emergence of two vagal systems: (1) an older circuit originating in the brainstem involved in the defensive strategies of immobilization such as fainting and dissociation and (2) a newer limbic circuit linking the heart to the face that is involved in both social engagement behaviors and in dampening reactivity in the sympathetic nervous system. These two aspects of the polyvagal system are respectively referred to as the dorsal vagus and the ventral vagus,

and each supports a different adaptive function.
- The *dorsal vagus* is a more primitive, early-developing "reptilian" or "vegetative" structure that oversees our primary defensive survival strategies and drives the freeze response. The dorsal vagus activates the impulse to hide or feign death. It shuts down metabolic activity during immobilization due to extreme terror.
- The *ventral vagus* is a later-developing "mammalian" limbic-based system that modulates sympathetic arousal through social engagement, with the goal of defusing aggression and tension. It provides safety through connection. The ventral vagus supports the ability to communicate via eye contact, facial expressions, tone of voice, and the ability to listen, all of which play important roles in our capacity for social engagement. The ventral vagus also calms the heart: the term vagal tone refers to the regulation of our heart rate. As the heartbeat slows,

we feel calmer and become more available for connection.

The Polyvagal Theory gives insight into the adaptive nature of our physiology. Porges sees the two branches of the vagal system as hierarchical. First, when social engagement is a possible choice, the newer ventral vagus directs our responses. If, however, safety through loving connection is not possible, as is the case with depressed, anxious, or dissociated mothers, the system falls back on the dorsal vagus: vagal tone decreases and the heart rate rises in preparation for survival.

The Polyvagal Theory is particularly useful to help us understand the Connection Survival Style. When there is early trauma, the older dorsal vagal defensive strategies of immobilization dominate, leading to freeze, collapse, and ultimately to dissociation. As a result, the ventral vagus fails to adequately develop and social development is impaired. Consequently, traumatized infants favor freeze and withdrawal over social engagement as a way of managing states of arousal.

This pattern has lifelong implications. On the physiological level, since the vagus nerve innervates the larynx, pharynx, heart, lungs, and the enteric nervous system (gut), the impact of early trauma on these organ systems leads to a variety of physical symptoms. On the psychological and behavioral level, the capacity for social engagement is severely compromised, leading to self-isolation and withdrawal from contact with others, as well as to the many psychological symptoms detailed in Chapters 2 and 8.

Building Blocks of Nervous System Organization

Within the brain are some 100 billion neurons, each capable of synaptic connection with 60,000 to 100,000 other neurons—a tremendous organization of neuronal networks with an almost infinite potential. When new information enters the nervous system, whether of internal or external origin, it activates unique patterns of interconnection, or neural assemblies, that are governed by specific laws. Since much of the work in NARM addresses the regulation of the nervous system, it is helpful to know some of the laws by which the nervous system grows, organizes, regulates, and changes.

Hebb's Law

This law is simple: cells that fire together, wire together. If two neurons are electrically active at the same time, they will automatically form a connection. If they are already weakly connected, the synapse between them will be strengthened. Neural firings gather all aspects of an experience together into a neural assembly that is encoded in memory. Indeed, it is believed that the firing *is* the memory.

This activity-dependent wiring together is the basic mechanism of all learning and adaptation. With new learning comes the growth of new neurons and the branching of dendrites that allow the brain to change and expand the established connections among existing neurons. We can conclude that at the physiological level, supporting growth and healing involves tapping into the processes that build and modify the cells of the nervous system and the firing patterns of neural assemblies. By working bottom-up—by specifically slowing down the pacing of a session in order to give attention to sensations and emotional responses as they are experienced in the moment—a NARM therapist makes room for new learning opportunities that can directly contribute to changing neural connections and building new networks.

Pruning

We are born with an overabundance of synapses, which represents the *potential* connections among neurons that infants might need in order to create internal maps and models of the world. In the neonatal period a pruning process begins: because the development of neural circuits depends on our experience, neural paths that are activated remain, whereas those that are not activated and incorporated into a developing structure are eliminated, leaving only the more adaptive synaptic configurations—a "use it or lose it" rule.

The nervous system is shaped by experience—either pruned or reinforced in response to safety and stress. When stress levels are consistently high, neural pathways connecting the limbic system to the cortex are pruned, while other circuits that are more adaptive to distressing interactions, are formed and strengthened. As a result, the neural landscape becomes vulnerable to emotional and social dysregulation. Adults whose brain and nervous system were patterned by distress at the beginning of life often feel helpless in the face of their symptoms; they do not have the neural circuits to imagine a different way of being. Thankfully, the brain is constantly changing. It is the goal of a resource-based therapy to stimulate and nurture the development of neural circuits that contribute to connection and stability.

Qualia and Reentry

Contrary to popular belief, the brain does not operate like a camera that takes in a whole scene. It is more like a feature detector that detects individual stimuli, (for example, edges, contours, line orientation, color, form, pitch, volume, and movement) and processes them in separate regions of the brain. The term *quale* (plural *qualia)* refers to discreet attributes of reality such as green, round, or hot; the experience of a quale (say, *green)* is generally never in isolation of other attributes *(long, sharp, cool.)* Given the absence of a computer-like central processor in the brain, each quale is processed in *its own separate region of the brain and has its own neural networks.* The experience of qualia is based in the wiring and activity of an individual's nervous system. Each and every perception is actively constructed from the building blocks of individual sensory cues under the guidance and influence of emotion, motivation, and prior experience. How a person experiences qualia is therefore highly personal and is believed to be a large part of what shapes individual consciousness.

Through a process known as reentry, the brain weaves together the information entering in different regions to create a full picture of what is happening. For example, information entering the visual cortex (*dark, red*) is automatically connected to information in the auditory cortex (*loud, sudden*) and vice versa: what we see influences what we hear, and what we hear influences what we see. The attention we give to qualia and our brain's capacity to blend them together comprise our perception of reality. It is believed that reentry could be the *unique, single-most-important feature of higher brain organization,* the vital component of integrated, complex cognitive tasks.

Under normal circumstances, all the aspects of an experience come together into one coherent whole. One of the markers of trauma is the failure to integrate the sensory imprints associated with an event into a coherent whole—a failure of the reentry function. When reentrant interactions are blocked, as they often are with trauma, unprocessed sensory information remains in disconnected fragments. For example, a client may be triggered by the color blue but have no other associations as to why this particular color triggers a stress response. As a result, incomplete memory fragments surface that do not allow sufficient recall for full processing. For a traumatized individual, missing qualia interfere with the capacity to put together a coherent narrative, and certain features of an event may become so prominent as to distort recall.

A number of somatically based interventions address the fragmentation caused by trauma. For example, a simple question such as "What else do you notice?" or "What is happening right now as you talk about this past experience?" encourages clients to open themselves to what may be missing in their recall and to bring back in connection what has been fragmented.

Pattern-Matching

With every new experience, the brain searches for a match between the incoming pattern of neuronal activity and patterns already stored in memory. This pattern-matching quest gives us the sense of recognition and familiarity. In essence, *perception happens through a comparison of past and present.*

Because perception evolved to facilitate adaptive and survival behaviors, economy and speed of processing are critical. The faster the brain detects food, foes, and mates, the better our chances of survival. This need for efficiency prompted the development of a split perceptual system within the brain's architecture.

- For quick survival-based responses, pattern-matching from minimal environmental cues uses the shortest possible route to transmit sensory stimuli directly to the amygdala, which is poised, like an alarm, to activate the body's fight-or-flight hormones. This quick-response emergency route bypasses the executive cortex, sacrificing accuracy and discrimination for speed. In a prey-predator world, this can make the difference between life and death.
- The second perceptual path seeks out detailed features for pattern-matching matching and is consequently much slower. Moving through the more complex executive cortex and on to the hippocampus, this pathway provides the sensory discrimination

that allows us to assess, regulate, and inhibit behaviors that, in the "hands" of the amygdala, are automatic responses based on summary information. This mechanism suggests that conscious awareness helps diminish fear and fight-flight-freeze responses.

The split perceptual system follows a pattern-matching protocol: (1) To minimize effort, the brain makes a quick assessment with just enough detail for a "good-enough" match. If danger is assessed, the amygdala responds to this minimal information. (2) If no match is found, the brain proceeds to seek more information until a match is found. (3) If still no match is found, a new category of experience is generated, the pattern of which is stored in memory for later matching.

Pattern-matching suggests an explanation for people's tendencies to confuse events in the present with events from the past or to repeat past painful experiences. Because the brain initially looks for a good-enough match between past and present events, we tend to jump to conclusions prematurely. We tend to "see" what we have seen before or predict that it will happen again. Neurologically, it is not so much that we repeat the same experience but that we interpret current situations with a bias toward what has occurred in the past. For example, a child, seeing an animal never previously encountered, such as a raccoon, might say "cat" because it fits the general pattern of "furry animal" already stored in memory. However, with conscious focus on detail, a new category of animal will be generated. Greater perceptual accuracy develops by encouraging conscious attention to details in order to create new categories of experience.

It follows that psychotherapy could be conceptualized as a method of treatment that pays conscious attention to increasingly specific details in order to develop greater perceptual accuracy, separate past from present, and, when necessary, generate new categories of experience.

The traumatized, hypervigilant brain forges ahead with pattern-matching before all the data have been gathered.

Traumatized individuals respond to triggering events as if they were being re-exposed to the original trauma, reacting to reminders of the trauma in a physiological way as if they were still living in the past. By mindfully focusing on the present moment, NARM interrupts the quick fight-flight-driven pattern-matching responses and challenges the accuracy of the client's predictive perceptions. By slowing the pace of a client's recall, interventions encourage sensory discrimination that supports a return to the present and a re-evaluation of identifications based on the past.

Windows of Sensitivity

The development of normal perception requires the brain to receive specific kinds of stimulation within particular time frames. For example, during the first year of life, there is a window of sensitivity for the development of attachment that mediates the capacity for self-regulation. Although in early life the brain has specific sensitive periods of development, its growth is thankfully not exclusively limited to these windows. Studies have shown that throughout our lives, repeated new stimuli trigger genes to transcribe and translate new proteins and stimulate the growth of new synapses. Over the life span, every part of the nerve cell can be altered by our ongoing experiences. This "plasticity" suggests that since the receptive properties of the brain and nervous system are clearly not fixed but open to change, providing a stimulus-rich environment is critical to healing. In NARM, the focus on accessing positive resources, supporting inquiry and open curiosity, and tracking the movement of connection, expansion, and aliveness cultivate positive affect and empowering cognitive states that support reconnection with the generative drive of the life force.

Plasticity and Permanence

It appears that the brain strikes a balance between circuit permanence and circuit plasticity. The brain's plasticity is an essential feature of our capacity for learning, change, and adaptation—that is, the solutions we develop to meet the problems posed by our needs.

For functions such as the learning of math facts or new vocabulary, the brain exhibits a lot of plasticity, thus facilitating new learning. However, in the emotional limbic circuits, the brain exhibits more circuit permanence and less plasticity, which stabilizes psychological development. It is because of circuit permanence that children develop long-lasting attachments and that we, as adults, continue to seek out and strongly respond to familiar sources of relational comfort and safety. The brain's plasticity is an essential feature of our capacity to learn and change, and its permanence stabilizes our psychological development, allowing us to establish long-lasting attachments. The brain is a malleable organ whose development and capacity for improvement and change are continuous and lifelong. We are not prisoners of our genes or of our environment, a hopeful message for anyone struggling with the effects of trauma.

The Endocrine System

The endocrine glands produce a chemical network of signals that keeps the entire body under balanced control and regulates vital metabolic activities. The endocrine system balances the delicate equilibrium, growth, and ongoing breakdown and regeneration of cells in the body by regulating the assimilation of nutrients and the elimination of waste. In other words, the maintenance of our health depends on the good function of the endocrine system. Its function is so closely associated with the nervous system that these two systems are often referred to as one: the neuroendocrine system.

Within the endocrine system are major glands located in different areas of the body: the pineal, hypothalamus, pituitary, thyroid and parathyroid, thymus, adrenals, pancreas, testes and ovaries. These glands produce hormones, chemical messengers that travel via the bloodstream to targeted organs carrying information vital to their good function. Each hormone is destined for a specific type of cell, which has a distinctly shaped receptor in which it can "dock." The cell waits for the delivery of the hormone's message to know what to do. If the hormone does not arrive, the cell remains inactive. When a hormone delivers its message, a chain reaction happens inside the cell that allows it to carry on its metabolic functions.

The Stress Response

Hans Selye, MD, PhD, first described the stress response in the 1950s. He introduced the General Adaptation Syndrome model describing how the body responds to external sources of stress and how psychological stress influences physical illness. Selye developed the theory that stress is a major cause of disease because of the long-term hormonal changes stress causes in the body. He determined that the body has a limited supply of adaptive energy with which to deal with stress and that this amount declines with continuous exposure. When there has been trauma, stress levels are chronically high and the body loses its capacity to adapt or recover, leading to adrenal fatigue and exhaustion.

Selye also found that the effects of stress depend not only on the magnitude and duration of the stressor, but also on the strategies individuals adopt to cope with it. This is particularly important to take into account in cases of early developmental trauma, where coping strategies often have not developed beyond those used by a helpless child.

Additionally there is now evidence that when at an early age, individuals become locked in the frozen, parasympathetically dominant state of conservation-withdrawal, the capacity for DNA repair is negatively affected and the vulnerability to illness is increased.

The Hypothalamic-Pituitary-Adrenal Axis

Selye's research clarified the biological consequences of the repeated activation of what has since become known as the hypothalamic-pituitary-adrenal (HPA) axis. He believed that the HPA system is at the core of the stress response.

The HPA axis manages the interaction between the nervous system and the endocrine system. It is useful to understand its function in trauma, since its wide range of functions affect almost every organ and tissue of the body, including the brain. The HPA axis is involved in the neurobiology of mood disorders and many illnesses, including anxiety disorder, bipolar disorder, insomnia, posttraumatic stress disorder, borderline personality disorder, attention-deficit/hyperactivity disorder (ADHD), major depressive episodes, burnout, chronic fatigue, fibromyalgia, irritable bowel syndrome, and alcoholism.

The HPA axis consists of a complex set of interactions among the *hypothalamus* (responsible for linking the nervous system to the pituitary), the *pituitary gland* (which secretes nine hormones that regulate homeostasis), and the *adrenal glands* (small, conical organs on top of the kidneys that release stress hormones). The HPA axis is critical to regulation: it helps regulate body temperature, digestion, the immune system, tissue function, growth and development, mood, sexuality, and energy usage.

In cases of developmental trauma, as neglect and abuse intensify, and as streams of stress hormones signal ongoing danger, the dysregulation of the HPA axis spirals. In a young child's vulnerable brain, not only does the continuous flood of stress hormones have a tragic dysregulating effect, it also deprives the body of the all-important wash of opioids that supports bonding and the feeling that all is well.

The Sympathetic-Adrenal-Medullary System

The mechanisms of the sympathetic-adrenal-medullary (SAM) system prepare the body for the massive output of energy that is required for the fight-flight response. In addition, the SAM response sets in motion the changes necessary for survival should there be injury.

The SAM response triggers a number of far-reaching changes in the body.

The *adrenal medulla* (the center of the adrenal gland) releases the hormones *adrenaline* (epinephrine) and *noradrenaline* (norepinephrine) into the bloodstream. These two hormones, which are potent stimulators of the sympathetic nervous system, are responsible for key changes in the body's homeostasis. Adrenaline and noradrenaline accelerate heart rate and respiration, increase the level of tension in the muscles, constrict blood vessels, divert blood away from the viscera into the muscles, increase blood pressure and blood sugar levels, and reduce gastrointestinal peristalsis. They also trigger pupil dilation, muscle twitching, and trembling; erect the hairs on the skin; and stop the flow of saliva. In anticipation of possible injury, elevated levels of adrenaline in the bloodstream release fibrinogen to speed up blood clotting and signal the brain to release endorphins and other endogenous opioids that are the body's natural painkillers.

These massive fluctuations in the HPA axis and SAM response are often accompanied by strong emotions: rage, disgust, terror or joy and the feeling that all is well. When NARM therapists support tracking changes in body sensations, they are encouraging clients to be present to, and not identified with, the effects of the fluctuations within the endocrine system.

Emotions

The functions of the internal body, more particularly the operation of the viscera—respiration, digestion, blood pressure, temperature control, reproduction, etc., which are all responsible for the maintenance of life—are of critical consequence to the world of subjective emotional experience. There is very little conscious control in the autonomic innervation of the viscera, yet visceral experience is at the core of our sense of identity and our ability to adapt. Infants react to negative emotional arousal by instinctively contracting. They manage high-intensity activation though deep contraction of the viscera and joints and through tension in the eyes, ears, and base of the skull. Adults who developed these patterns in childhood are habituated to them and continue to use these same patterns of muscular tension and visceral contraction throughout life.

Emotional arousal, or when an event overpowers our sense of safety, causes a variety of brain alterations; high levels of emotions, as well as lack of emotion, lead to physical changes that contribute to autonomic dysregulation and psychosomatic disorders.

- In response to external danger, emotional processing shifts away from the frontal cortex, which is responsible for focused attention, motivation, and monitoring of goals, to the posterior cortex, responsible for vigilance.
- Intense emotion and stress-related illness are often accompanied by cognitive complaints such as impaired memory, diminished concentration, and difficulty thinking coherently. Reduced frontal activity seems to contribute to the apathy and lack of concentration associated with disorders such as major depression.
- In chronic states of high autonomic arousal, constant elevated levels of

cortisol can impair the immune system, contribute to ulcer formations, lead to diminished activity or even atrophy of hippocampal cells, and cause damage to body tissues in the viscera and cardiovascular system.
- High emotional arousal can also trigger the physical symptoms of anxiety and panic, such as muscle tension, heart palpitation, increased blood pressure, and difficulty breathing; in turn, the autonomic dysregulation of the lungs and intestinal function may play a role in such conditions as asthma and irritable bowel syndrome.

The list of dysfunctions caused by visceral/emotional dysregulation continues to grow. Obsessions and compulsions seem to be caused by a fixed neural switch in a brain area that monitors the environment for danger; addictions, eating disorders, and alcoholism stem from dysfunction in the brain's reward system. Disorders on the anxiety spectrum (anxiety, panic, phobias), disorders of affect regulation (bipolar, dysthymic), borderline personality disorder, and many others are increasingly seen as rooted in the neurobiologically induced affective chaos that may have its origins in early failures of attachment or breakdowns of the environment. These internal body imbalances draw an individual's attention to his or her internal world and override, sometimes dangerously, his or her ability to tend to the external world.

Memory

Much of what we take for granted as "the way the world is," is in fact the world as we remember it. Remembering is a reconstructive process, and every time we recall a memory, it is received in the brain as new information. Since a retrieved memory is not an exact replica of the past, retelling painful memories from a safe and resourced place opens opportunities to reduce their associated pain. Appropriate titration in the safe context of the present moment and in the presence of an empathic therapist initiates new neural firings that add positive associations into the old memories. These new firings encode feelings of safety and comfort into the traumatic recall, thereby creating opportunities for the modification and transformation of our trauma responses.

Explicit and Implicit Memory

We do not have to be conscious of a memory in order for it to actively influence our thinking, feeling, and behavior. Our long-term memory is divided into two main branches: explicit, or consciously processed memory, and *implicit,* or unconsciously processed memory.

- *Explicit Memory.* Usually, when we think of memory, we think of the explicit branch, which holds all the sights, sounds, smells, conversations, as well as thoughts and images of which we are conscious. It holds personal and general facts that underlie our knowledge of the world—date of birth, who is president—and the autobiographical memory of specific personal events that uniquely define our lives—yesterday's visit to a friend, last year's birthday celebration.

Explicit memory is readily made conscious through images and words.
- *Implicit Memory.* The implicit branch stores information that is out of our conscious awareness and verbal experience. Consequently, even though it constantly influences our current functioning, it does not feel like memory to us. It feels more like who we are. Stored in implicit memory are the memory of shapes and forms; the bodily memory of motor skills, habits, and routines; and the memory of our emotional and relational responses. Because implicit memory is non-conceptual and nonlinguistic, it is difficult to investigate its content with verbal methods. Techniques that use a bottom-up approach and make room for empathic resonance are better suited to explore experiences encoded in implicit memory.

Most authors who address issues of somatization agree that they are rooted in failures of infant-caregiver attunement and that these failures are imprinted in implicit memory. The fundamental relationship between the brain-mind-body, particularly when it comes to the processes that establish the underlying capacity for self-regulation, occur rapidly and autonomously, beneath conscious awareness. It is by facilitating a felt sense awareness that nonverbal experiences can become known, thereby developing the capacity for self-knowledge and organization.

Implicit Relational Knowing

How is it that we instinctively recognize a safe person, and how is it that we know, at a "gut level," the authenticity or falseness of a new acquaintance? Infant observation studies suggest that infants are born with a great High emotional arousal can also trigger the physical symptoms of deal of relational knowing. They show anticipation of contact and are upset with violations of expected loving connection. These types of relational patterns are seen to be true in all infants. This universal human experience is anchored in what is now called implicit relational knowing. As adults, we experience a visceral recognition and sense of heartful expansion during authentic person-to-person connection and a visceral distress when connection fails. The joy that rises in moments of authentic meeting, of meaningful connection, is recognized by all humans as central to the feelings of aliveness that infuse our desire to live. Much of adults' memories of relational trauma involve stories of the outrage they experienced in the face of what they viscerally knew to be a violation of natural goodness.

Emotions, Memory, and Trauma

Transforming what we see, hear, feel, and think into memory is directly related to the degree of attention we give to the information we receive. This degree of attention is in relation to the pleasure or aversion we feel in a given situation. When retrieving a memory, the richness or paucity of the emotions associated with that memory affects the content and quality of what we remember. To grasp the potent hold of emotions on our thoughts, we must remember that the rational cortex is rooted in the earlier emotional limbic system; cortical and limbic brains are inseparably intertwined. In effect, we have two minds—one that thinks and one that feels—the classic duality of the rational head and emotional heart. The emotional brain is the foundation upon which the thinking brain is built.

Although emotional arousal normally enhances our capacity to remember, excessively high levels of emotional arousal impair memory. In the case of severe trauma and posttraumatic stress disorder, high levels of circulating cortisol can cause cell damage or even complete shutdown in the hippo campal system, precipitating impairments in explicit memory. In such cases, traumatized individuals cannot express what happened to them in words, and their memories manifest implicitly as dissociative behaviors, startle responses, nightmares, and visual and somatic flashbacks.

State-Dependent Memory

It has been clearly demonstrated that an experience learned in one context, either inner (mood and emotions) or outer (environment, location), is more easily recalled when we are in a similar inner-outer environment. We are, for example, more likely to recall an event that was encoded in a sad mood if we are feeling sad. The closer the similarity between a memory and the state we are in at the moment of recall, the more the memory is enhanced and the greater the chance that the memory will be relived rather than recalled. This close relationship between the state we are in at the time of encoding and the one at the time of remembering is called state-dependent learning and memory.

When working with trauma, in order to avoid harmful regressions and traumatizing reliving of past experiences, managing state-dependent memory is particularly important. This is why in NARM, the focus on working with the dual awareness of past and present is an important tool to avoid the danger of reliving rather than remembering a trauma.

SECTION II: UNDERSTANDING TRAUMA RESPONSES

In the face of threat, there are predictable biological responses that are shared by humans and animals alike. Here, we describe four major responses that are particularly relevant to developmental trauma: the defensive-orienting response, hypervigilance, the fight-flight-freeze response, and the exploratory-orienting response.

The Defensive-Orienting Response

The defensive-orienting response is nature's first reaction to threat. The following short, guided fantasy, adapted from Somatic Experiencing, helps access the direct experience of the defensive-orienting response. As you go through the exercise, it is important to track your bodily experience and reactions:

Imagine you are home alone, relaxed in bed, reading a book. You are not expecting anyone. Suddenly you hear a very loud noise. What is the first thing that you notice in your body?

Most people report contraction and arousal. This is the startle-arrest response. When faced with possible or actual threat, the body goes into an arrest response: we hold our breath, we become completely still, all extraneous activities stop. We focus attention on our senses, particularly vision and hearing. Usual comments to this exercise are: "I perk my ears up" or "I begin to scan." Why would we do that?

Obviously, we are hardwired to identify the nature of the threat. We want to know what it is and where it is coming from. We use our eyes and ears to orient ourselves to the source of the threat. Primarily using our senses of vision and hearing, we search for the source of the real or possible danger. Why is this important?

Identifying the nature of the threat leads to one of three reactions: fight, flight, or freeze. If actual danger is located, there are three available strategies: fighting the danger, running away from it, or remaining completely still so as to be invisible.

Imagine now that you identify the source of the threat as merely the wind banging a tree limb against the window. What happens in your body now?

You begin to relax. Bodily tension, particularly in your neck, shoulders, and eyes, dissipates. When we realize that there is no threat, there is a return to a state of relaxation.

When the defensive-orienting response remains incomplete in the nervous system, individuals live with a continual sense of threat. In a reaction of hypervigilance, they are constantly looking for danger. Until the defense-orienting response is completed, people can spend their entire lives in this state.

Hypervigilance

When individuals are stuck in an unresolved, persistent defensive-orienting response, they continue to scan the environment for danger even when the external threat is no longer present. This continuous scanning, traditionally called hypervigilance, is the result of an attempt to locate danger, not realizing that the source of the danger no longer exists externally. It is, however, still driven internally by undischarged high arousal in the nervous system. (The related symptom of hypovigilance, which consists of a diminished and inadequate awareness of threat, is discussed later under dissociative reactions.) Individuals with early developmental trauma are more vulnerable to later traumas because of their narrowed range of resiliency and lack of access to their aggression, including the fight-flight response. The more extreme the early trauma, the less resilient they are likely to be, and the more severe their symptoms.

The Fight-Flight-Freeze Response

Essentially, the goal of the fight-flight response is to prepare us to defend ourselves in a situation of threat or to run away if we cannot defend ourselves. The fight-flight response is mediated by *high arousal* in the sympathetic branch of the autonomic nervous system as it prepares the body for self-protection and survival. The freeze response is mediated by the parasympathetic branch of the autonomic nervous system. There are two aspects to the freeze response: (1) freeze as a highly charged but immobile defensive maneuver and protective reaction, which is used by all animals, including humans, to avoid being noticed by a predator and (2) freeze as a collapsed fallback position when fight-flight is not possible.

A common metaphor used to explain fight-flight-freeze is to compare the sympathetic branch of the autonomic nervous system to the gas pedal of a car and the parasympathetic branch to the brakes. In trauma, the sympathetic branch is fully engaged (that is, our foot is pressing the gas pedal to the floor) to mobilize massive amounts of fight-flight survival energy. At the same time, the parasympathetic branch is applying the brakes in an attempt to modulate the dangerously high sympathetic arousal. In essence, both the gas pedal and the brakes are simultaneously pressed to the floorboard. The result is high tonus in both branches of the autonomic nervous system: the engine is turning at high speed but the brakes are fully engaged, leaving the car at a standstill. This standstill involving high tonus in both branches of the autonomic nervous system is a particular type of freeze response called tonic immobility. The state of *tonic immobility* should not be confused with a collapse response, which is a type of freeze in which the parasympathetic branch of the autonomic nervous system is dominant.

The Exploratory-Orienting Response

In the presence of safety, all animals, including humans, return to what is called the *exploratory-orienting response*. Curiosity is the non-traumatized body's natural movement outward as it is motivated by the desire to explore its surroundings when there is no threat or sense of threat. To see the exploratory-orienting response in action, simply observe any healthy toddler, puppy, or kitten. The world is their oyster: they are curious about *everything,* and their exploration is joyful and full of discovery. This state of open curiosity is the normal non-traumatized state. It becomes available again when a person completes the biological sequence of the defensive-orienting response.

SECTION III: THE IMPACT OF TRAUMA ON EARLY DEVELOPMENT

Early trauma is overwhelming, disorganizing, and painful. It creates high levels of systemic arousal and stress that, when ongoing and undischarged, are managed in the body through visceral dysregulation, muscular contraction, and the dissociative processes of numbing, splitting, and fragmentation.

Shock Trauma versus Developmental Trauma

Shock trauma—the impact of acute, devastating incidents that leave an individual frozen in fear and frozen in time—is clinically recognized and treated under the diagnosis of posttraumatic stress disorder (PTSD). In single-event shock trauma, the defensive-orienting response is overwhelmed, completion of fight-flight is not possible, and individuals stay stuck in an incomplete defensive-orienting response. The goal of therapy is to help individuals come out of freeze and complete the fight-flight responses.

Developmental trauma causes ongoing autonomic activation that forms chronic patterns that lead to physiological and psychological developmental deficits. In developmental trauma—which can include specific shock traumas at an early age, profound ongoing misattunement such as in attachment trauma, as well as ongoing abuse and/or neglect—the physiological response may be similar to that in shock trauma, but the dynamics of the trauma itself are quite different. Commonly, with developmental trauma, there is no single traumatizing event, but rather, ongoing experiences of neglect, abuse, and misattunement. The early nature and chronicity of developmental trauma, along with the relational element when parents are the perpetrators, create the therapeutic challenges that are addressed in this book.

Current studies in developmental traumatology show that the cumulative effects of chronic early abuse and neglect adversely influence brain development and negatively impact the nervous system, endocrine system, and memory. Many studies show that trauma of a relational nature is more impactful than trauma from nonhuman or inanimate sources. In fact, it is now believed that severe relational trauma can be so powerful as to override every aspect of an individual's capacity to cope.

Because of the lifelong psychological and physiological deficits that result from relational abuse, neglect, and dysregulated attachment, a new differential diagnosis of developmental trauma is being considered. In a call for this new diagnostic category, Bessel van der Kolk, MD, and others have shown that trauma has its most pervasive impact during the first decade of life. Abused infants and children often experience a broad spectrum of developmental delays, including cognitive, language, motor, and socialization skills. The diagnostic criteria for PTSD is not sensitive to developmental issues and therefore does not adequately describe the effect of ongoing early trauma, abuse, and neglect on child development. Chronic family stressors and relational trauma, particularly early in life, increase the risk for psychological, social, and physiological disturbances whose symptoms and treatment differ significantly from the traditional clinical approach to PTSD. The newly proposed diagnosis of developmental trauma addresses several key aspects unique to *ongoing* trauma occurring early in life. As we demonstrate in this book, developmental trauma can lead to long-lasting changes in neurobiology, behavior, development, and physical health, resulting in identity distortions and systemic dysregulation.

Developmental trauma may well be one of the most important public health issues in the world today. It is estimated that in the United States alone it affects nearly three million children yearly. Because PTSD does not factor in developmental issues, and because developmental trauma is not a recognized diagnosis, children are often misdiagnosed with ADHD and bipolar disorder. Large populations of children who could benefit from treatment are missed, mislabeled, or treated incorrectly based on an inaccurate diagnosis. A recognized diagnosis would open needed avenues of funding for the research and development of appropriate treatments for this critical area of human development.

The Impact of Chronic High Arousal on Early Life

One of the strategies used by animals in response to threat is to run for safety. Animals run to their burrows, flee to their caves or to any other safe place. When infants or small children experience early shock or attachment trauma, the threat is inescapable. Whether the threat is intrauterine or takes place at birth or later in life, there is no possible safety independent of that provided by the caregivers. Infants are completely dependent, and when their caregivers, for whatever reason, are unable to provide safety or are the source of the threat, infants experience the only home they have as unsafe. This sets up a pattern for a lifelong sense that the world is unsafe. *The earlier the trauma, the more global the impact on the physiology and psychology.*

When there has been early trauma and developmental wounding, a person may become "stuck" in the defensive-orienting response. The problem for human beings is that the high arousal that gears us up for fight-flight, when not discharged, creates a sense of threat that triggers more defensive-orienting and sets up an ongoing distress cycle that affects all of the body's systems. Strategies to resolve the sense of threat once real threat has passed, must address the source of the threat that is now in the nervous system itself as well as held in memory and in every cell of the body.

The Effects of Chronic Threat

When threat is chronic, when danger never goes away and there is no possible resolution, as is the case in abusive families, the entire organism remains in a defensive-orienting response and the nervous system remains locked in a state of high sympathetic arousal and vigilance. In cases of early or severe trauma, when infants cannot run from threat or fight back, arousal levels can be so dangerously high that they threaten to overload the nervous system, and often do so. Locked in perpetual, painful high arousal, the only alternative, the fallback position, is to go into a freeze state, which infants and small children accomplish by numbing themselves. Until the defensive-orienting response is completed and the high levels of arousal are discharged from the nervous system, the environment continues to feel unsafe even when the actual threat is gone. Being locked in an unresolved defensive-orienting and freeze response can become a lifelong state, as we see in individuals with the Connection Survival Style.

As Peter Levine, PhD, has documented, tonic immobility and other kinds of freeze responses are intended to be time-limited. When the threat has passed, animals return to normal functioning by allowing their bodies to tremble in order to shake off the high sympathetic arousal. In the face of chronic threat, however, when a fetus, infant, or child remains in a persistent freeze state, he or she is living in a parasympathetically dominant state of collapse. When collapse and threat continue, individuals seek comfort from this unbearable state by detaching their consciousness from their ongoing painful experience. They disconnect from bodily experience and from the threatening environment. This disconnection is the beginning of what can become a lifelong dissociative pattern.

Range of Resiliency

In Somatic Experiencing®, the term *range of resiliency* is used to describe an individual's overall capacity to cope. Included in that definition is a person's capacity to self-regulate and self-soothe. In NARM, range of resiliency also includes a person's access to his or her core energy or basic life force.

High levels of arousal, freeze, and dissociation held in the body foreclose a person's access to his or her life force and create a diminished range of resiliency. The tragedy of early trauma is that when babies resort to freeze and dissociation before the brain and nervous system have fully developed, their range of resiliency becomes drastically narrowed. In addition to the normal challenges of childhood, meeting later developmental tasks becomes that much more difficult. Being stuck in freeze-dissociation, these individuals have less access to healthy aggression, including the fight-flight response. In addition, their capacity for social engagement is strongly impaired, leaving them much more vulnerable and less able to cope with life challenges and later trauma.

Coherence

Coherence refers to how each part of a system behaves in relationship to the others and to the whole. Coherence is a reflection of the positive cooperation within a system and between systems, and is experienced as a sense of ease, organization, and unity throughout the whole body. Coherence is the result of the smooth interplay between various systems of the body and often results from the integration of internal and external resources.

In the context of development, external resources are those elements of our early environment that are experienced as supportive, that help us learn to self-regulate, that provide a sense of safety, meaning, and continuity to our life. Inborn internal resources involve genetic resiliency and general hardiness. Additional internal resources develop as a result of supportive positive life experiences.

As children develop, internal resources and the availability of ongoing external resources progressively support coherency and organization on all levels of being. Individuals who are unable to integrate their traumatic experiences often lose their capacity to assimilate new experiences, and their development stops at a certain point. The psychological consequence of trauma is the breakdown of the adaptive processes that normally lead to the maintenance of an integrated coherent, continuous, and unified sense of self.

Traditional psychology focuses on the importance of a coherent narrative. Understanding that a coherent narrative is a reflection of somatic coherence helps develop a positive healing cycle in which increasing somatic coherency supports an increasingly coherent narrative bottom-up, and an increasingly coherent narrative reinforces somatic coherency top-down.

COHERENCE	ACTIVATION
Breath is slow and deep	Breath is rapid and strained

No bracing in muscles	Muscles are braced or slack
Breath moves through whole body in steady rhythmic wave	Breath is disconnected and does not flow between body areas

TABLE 7.2: Some Physiological Markers of the Differences between Coherence and Activation

CONCLUSION

NARM is a scientifically informed approach to the experience of self, embodied self, and self-in-relationship. Through the use of somatic mindfulness, NARM calls upon the body's natural regulatory mechanisms to support the brain's relationship to and interpretation of sensory experience. Somatic mindfulness is a bottom-up, nonverbal skill for self-reflection that helps us examine the internal relationships between body, brain, and self. It supports being present to, but not identified with, shame- and pride-based identifications. By exploring the links between our in-the-moment conscious experience and our unconsciously held in-the-gut encoded memories, NARM supports the capacity for regulation. By helping clients build tolerance for stress and increased levels of arousal, NARM seeks to expand the neural networks of descending and ascending communication that organize experience. In this way we can better know what we are feeling about our thoughts and what we think about our feelings.

NARM principles, tools, and techniques, described in Chapter 10, contribute unique approaches to stabilizing nervous system activation by encouraging new neurological connections, facilitating neural interconnectivity, and nurturing neurological deficits. For example, by making resourcing central to NARM therapy while supporting greater compassion for ourselves and others, treatment is delivered in a context of support, accessing the brain-building capacity of positive experiences. Many of the disorders that have been seen as purely psychological are now being reframed to include neurobiological correlates and mechanisms. Taking into consideration that trauma can damage the brain itself, NARM supports the development of skill-building techniques that bring organization and regulation to impaired functioning.

8

The Beginning of Our Identity

Understanding the Connection Survival Style

When there is early trauma, the ensuing biological dysregulation forms the shaky foundation upon which the psychological self is built.
When individuals have had to cope with early threat and the resulting high arousal of unresolved anger and incomplete fight-flight responses, adaptive survival mechanisms develop on every level of experience: behavioral, emotional, relational, physical, and physiological. The seemingly diverse issues presented in Table 8.1 reflect some of the many symptoms that an individual with the Connection Survival Style may develop. These varied symptoms reflect the systemic dysregulation and developmental posttraumatic stress that affect people

who experience early trauma. As we will see, this systemic dysregulation disrupts the capacity for connection and social engagement and is the thread that links the many physical, emotional, behavioral, and cognitive symptoms of individuals who have experienced early developmental/relational trauma.

Early trauma and its associated physiological dysregulation are often at the root of psychological difficulties such as low self-esteem, chronic anxiety, and depression. The conscious and unconscious shame-based identifications that result from early trauma center around feelings of not belonging, of feeling unwelcomed, rejected, unlovable, bad, wrong, and even sometimes alien or not quite human. Individuals with the Connection Survival Style experience themselves as outsiders, disconnected from themselves and other human beings. Not able to see that the traumatic experiences that shaped their identity are due to environmental failures that were beyond their control, individuals with this adaptive survival style view themselves as the source of the pain they feel.

Individuals with early trauma experience symptoms on a continuum of less to greater dysfunction depending on the degree of trauma and the coping survival strategies they have developed. Since early trauma is more widespread than commonly recognized, most adults are affected by some elements of the Connection Survival Style. Those on the more symptomatic end of the continuum have experienced years of emotional struggle as well as many challenging physiological problems. Their efforts to understand and come to terms with their deep-seated physiological and emotional distress often leave them filled with shame and self-hatred. Individuals with less obvious features of this survival style may not consciously realize that they experience a diminished capacity for joy, expansion, and intimate relationship. If they are aware of their difficulties, they usually do not understand their source. Managing the physiological and psychological fallout of early trauma can require so much energy that there is often not enough left over to enjoy life. Early trauma is difficult and confusing not only for those who have experienced it but also for those who treat it.

THE BEGINNING OF OUR IDENTITY

In NARM, Connection is the name given to the first stage of human development and the first organizing life principle. The degree to which we feel received, loved, and welcomed into the world makes up the cornerstone of our identity. When our capacity for connection is in place, we experience a right to be that becomes the foundation upon which our healthy self and our vital relationship to life is built. The Connection Survival Style develops as a way of coping with early shock, developmental and/or attachment trauma, and as a result of feeling unloved, unprotected, and unsupported in the first stage of life. In reaction to trauma, infants experience their environment as threatening and dangerous; their reaction is to cling to others or to withdraw into themselves. Their capacity to enjoy life is compromised from the very beginning, and as a result, they do not develop a full sense of self. Early trauma compromises their sense of safety, their right to exist and be in the world, and their capacity for connection. Therefore, they do not learn what it feels like to have a sense of self, to be connected to their body, and they are left frightened of intimate connection.

Do you prefer to recharge your batteries by being alone rather than with other people?	Yes	No
Did you need glasses at an early age?	Yes	No
Do you suffer from environmental sensitivities or multiple allergies?	Yes	No
Do you have migraines, chronic fatigue syndrome, irritable bowel syndrome, or fibromyalgia?	Yes	No
Did you experience prenatal trauma such as intrauterine surgeries, prematurity with incubation, or traumatic events during gestation?	Yes	No
Were there complications at your birth?	Yes	No
Have you had problems maintaining relationships?	Yes	No
Were you adopted?	Yes	No
Do you have difficulty knowing what you are feeling?	Yes	No
Would others describe you as more intellectual than emotional?	Yes	No

Do you have disdain for people who are emotional?	Yes	No
Are you particularly sensitive to cold?	Yes	No
Do you often have the feeling that life is overwhelming and you don't have the energy to deal with it?	Yes	No
Do you prefer working in situations that require theoretical or mechanical skills rather than people skills?	Yes	No
Are you troubled by the persistent feeling that you don't belong?	Yes	No
Are you always looking for the why of things?	Yes	No
Are you uncomfortable in groups or social situations?	Yes	No
Does the world seem like a dangerous place to you?	Yes	No

TABLE 8.1: Recognizing the Symptoms of Early Trauma

The identity of adults with early trauma is shaped by the distress and dysregulation they experienced in early life. Our earliest trauma and attachment experiences form a template for lifelong psychological, physiological, and relational patterns. Difficulties in the initial Connection stage of development undermine healthy psychological progression through all later stages of development, impacting self-image, self-esteem, and the capacity for healthy relationships. Trauma in the Connection stage becomes the basis for diverse cognitive, emotional, and physiological problems. Table 8.2 lists common sources of the two principle kinds of early trauma: developmental/relational and shock trauma.

The Distress Cycle in the Connection Stage

During this first stage of life, the fetus and infant are completely dependent on caregivers and on a benevolent environment. As a result of this complete vulnerability, an infant's reaction to early developmental or shock trauma is one of overwhelmingly high arousal and terror. The vulnerable infant, who can neither fight nor flee, cannot discharge the high arousal and responds to threat with physiological constriction, contraction, core withdrawal, and immobility/freeze. Anyone who has pricked an amoeba and seen it contract and close in on itself has witnessed this process of contraction and withdrawal. As with all living organisms, constriction, contraction, withdrawal, and freeze are the primitive defense mechanisms infants utilize to manage the high arousal of terrifying early trauma. In the infant, this combination of high arousal, contraction, and freeze creates systemic dysregulation that affects all of the body's biological systems. The underlying biological dysregulation of early trauma is the shaky foundation upon which the psychological self is built.

Early Developmental and Shock Trauma Held in Implicit Memory

Both early attachment failures and shock trauma before an infant is six months old can have a lifelong impact on an individual's health and capacity for relationship. Neuroscience confirms that early trauma is particularly damaging. Since the hippocampus is responsible for discrete memory, when trauma occurs early in the development of the neocortex and before the hippocampus comes online, many individuals show symptoms of developmental posttraumatic stress *yet have no conscious memories of traumatic events.* Early trauma is held *implicitly* in the body and brain, resulting in a systemic dysregulation that is confusing for people who exhibit symptoms of traumas they cannot remember. It is equally confusing for the clinicians who want to help them.

Early Events That May Cause Long-Term Traumatic Reactions

From Conception to 6 Months after Birth (partial list)

Attachment and Developmental Trauma
- Being carried in the womb of a mother who does not want you
- Being carried in the womb of a traumatized, dissociated, depressed, or anxious mother
- Serious consideration of abortion
- Mother abusing alcohol or drugs during the pregnancy
- Feeling rejected, blamed, or even hated by one or both parents

- One or both parents struggling with Connection issues themselves
- Attachment attempts with a dissociated, chronically depressed, anxious, or angry mother
- A psychotic or borderline mother
- Being made to feel like a burden
- Physical or emotional abuse
- Neglect
- Adoption

Shock Trauma
- Attempted abortion
- Mother's death in childbirth
- Premature birth
- Long, painful delivery
- Extended incubation with insufficient physical contact
- Early surgeries
- Significant traumatic events for the mother or other members of the family
- Death in the family
- Traumatic loss and bereavement
- Being born into wartime, depression, significant poverty
- Intergenerational trauma such as being born to Holocaust survivors
- Natural disasters

> ***
> **TABLE 8.2:** Early Sources of Trauma

The internal experience of adults traumatized in the Connection stage is one of constant underlying dread and terror. Whether conscious or unconscious, dread and terror are always in the background of their experience. In the adult with the Connection Survival Style, the nervous system has remained in a continual sympathetically dominant global high arousal. It is this global high arousal that drives and reinforces their profound and persistent feeling of threat. The sense of threat, together with the feeling of danger and lack of safety that accompany it, trigger hypervigilance (an incomplete defensive-orienting response): ongoing feelings of high arousal, lack of safety, continuous sense of danger, and hypervigilance function together in an interconnected closed system, one reinforcing the other. Although not as obvious, individuals who have collapsed into freeze and dissociation have the same underlying levels of high arousal.

The lifelong impact of early trauma is generally underestimated by medical and psychological professionals. It was not long ago that physicians believed that infants, because they have no explicit memory until about eighteen months of age, would not remember any early trauma that happened to them. From today's perspective, it seems bizarre that it was only in 1988 that the American Medical Association first officially recognized that infants feel pain. As a result of the belief that infants do not remember trauma and do not experience pain, surgeries performed on neonates often involved curariform paralysis using a medication that kept these young patients from moving but did not deaden their pain. Children exposed to this kind of experience felt pain and panic while frozen and helpless. Although this kind of surgical trauma is extreme and no longer happens, it is important that parents and medical professionals not underestimate the effects of early surgeries and other traumas on a young child's nervous system and identity.

THE IMPACT OF EARLY TRAUMA

It is useful to distinguish four phases during which traumatic experiences form the Connection Survival Style: (1) prenatal trauma and prenatal attachment; (2) birth trauma; (3) perinatal trauma; and (4) attachment and relational trauma, which include neglect, abuse, and ongoing threat. Each phase flows into and influences the next. Early trauma impacts the body, nervous system, and developing psyche, and its effects are cumulative. Trauma experienced in an early phase of development makes a child more vulnerable to trauma in later phases of development. For example, prenatal trauma can make birth more difficult, and a traumatic birth can affect the subsequent process of attachment.

The topics of prenatal and perinatal trauma, neglect, abuse, and adoption would require books of their own to do them justice. This chapter can only highlight some of the significant elements in each of these areas and describe how they are relevant to the development of the Connection Survival Style.

Symptoms that are present in varying degrees when there is trauma in the first four phases of development are:
- A sense of constant threat
- High arousal
- A thwarted fight response
- Freeze-dissociation
- Numbing, splitting, fragmentation
- Acting in and acting out of aggression
- Diminished aliveness

It is important to understand that these symptoms may occur simultaneously, loop back upon themselves, and continuously reinforce one another.

Prenatal Trauma and Prenatal Attachment

The prenatal period is one of the least understood yet most significant phases of human development. Within a period of nine months, growth proceeds from a single cell to a fully formed infant. Until recently, the gestation process was viewed as primarily genetically determined, and prenatal development was considered to be relatively immune to external influences. As technology has advanced, a more sophisticated examination of the gestation process has become possible. It is now apparent that birth is not the beginning of a baby's awareness, and that events in utero, both physiological and psychological, influence future development. It is now known that environmental influences, including the mother's capacity to attach to her unborn baby, affect the developing fetus.

Attachment Theory has focused on the relationship of the mother and infant after birth. Prenatal and perinatal specialists have been working to extend this focus to include the importance of the attachment process and other environmental influences before birth. Women have intuitively known for thousands of years that experiences during pregnancy impact their developing fetus. It is only recently that scientific evidence supports what women have always known.

The Impact of Family and Environment on Fetal Development

Factors in prenatal trauma include:
- The mother's emotional and physiological health
- The mother's relationship to her own pregnant body and to her developing baby
- The relationship of the father to the pregnancy
- The atmosphere in the family
- The relationship between the mother and father
- The wild card of fate, such as being born in wartime

When persistent biological distress is part of fetal development, the distress is held in implicit memory at the core of that individual's experience. Prenatal psychobiological distress often underlies persistent anxiety and depressive states that have no other obvious etiology and are an important characteristic of the developmental posttraumatic stress disorder that affects individuals with the Connection Survival Style.

The womb is the universe for the fetus, the first experience of existence. Initially, it was thought that the womb formed a barrier that kept the fetus safe from influences that could harm its development. However, the thalidomide tragedy of the 1950s proved this to be false. Thalidomide was a tranquilizer/sedative thought to be safe for pregnant mothers. Its toxic effect was dramatic: it resulted in the birth of children with severe limb abnormalities. The thalidomide tragedy forced the realization that the fetus could be severely *physically* traumatized in utero and its development permanently affected by external influences.

In 2005, *The Journal of Clinical Endocrinology and Metabolism* published a seminal study by Yehuda et al. documenting the transmission of posttraumatic stress disorder (PTSD) directly to the fetuses of pregnant women exposed to the World Trade Center attack. Women who were diagnosed with PTSD, as identified by specific biological markers, gave birth to infants who showed the same biological markers. This study clearly documents that a mother's psychological and physiological experiences influence the fetus in the womb and impact its development. The empirical data of Yehuda et al. support the reality of prenatal trauma and have developmental implications that can be expanded beyond obvious shock trauma events such as 9/11. If a mother is chronically depressed, angry, anxious, dissociated, or exposed to continuous stressors during pregnancy, the experience has an effect on the baby. Additionally, physiological stressors, such as drugs, alcohol, and even dietary deficiencies, create distress in the mother's system. The fetus reacts to the mother's states of distress with its own distress. The only way the fetus can cope when mother experiences chronic distress states is by going into contraction, withdrawal, and freeze. Instead of an expansive nurturing environment, the womb becomes a toxic, threatening place in which the fetus is trapped. Biological distress lies at the foundation of psychological distress. *Early chronic physiological distress undermines subsequent psychological development, creating psychological symptoms that may not become apparent until later in life.*

Having experienced prenatal trauma, the nervous system of an individual with the Connection Survival Style develops around a core contraction/withdrawal and freeze/paralysis response. The fetus, as is seen clearly in videos taken in utero, goes into physiological contraction and withdrawal when it experiences stress or threat. The contraction/withdrawal reflex and the related fear/paralysis reflex are part of nature's wisdom and a defensive capacity shared by animals and human alike. Even one-celled amoebas visibly contract and withdraw into themselves when pricked by a pin. The intensity and duration of withdrawal increase with repetition and the chronicity of threat. This point is relevant to the experience of the fetus when it endures chronic and repeated stressors. Because the fetus goes into a parasympathetically dominant freeze state before the nervous system is fully formed, physiological resiliency is impaired and subsequent psychological resiliency does not develop adequately.

The disturbance at this stage is global and is referred to in Somatic Experiencing® (SE) as global high intensity activation (GHIA). GHIA is understood in SE to refer not only to activation in the autonomic nervous system but also in the central nervous system. In NARM, we use this term to include all the major systems of the body. GHIA affects every system and every cell within these systems: skin and connective tissues, brain chemistry, organ systems, nervous and endocrine systems, and the immune system.

Birth Trauma

Birth trauma has been widely researched and written about. The emphasis in this book is not to elaborate on what has already been written, but to point out that unresolved birth trauma and the resulting coping mechanisms leads to the development of the Connection Survival Style. As with prenatal trauma, traumatic birth experiences, such as being born with the umbilical cord wrapped around the neck, lengthy painful delivery, Cesarean birth, forceps delivery, and breach birth, can trigger profound threat reactions of high arousal, contraction/withdrawal, and fear/paralysis responses in the newborn, all precursors of the Connection Survival Style.

Premature Birth

Even with loving parents who are fully capable of strong attachment, trauma can find its way into an infant's life. Historically, incubation for premature infants was itself the source of profound trauma. Tragically, until relatively recently, it was not known that premature infants needed significant, caring physical touch and that touch has a powerful organizing impact on the nascent organism. As a result, in the past, babies were left in their incubator without adequate nurturing touch. Although loving parents can mitigate such a traumatic beginning, the effects of inadequate contact can remain in the physiology and psychology of the developing child and later, in the adult.

Traumatic Symbiosis

Margaret Mahler, MD, used the expression *dual unity* to describe the early period of development in which mother and child are merged in such a way that they function as one. Following Mahler's thinking, and consistent with Yehuda et al.'s research, NARM holds that in the merged state between mother and baby, there is an energetic exchange wherein even subclinical states of chronic depression, anxiety, and dissociation in the mother leave physiological traces in the baby's core experience. NARM uses the term *traumatic symbiosis* to describe this process, which impacts the physiology and in turn the psychology of the developing baby. The understanding of traumatic symbiosis informs later clinical interventions. Much of the distress that adults with the Connection Survival Style describe is really only partly their own distress and often is the result of maternal distress and other environmental failures.

Perinatal Trauma

Attachment Theory, beginning with John Bowlby and continuing to the present day, focuses on the importance of successful early attachment for the development of the capacity for healthy relationships. The focus in this chapter is to elaborate on how inadequate attachment, particularly during the first six months of life, is experienced as traumatizing. We include coping with attachment trauma as one of the primary precipitating factors in the development of the Connection Survival Style. As Daniel Siegel, MD, and Mary Hartzell communicate in their book *Parenting from the Inside Out:*

> For those whose histories included a sense of emotional unavailability and a lack of attuned, nurturing parenting, there may have been an adaptation that minimizes the importance of interpersonal relationships and the communication of emotion.... As this adaptive response continues, children may have a decreased connection not only to their parents but to other

people as well.... In addition there may be a decreased access to and awareness of their own emotions. (pp.134–135)

Attachment and Self-Regulation

Although there is valuable confirmation and support from the neurosciences on the impact of inadequate attachment and attachment failure on the brain, there has been a significant disconnect between neuroscientifically based Attachment Theory and somatically oriented psychotherapies. Since re-regulation is best supported by referencing the body, and since the importance of the body is often not understood in traditional therapies, this lack of somatic understanding limits the effectiveness of many current clinical interventions. NARM attempts to bridge this gap by grounding Attachment Theory in bodily experience and working with the mindful awareness of adaptive survival styles.

Infants need loving parents in order to learn to regulate the various forms of arousal their vulnerable nervous system experiences. A mother must be able to respond to and match her infant's positive emotions and join in the joy and excitement of their shared play. It is through these attuned interactions that children develop secure attachments and acquire the resources and autonomic resiliency that lead to a capacity to live life fully. Resources and autonomic resiliency will help individuals effectively cope with the later challenges and traumas that life brings. It is through loving contact that infants learn to modulate their levels of arousal and through which the capacity for social engagement develops. Ideally, the infant learns autonomic self-regulation from attuned mothers and caregivers who provide a framework for successful attachment. Unsuccessful attachment, neglect, and the absence of loving connection are traumatic and leave a legacy of impaired capacity for self-regulation that can last a lifetime.

The Interplay of Shock and Developmental Trauma

In the earliest stages of development, there is a continuous interplay between shock trauma and developmental trauma. Shock traumas, including early surgery, an infant's or mother's illness, death in the family, and global events such as being born into wartime, have a disruptive effect on the attachment process. In these situations infants are affected not only by the shock itself, but also by how the shock negatively impacts the attachment process.

An example of the interplay between shock and developmental trauma can be seen in infants who have experienced prenatal trauma. At birth the already-traumatized infant is in a disorganized and dysregulated state. Studies show that it is more difficult for a mother to bond with a distressed baby. A traumatized infant presents the mother with significant regulation and attachment challenges that do not exist in a non-traumatized newborn.

Relational Trauma: Neglect, Abuse, Ongoing Threat

Some infants are born to parents who do not have the maturity or capacity to properly care for them.

Other infants and children are blamed and made responsible for their parents' frustrations, pain, and unresolved psychological issues.

When parents are emotionally inaccessible, neglectful, or abusive, infants respond to the ongoing negative relationship with a sense of threat and high arousal. Infants with neglectful and abusive parents live in ongoing dysregulated states that severely tax their developing nervous system. Early relational trauma has a serious impact on the infant's capacity for connection. In infants, states of threat and distress are expressed through crying and screaming, reflecting sympathetic hyper-arousal that is accompanied by elevated levels of stress hormones. Not only is the attachment process severely disrupted, but the developing brain is affected at a critical formative period. The effects of early relational trauma leave infants without resources for self-regulation and at the mercy of distressed and disorganized states that are the precursors of the Connection Survival Style.

The Unwanted Child

Unfortunately, some infants are born to parents who do not want them and openly reject them. They are seen as an imposition; their very existence is rejected. When infants experience such profound rejection, they internally withdraw, collapse, and fail to develop the necessary neural pathways for connection. Babies manage such rejection by limiting or shutting down their aliveness and by dissociating. The impact of growing up in a family where they feel hated creates an impossible challenge, and they react to the ongoing threat by disconnecting both from the environment and from their internal experience, engaging the primary adaptive mechanisms of the Connection Survival Style.

The Abused Child and the Hated Child

Children who grow up in an atmosphere where there is continuous threat of physical and/or emotional abuse, or those who are on the receiving end of real hatred, cannot flee and cannot fight back. When the caregivers who are supposed to love and protect them are the source of threat, an impossible dynamic is created. The child's only option is to freeze and dissociate, a pattern that develops into the Connection Survival Style and continues into adulthood.

Children who are hated learn to hate themselves. Children on the receiving end of rage and abuse have the dual challenge of needing to endure both the terror of abuse and the impossible dilemma of managing their own rage toward the parents they also love. The normal biological response to abuse and threat is deep rage and a powerful fight response. When the object of that rage is the beloved parent upon whom the child is completely dependent, children's fear of their own rage adds to the sense of threat. In order to protect themselves and the attachment relationship children split off their rage and hatred. It is life saving to use splitting as a survival mechanism, but this adaptation comes at a great price. The child's need to protect the image of the parent by becoming the "bad object" can leave a lifelong legacy of shame.

Splitting off rage is a powerful energetic process resulting in diminished access to strength, self-assertion, self-expression, and the life force itself (see Figure 1.2). Usually, the split-off rage is turned against the self, creating a wide range of symptoms. When abuse is persistent and ongoing, the splitting and disconnection trigger the adaptations of the Connection Survival Style.

Neglect

Neglect is often a more challenging traumatic experience than is overt abuse. Neglect is the absence of necessary elements for life rather than the presence of definable threat. Insufficient holding, attunement, nourishment, attachment, and touch are experienced as a profound but undefinable threat.

When there is early neglect, it is held in implicit memory in the brain and body and becomes one of the core psychological features of individuals with this early survival style. At first, when needs are not met, infants will protest, but when neglect of basic needs is chronic, infants resign themselves and physiologically shut down. Traditionally, the term failure to thrive is used to describe infants who perish from neglect, such as the infants left untouched in Romanian orphanages. Individuals who experience neglect and survive do so by disconnecting from their bodies, going into freeze and dissociation.

Adoption

It is not unusual for individuals who were adopted to develop the Connection Survival Style as a way of adapting to early trauma and loss. Adoption presents the infant with particular challenges; it is not just the trauma of separation after birth that affects the infant. The trauma of adoption can begin prenatally when the mother does not emotionally attach to her developing fetus. The need of adopted adults to seek out their biological parents can be explained at least in part as a way of trying to come to terms with early attachment trauma and the associated feelings of disconnection. Being placed in a foster home for a significant length of time before being adopted or repeatedly being passed on to different foster homes can be the source of significant attachment trauma. Adoptive mothers may feel rejected by their traumatized infants' inability to attach, which in turn may cause them to withdraw from their infant in subtle or overt ways. Early placement into a loving family can mitigate previous attachment trauma. Nonetheless, clinicians who work with adults who were adopted as infants will recognize the dysfunctional relational patterns that sometimes remain in place for adoptees even when their adoptive families were quite loving and capable of healthy attachment.

THE CONNECTION SURVIVAL STYLE: THE ADULT EXPERIENCE

When early life experience has been traumatic, the trauma lives on in the form of ongoing high-arousal states in the nervous system. Unresolved high arousal becomes the source of a relentless, nameless dread, a continuous sense of impending doom that never gets resolved. Since early trauma is fairly commonplace, most adults experience some elements of the Connection Survival Style. The following descriptions focus on the more severe end of the continuum but nonetheless are relevant to most of us.

Adults who develop the Connection Survival Style are engaged in a lifelong struggle, conscious or unconscious, to manage their high levels of arousal. They struggle with dissociative responses that disconnect them from their body, with the vulnerability of energetic boundary rupture, and with the psychological and physiological dysregulation that accompany such struggles. As a result of having gone into freeze at an early age, the infant, child, and later the adult is left with a narrowed range of resiliency and a compromised capacity for self-regulation. Individuals feel awkward within themselves and shy away from social contact: they narrow their lives in order to avoid stress and manage their anxiety.

Physically, adults with the Connection Survival Style present with diminished aliveness, sometimes with a lifeless, absent look and at other times with a chronically fearful look. Overall, individuals with the Connection Survival Style have a frozen, under-energized appearance—pallid complexion and a lack of vibrancy, passion, and fire. Underneath this shut-down exterior is an extremely sensitive, often hypersensitive being. Their bodies are braced, contracted, and tight. The psychological fragmentation they experience can be observed in their body as an overall underdevelopment and lack of symmetry.

Identifying the Organizing Life Principle

Individuals with the Connection Survival Style often feel relief at understanding that their difficult symptoms have a common thread, what we call *an organizing principle.* Their struggle with high levels of anxiety, psychological and physiological problems, chronic low self-esteem, shame, and dissociation with its related difficulties all constellate around the organizing principle of connection—the simultaneous experience of both the *desire* for connection and the *fear* of connection.

On the more extreme end of the spectrum are individuals who have no conscious desire for connection. Connection is experienced as threatening, and connection with emotions and the bodily self is experienced as painful and uncomfortable. Nonetheless, no matter how deeply out of consciousness the desire for connection is buried, it is always there. Since the need for connection is at the core of our human existence, individuals who are no longer in touch with this need—and even seemingly experience the opposite need to disconnect—have had to shut down the most basic element of their humanity. As a result, the more disconnected individuals are from their desire for connection, the more psychologically and physiologically symptomatic they tend to be. Low self-esteem and poor self-image; pathological shame and guilt; phobias;

anxieties, including a generalized fear that something bad is going to happen; and many other symptoms are commonly experienced by individuals struggling with the Connection Survival Style. It is essential to understand the organizing life principle of connection to work effectively with these seemingly diverse symptoms.

Distress in Search of an Explanation

Early trauma creates profound distress and disorganization in the nervous system on all levels of bodily function and ultimately leads to distortions of identity. The relentless overall feeling that something bad is going to happen reflects the reality that something bad has already happened and is being carried forward unconsciously.

Nameless Dread

Individuals with the Connection Survival Style create specific content to name the feeling that something bad is going to happen, a state of hypervigilance characterized in NARM as nameless dread. A named and identified threat is better than nameless dread. Naming and creating a narrative for the nameless dread is the Connection individual's attempt to explain the internalized arousal resulting from early trauma. These attempts can be seen in such symptoms as chronic shame, diverse phobias, and pathological fear of death, to name but a few.

The diverse fears, elaborate rituals, and obsessive thinking that characterize obsessive-compulsive disorder (OCD) can be understood through the prism of this mechanism as an attempt to name and manage nameless dread. There is relief in seemingly identifying the source of a nameless dread. People with OCD, not being consciously aware of the profound high arousal in their nervous system, find a certain comfort in identifying a threat: "If I shake hands, I'll get germs and get sick"; on hearing a loud thump while driving—"Did I just hit somebody?"; having checked several times, they perseverate—"Maybe I did not lock the door" or "Maybe I left the stove on." Attempting to identify their sense of threat and developing elaborate rituals to manage the threat, as painful as it may be, feel preferable to the nameless dread. Therapies that work only with the behaviors and irrational thinking but do not address the underlying high activation miss the most important element of this trauma reaction.

The defensive-orienting response (see p.115) is a specific sequence of biological reactions characterizing how human beings respond to threat. A basic element of the defensive-orienting response is its alerting function: the body is hardwired to search for any source of threat. This is a natural survival mechanism. Individuals with early trauma are locked in an uncompleted defensive-orienting response. Having an ongoing sense that something is wrong, they look for the source of the threat they feel. Not realizing that the danger they once experienced in their environment is now being carried forward as high arousal in their nervous system, traumatized individuals have the tendency to project onto the current environment what has become an ongoing internal state. These individuals try to locate the danger, but because the danger is now internally generated and no longer coming from the environment, a pernicious cycle develops. The mind attempts to make sense of this internal biological dysregulation by finding an external cause for the continuous state of inner arousal. It brings short-term comfort to name a fear even if it is inaccurate, but it creates even more long-term distress.

The Designated Issue

Many individuals with the Connection Survival Style, not knowing the actual source of their distress, create explanations that are designed to help them make sense of their symptoms. Once the nameless dread has been named, it becomes what in NARM is called the designated issue. The designated issue can be fear of death, a phobia, real or perceived physical deficiencies such as being overweight or other perceived "defects," as well as real or perceived psychological or cognitive deficiencies such as dyslexia or not feeling smart enough. The pitfall is that because of chronic dysregulation, many individuals do develop real physical problems that then become the focus of their lives. *Designated issues, whether or not they have a basis in physical reality, come to dominate a person's life, covering the deeper distress and masking the underlying core disconnection.*

Unfortunately, creating a designated issue ultimately causes more distress. Designated issues may take many forms and occupy a person's attention, becoming the focus for his or her lifelong struggle. The designated issue functions protectively, giving a frame of reference for the underlying feeling of distress. Individuals with the Connection Survival Style believe that if only their "problem" could be solved, then they would be happy. The content of the designated issues must be heard and addressed, but ultimately, designated issues are of secondary importance to the primary theme of disconnection and dysregulation.

Paradoxically, solving the "problem" of the designated issue represents a greater threat than not solving it. For example, those clients who designate being overweight as their life issue find that when they successfully lose the weight, they cannot tolerate the vulnerability and emotionality of being thinner. Focusing on the designated issue diverts attention from the underlying unrecognized high arousal, dysregulation, and disconnection that drive the nameless dread. When this underlying high arousal has not been addressed, individuals feel the nameless dread more intensely when they no longer have the designated issue as a frame of reference.

Self-Image and Self-Esteem

Self-image and self-esteem problems often begin in the difficulties of this first developmental phase. The original holding environment, which includes caregiver relationships, becomes a significant part of the template of who we come to believe ourselves to be. An infant feels no separation between self and environment; both the successes and the failures of the early holding environment are internalized and form the core of our self-image and self-esteem. As such, early trauma and attachment difficulties have a negative impact on our sense of self.

Shame and Self-Hatred

Individuals with the Connection Survival Style, more than any other survival style, have experienced profound early environmental failure. The experience of a deficient early holding environment is often at the root of the adult's low self-esteem. Lifelong feelings of shame and deficiency are typically found to accompany the distress states caused by early trauma. Infants cannot experience themselves as being "a good person in a bad situation." Failure of the holding environment is experienced as failure of the self. Infants who experience early trauma of any kind experience the early environmental failure as if there were something wrong with *them.* Later cognitions such as "There is something basically wrong with me" or "I am bad" are built upon the early somatic sensation "I *feel* bad."

The precursors of chronic shame, low self-esteem, and other distortions of the self often begin in the Connection phase. The internalized environmental failure, held as distress in implicit memory, creates the strong distortions of the sense of self and leads individuals to feel chronically unloved, unlovable, and without value. Simply understanding that their shame *reflects the environmental failure they experienced* rather than who they are has helped many people who suffer from lifelong patterns of low self-esteem, shame, and a sense of worthlessness to see themselves in a new, more compassionate way.

The Search for Meaning

A common refrain from individuals with the Connection Survival Style is "Life has no meaning" or "What's the point?" or "We'll all be dead eventually anyway—what does it matter?" Searching for meaning, for the *why of* existence, is one of the primary coping mechanisms that both the thinking and spiritualizing subtypes of the Connection Survival Style use to manage their sense of disconnection and the despair that disconnection brings. When a baby's introduction to the world has been unwelcoming, painful, and traumatic, the world is experienced as cold and unloving. Seeing the world in this way, thinking subtypes try to ignore it by living in the realm of ideas and searching for meaning through the intellect. Spiritualizing subtypes believe that even though the world is a cold, unloving place, at least God (or the Buddha or a higher power) loves them, and they search for meaning through some form of transcendent connection.

Because of their early trauma, both thinking and spiritualizing subtypes disconnect from and bypass bodily experience and close personal relationships. Bypassing the body is a defensive process that cannot be sustained long term because the dysregulation of the body eventually leads to symptoms that cannot be ignored. The coping mechanisms of intellectualizing and spiritualizing ultimately create more disconnection. NARM holds that the key to meaning in life and connection to the spiritual can most effectively be found when our biology is regulated and our capacity for connection is developed. It is through connection that coherency of mind, body, and spirit, expansion, engaged relationship, and aliveness are possible.

Dissociation: Bearing the Unbearable

When trauma is early or severe, some individuals completely disconnect by numbing all sensation and emotion. Disconnection from the bodily self, emotions, and other people is traditionally called *dissociation.* By dissociating—that is, by keeping threat from overwhelming consciousness—a traumatized individual can continue to function. Adults with early trauma have turned away from their body and retreated into the mind or live primarily in energetic or spiritual realms. When individuals are dissociated, they have little or no awareness that they are dissociated: they become aware of their dissociation only as they come out of it.

A Universal Human Response

Dissociation is often misunderstood and pathologized. Dissociation is a human response. In reaction to trauma, the dissociative process is a lifesaving mechanism that helps human beings bear experiences that would otherwise be unbearable. If human beings did not have the capacity to dissociate, many individuals would not have survived the hardships of their lives. Given the history of human suffering, it is doubtful that our species would have made it this far without the capacity to dissociate.

Dissociation is an everyday life process and affects everyone; it is part of the continuum of existence and as such is a universal human issue, not simply a pathology. We are all disconnected and dissociated to one degree or another. For example, arriving at a destination without any memory of having driven there is an everyday experience of dissociation. Though not necessarily pathological, this experience helps us see how we can be dissociated and still function.

It is a paradigm shift to think of dissociation as a *bodily* process; in NARM dissociation is seen as more *physiological* than psychological. The process of living fully in the body is functionally the same as being fully present in the moment. The body lives only in the present moment. In the mind, we can remember the past or think about the future, but we can be in the present moment only by being fully connected to the body. The more disconnected we are from our body, the less we are in the present moment. Not living in the present moment, we live life through the filter of past experience, particularly through the filter of unresolved traumas. NARM holds that the path of healing is a path of reconnection and that the way to be more fully in the present is to resolve our developmental and shock traumas.

Compassionate understanding of the pain and fear that drive the dissociative process is critical to healing the Connection dynamic. Having undergone the earliest and most difficult traumas, individuals with the Connection Survival Style tend to be less in their body and therefore less in the present moment. Because of their early trauma, dissociation is often the *only* state individuals with the Connection Survival Style have ever known. It is more challenging, though not impossible, to help individuals discover their body when they have never experienced it.

The Energetics of Dissociation

Early-traumatized individuals energetically disconnect from the ground. Their energy and self-awareness are pulled up from the ground, out of the body, and focused in the head. In NARM they are the thinking subtypes of the Connection Survival Style. When individuals with this coping style are asked what they feel, they will tell you what they think. Spiritualizing subtypes disconnect from the body completely so that body and emotional awareness are limited or nonexistent. These individuals keep their awareness in the energetic field. Even though they can be very attuned energetically, there is so much dysregulation in their nervous system that they are uncomfortable in their bodies and prefer to live on a more esoteric or ethereal realm.

Dissociation as a Lifestyle

When adults with early trauma continue to dissociate, this life-saving mechanism comes to function automatically even though it has outlived its usefulness and is now creating more distress. In short, the dissociative response develops into a lifestyle. Dissociated individuals develop a pattern of living that minimizes relating with other human beings. Friends, career, and relationships are developed to limit connection because too much human contact challenges the disconnective process of dissociation. Dissociative lifestyles are sometimes diagnosed as social phobia without understanding the global high arousal that drives the phobia.

Disconnection sets up a pernicious cycle. To manage early trauma, children disconnect from their bodies, emotions, and aggression, foreclosing their vitality and aliveness. They also disconnect from other people. This disconnection, though life saving, produces long-term distress because they feel exiled from self and others. Seeing other people live in what one client called "the circle of love" and the distress of feeling "on the outside looking in" heighten both shame and alienation.

The Dissociative Continuum: Numbing, Splitting, Fragmentation

NARM views dissociation on a continuum ranging from numbing to splitting to fragmentation. Just as a coyote with its leg caught in a trap chews it off in order to escape, in attempting to manage early trauma, the organism *gives up its unity in order to save itself.* Numbing, splitting, and fragmentation create disorganization on all levels of experience. Unmanageable levels of overload that overwhelm the organism's capacity to process are experienced as distress, and when distress becomes unbearable, the organism manages first by numbing, then by splitting, and finally by fragmenting. These life-saving dissociative processes exact a terrible cost.

Numbing

It is useful to differentiate between two types of numbing experiences: what NARM calls the *dimmer switch state* and the *breaker switch state.*

The dimmer switch state: Many individuals, looking back on their experience of dissociation, report that they felt as if they had been swaddled with bandages or gauze that had the effect of diminishing the intensity of all their experience, particularly their emotions. Some have used the metaphor of coming out of a trance state, others as having been on Novocain. It is not that they had no feeling at all, it is just that all feeling had been dulled or muted. The experience of coming out of this dimmer switch state is consistently described as feeling the body more acutely; literally seeing things more clearly, including brighter colors, more visual acuity, and being more present and aware of one's surroundings.

The breaker switch state: The breaker switch state, commonly called "shock," occurs when all emotion and sensation shut off, literally as if a breaker switch had been thrown. In the therapeutic process, a surprising number of clients say that they feel nothing when asked what they feel in the body. The question itself, "What do you feel in your body?" is confusing and anxiety producing.

Splitting

It is natural to react to an inadequately supportive or threatening environment with increasingly aggressive strategies: first protest, then anger, and finally, when those are not successful, rage. The problem is that for a vulnerable and dependent infant or child, expressing aggression may create more danger. Dissociation, in addition to numbing the pain created by parental failure, also helps children disconnect from their own aggressive reaction to that parental failure. In addition to managing the external threat, infants and children must also manage their own internal aggressive impulses. They manage by splitting off, disowning, and projecting these aggressive impulses.

Melanie Klein and other psychoanalysts view splitting primarily as a psychological response to the frustration a child experiences when early drives are not met. NARM sees split-off aggression as the result of early trauma—not only as a psychological process but also as a physiological process. Hate, rage, and the fight response that children feel toward neglectful or abusive parents is managed through psychological splitting and *physiological shutdown;* there is a functional unity between the process of psychological splitting and physiological shutdown. From conception, physiological splitting is one of the primary protective mechanisms used to manage the overwhelming charge of such intrusive intrauterine threats as surgical procedures, chemical toxicity, and traumas experienced by the mother. In later life, this early high sympathetic arousal is experienced, consciously or unconsciously, as aggression, rage, and hatred.

In addition, NARM maintains that persistent destructive and aggressive feelings on the part of a child are not normal to development; they are a response to early trauma, particularly the relational traumas of neglect or abuse. Abused and neglected infants and children split off aggressive impulses toward their parents in order to maintain their loving feelings for them, and to protect the attachment relationship which is as essential as food or air. No matter how neglected or abused children are, they endeavor to protect the love they have for their parents by disowning the conscious awareness of their hurt and their angry reaction to that hurt. Therapists who work with children are used to hearing abused children defend their parents and blame themselves for the abuse they have experienced. A common refrain from abused children is "My dad didn't really mean it; he was just having a bad day" or "I slipped and got this black eye." Protecting the image of the parent can continue into adulthood; a client who was severely abused as a child once said, "My dad wasn't abusive.... He took the strap to us a couple of times a week but only when we needed it."

Aggression: Acting In and Acting Out

When children split off significant aggressive impulses, they see only two possibilities: to identify as good but powerless—acting in—or as bad but powerful—acting out (Table 8.3).

- *Acting in.* On one level abused children see themselves as good but powerless; on another, they experience parental abuse as their own failure, turning their aggressive reactions against themselves. Children unconsciously think, "Only abusers have anger. I don't want to be like the abuser, so I won't feel any anger." They still carry anger, of course, but it is split off and turned against the self.

  Early-traumatized and abused children, without access to their aggression and fight response, feel like outsiders. Their identification with being good but powerless sets them up to be victims. Not able to fight back, these are the children who are picked on by other children who sense their vulnerability; this reinforces their experience as victims. As adults with little or no access to their own aggression, they remain identified with a feeling of powerlessness and continue to disown and project their split-off anger and rage. These individuals reenact the role of victim by continuing to act in their aggression against themselves and become psychologically and physiologically symptomatic.

Individuals with the Connection Survival Style act in their anger in the form of self-hatred. They hate themselves for feeling unloved and unlovable, for never feeling that they fit in; they believe that there is something basically wrong with them and that the abuse and neglect they experience is their fault. They hate themselves for their perceived physical flaws and their psychological symptoms. They often feel that their body is their enemy. They hate their body for the fear and distress they experience and may focus their hatred on some real or imagined physical inadequacy: "If it weren't for my nose [hips, fat, skin, hair, shortness, tallness, small breasts, etc.], then I would be happy."

The Distortions of Healthy Aggression

Expression of a core need...

→Meets with frustration

→Triggering protest

→The protest is unsuccessful or penalized

→The protest escalates to anger

→The anger becomes overwhelming or is punished and split off:

- The anger is turned against the self: acting in
- The anger is turned against the environment: acting out

TABLE 8.3: Distortions of Healthy Aggression

Adults with the Connection Survival Style have split off significant amounts of aggression. They present as meek and mild, sometimes very cerebral and sometimes otherworldly and ethereal. They don't know that they are angry except toward themselves, often to the point of self-hatred. Integrating their split-off aggression—learning neither to act it in nor act it out, transforming it into healthy aggression—is key to reconnection with the bodily self and the world, to increased aliveness, and to coming out of dissociation. They fear that if they allow themselves to feel their anger, they might hurt someone.

For individuals with the Connection Survival Style, the therapeutic key is to get in touch with and reintegrate the split-off aggression *slowly.* Integrated, healthy aggression leads to increased capacity for self-expression, strength, and individuation (Figure i.2).

- *Acting out.* Some individuals with early trauma, particularly when they have a history of abuse, begin acting out their aggression as children; initially they act out against younger children or animals. As adults, power and control become primary themes in their lives: these individuals identify with the bad/powerful aspect of the split and act out as abusers and perpetrators. The bad/powerful aspect of the split is expressed as anger against the world: "Life is a jungle"; "It's about the survival of the fittest"; "I give ulcers, I don't get ulcers";"Winning is everything"; "Fuck them before they fuck you." In these cases, continually acting out aggression develops into what later becomes the Trust Survival Style (see Chapter 4).

Some individuals spend most of their lives acting in, living a lifetime of despair and self-hatred, for the most part disconnected from their anger. In a minority of cases, the aggression that has been turned against the self erupts and is acted out against the environment, sometimes in a violent way. A refrain sometimes heard after an episode of family violence is: "He was such a meek and mild guy. We would never have thought that he could do such a thing."

Fragmentation

Many individuals with the Connection Survival Style, without going to the extreme of developing a personality disorder, use fragmentation as a coping mechanism to manage overwhelmingly high levels of arousal and painful emotions. On a biological level, fragmentation creates a lack of coherency in all systems of the body. When trauma is particularly severe and/or ongoing, the dissociative response is correspondingly more extreme: from a psychobiological perspective, individuals use fragmentation as the coping mechanism of last resort. On psychological and behavioral levels, fragmentation can be gauged by the lack of consistency and degree of disorganization in all aspects of life. Some people lead chaotic lives, are unable to hold steady jobs, and have chaotic relationships. Fragmented individuals cannot organize a coherent narrative of their lives. Fragmentation, in one of its most pathological forms, is diagnosed as dissociative identity disorder, formerly called multiple personality disorder.

The Interaction of Physical Structure and Physiological Function

In this section we consider two interrelated dimensions of bodily experience: physiological function and physical structure. *Physiological function* relates to the internal workings of all systems of the body, and *physical structure* describes patterns of tension and collapse that can be seen in a person's musculature and physical appearance. In humans, as in all living organisms, there are continual feedback loops between physical structure and physiological function that affect every system in the body, down to the cellular level. Each adaptive survival style has characteristic patterns of hyperarousal, such as tension and bracing, as well as patterns of hypoarousal, such as collapse, that affect both physical structure and physiological function in specific ways.

The Regulation and Dysregulation of Energy

We cannot understand the adaptive coping process of the Connection Survival Style without first understanding the impact of the stress response on the body's flow of energy. For non-traumatized adults, one of the natural ways of managing the high arousal of threat is through muscular contraction and mobilization as well as through visceral constriction. As mentioned earlier, these reactions are designed to be time-limited responses that are discharged when the threat is over. However, the physiological challenge for individuals with the Connection Survival Style is that threat was experienced before the brain, nervous system, and musculature were well developed. Fetuses and infants are primarily visceral systems and central nervous systems without a developed musculature. The only protective responses available to them are to shut down and freeze the central nervous system and visceral system.

Energy flow in the body is managed by contractions of the transverse tissues called diaphragms. The most well-know diaphragm is the respiratory diaphragm. For individuals with the Connection Survival Style, the high arousal of early trauma is managed through powerful, chronic contraction in all the diaphragms of the body, most prominently in the respiratory diaphragm but also the diaphragms at the base of the skull and in the eyes, feet, and joints. There is also, as Porges has documented, a freeze response mediated by the dorsal aspect of the vagus nerve. These contractions and freeze responses result in severe disruption of energy flow in the body. This systemic inhibition of energy helps us understand why any upsurge of sensation, emotion, or feeling can be so difficult for individuals with the Connection Survival Style. It also helps us see why therapeutic approaches that do not address physiological dysregulation are limited in their effectiveness when working with early trauma.

Impairment of the Social Engagement System (SES)

Developmentally, the dorsal aspect of the vagal system develops first, followed by the ventral aspect, which is directly involved in social engagement, the capacity to connect with other human beings. When the dorsal vagal system reacts to manage early trauma, the ventral aspect does not develop adequately and can remain impaired throughout life. In individuals with the Connection Survival Style, the physiological impairment of the SES is directly observable in the lack of emotion and expressiveness in the face, the lack of contact and engagement in the eyes, and behaviorally, in the social anxiety and withdrawal they experience.

Systemic Dysregulation and Chronic Health Issues

The impact of early, chronic developmental and shock trauma on health leads to poorly understood and often lifelong ramifications. Early trauma creates pervasive systemic distress that leaves a person vulnerable to disease processes that may not appear until later in life. For example, the role of systemic inflammatory processes in the development of many diseases is a primary focus of current medical research. Though it has not yet been scientifically validated, NARM maintains that one of the poorly understood links in the development of systemic inflammation is trauma, particularly early trauma. With inadequate parenting, infants are subject to chronic, cumulative, and unpredictable stress. The resulting combination of undischarged high arousal, freeze, and dissociative strategies create profound dysregulation in all the systems of the body, particularly in the brain and in the nervous, endocrine, vascular, and digestive systems. This systemic dysregulation is a significant part of the life experience of individuals with the Connection Survival Style and leaves them vulnerable to numerous disease processes.

> **The Impact of Early Trauma on Health**
> Undischarged High Arousal→Contraction/Freeze→Systemic Dysregulation→Chronic Health Issues

TABLE 8.4: Effects of Early Trauma on Health

The Impact of Early Trauma on Energetic Boundaries

The word *boundaries* is widely used in psychology and somatic psychotherapy, but its meaning is often unclear. Our skin is a boundary; it is our *physical* boundary. There is also an *energetic* dimension to boundaries. Our energetic boundaries constitute the three-dimensional space that surrounds us: above us, below us, and around us. Because energetic boundaries are invisible, it is not generally understood that they are real and have profound implications in our lives. Energetic boundaries buffer us from the outside world and help us regulate our interface with other people. Each of us has a sense of our own space and what is comfortable to us within and around that space. For example, everyone has had the experience of someone standing too close and wanting distance from that person; this is an everyday experience of boundary impingement. Just as the skin marks the boundary between the body's inside and outside, the energetic boundary defines personal space. And just as a cut or a blow to the skin is painful, we experience an energetic boundary impingement or rupture as threatening and anxiety provoking.

Intact energetic boundaries are accompanied by a feeling of personal safety and a capacity to set appropriate limits. We normally become aware of boundaries only in their absence or when they are impinged upon or ruptured. Since we are not usually consciously aware of our energetic boundaries, the experience of a boundary rupture can be puzzling and distressing. Traumatic events that occur before an individual can orient to danger leave that individual with the internal sense that danger can come from anywhere, at anytime. When there is chronic early threat, boundaries often never form adequately and become severely compromised; when boundaries are compromised or missing, we become symptomatic.

In the Connection stage of development, trauma compromises boundary development and creates boundary ruptures. The inability to develop adequate energetic boundaries has profound implications. Many of the psychological and physiological symptoms of the Connection Survival Style can be better understood from the perspective of compromised energetic boundaries. Connection individuals' struggle with compromised boundaries is often misunderstood and pathologized: they feel crazy because of their extreme sensitivity to environmental triggers. Practitioners, friends, and family often reinforce these individuals' negative feelings by communicating that it is "all in their head." It is not. Table 8.5 lists the characteristics of healthy versus compromised energetic boundaries.

Easily Overwhelmed

People with significantly compromised energetic boundaries describe themselves as feeling raw, sometimes without a skin. Compromised energetic boundaries lead to the feeling of being flooded by environmental stimuli, particularly by human contact. Conversely, such damaged boundaries can also lead to the feeling of "spilling out" into the environment, not knowing the difference between self and other, inner from outer experience. The inability of a traumatized person who does not have adequate energetic boundaries to filter external stimuli makes the world seem continuously threatening. Compromised energetic boundaries are one cause of the continual sense of threat and high arousal that lead to hypervigilance.

The Need to Isolate

Because of the breach in their energetic boundaries, individuals with the Connection Survival Style use interpersonal distance and self-isolation as a protective mechanism, as a substitute for their compromised boundaries. They develop life strategies to minimize contact with other human beings. Adequate energetic boundaries are among the missing resources for socially phobic individuals.

Examples of Healthy Energetic Boundaries
- Feeling comfortable in one's own body
- Feeling an implicit sense of safety in the world
- Feeling a clear sense of self and other
- Being able to say no and set limits
- Knowing the difference between self and other

Examples of Compromised Energetic Boundaries
- Extreme sensitivity to other people's emotions
- A raw feeling of walking around without "skin"
- Energetic merging with other people, animals, and the environment
- The sense that danger can come from anywhere at anytime

• Hypervigilance and/or hypovigilance in general or in specific directional vectors such as from behind
• Environmental sensitivities and allergies
• Feeling uncomfortable in groups or crowds
• Agoraphobia

***

TABLE 8.5: Characteristics of Healthy and Compromised Energetic Boundaries

Environmental Sensitivities

Intact energetic boundaries function to filter environmental stimuli. Inadequate or compromised boundaries, on the other hand, allow for an extreme sensitivity to external stimuli: human contact, sounds, light, touch, toxins, allergens, smells, and even electromagnetic activity. As energetic boundaries form, many individuals with the Connection Survival Style report a decrease of their sensitivities to environmental stimuli.

The Physiology of Projection

Commonly, projection is viewed as a psychological process and considered a "primitive" defense mechanism. In NARM, projection and the role of the eyes in the projection process are understood from the perspective of the functional unity between a person's psychology and physiology. Most therapists are surprised to discover that projection, which is normally considered a psychological defense mechanism, is a physiologically based process that has profound psychological implications. Hans Selye and his groundbreaking research on the stress response documented that with high levels of psychological stress, there is a narrowing of the visual field: tunnel vision is part of a survival response that provides focus when life is threatened. Individuals with the Connection Survival Style, having lived with an almost continual experience of threat, have chronic narrowing and other distortions of the visual field.

The eyes reflect a person's emotional state. It is said that the eyes are the windows to the soul. This may or may not be true, but they are definitely windows into the nervous system: in the eyes we can see aliveness, availability, enthusiasm, joy, or, on the contrary, we can see fear, deadness, absence, distance, dullness, depression, or disconnection. The eyes of individuals with the Connection Survival Style reflect the difficulty they have with making contact. They may avoid eye contact in general, or their eyes may be out of focus, giving them a distant or unavailable look. Their eyes may look lifeless, sleepy, or wide with fright. The lack of presence and the undeveloped social engagement system give the eye region, and sometimes the whole face, a sallow, waxen quality. In addition to the eyes, the diaphragms at the crown of the head and cranial base are extremely constricted. Connection clients commonly complain: "I sometimes feel like I have a clamp on my head that just gets tighter and tighter when I get upset." Tension in these diaphragms causes headaches, one of the most common physical complaints of the Connection Survival Style.

The Ocular Block

How contraction in the eyes and cervical areas abet withdrawal from experience was understood by Reich as an actual blocking of the diaphragms at the cranial base, the tentorium, and in the region where the optic nerves cross. In Reichian theory, what is called the eye block engenders a depression of all bodily functions and a systemic reduction of energy available to the organism. To the degree that there is contraction and disengagement in the eyes, we do not see the reality of our environment. When we are not present to who or what is directly in our vision, we live in fantasy. For example, if a child is bitten by a dog, all dogs may become trauma triggers. If the adult that child becomes sees all dogs as dangerous, that individual is not using his or her eyes. He or she is not able to distinguish in the present moment which dogs are dangerous and which dogs are not. The ideal of seeing the world accurately is related to the process of being present, in the moment and in the body.

Transference and the Ocular Block

Transference is a projective process related to the ocular block. It is a nearly universal human phenomenon that affects all of us. For example, when a man responds to another person as if he or she were his mother, he is literally not seeing the other person; he is not using his eyes. As a result, he is living in a fantasy; he is responding from his adaptive survival style to unresolved past experience.

The resolution for transference and trauma triggers is to see what is actually in front of us without an overlay of fantasy or projection. One of the most effective ways to help individuals with projective patterns is to invite them to engage their eyes, to orient themselves to their environment in the present moment. As soon as individuals begin to use their orienting response, they become more present, and projections begin to dissolve. Because of their early trauma, individuals with the Connection Survival Style have the greatest tendency to use projection as a coping mechanism. The process of resolving projections takes time of course, but understanding the functional unity between the physiology and the psychology of projection gives therapists a significant tool to interrupt and help resolve projective distortions.

CONCLUSION

The complementary and interwoven elements of experience discussed in this chapter identify the issues that need to be addressed to support the healing cycle for individuals with the Connection Survival Style:

- Working through early trauma
- Developing the right to "be"
- Supporting the ventral vagus and social engagement system
- Increasing the capacity for attachment, connection, and relationship
- Developing self-regulation
- Working through self-hatred, self-judgments, and identity distortions
- Tolerating increasing aliveness
- Seeing through the illusion of "designated issues"
- Coming out of dissociation

- Integrating aggression
- Being present in the body
- Repairing boundary ruptures
- Dissolving the ocular block and reestablishing the exploratory-orienting orienting response
- Working through projection
- Learning to live in the present moment

How to work with these elements from a clinical and personal growth perspective is elaborated in Chapter 10.

9

Transcript of a NARM™ Therapy Session with Commentary

This session transcript and commentary present many key elements of NARM therapy with the Connection Survival Style. For the sake of clarity, the transcript has been slightly edited.

Carla was a participant in one of my (Larry's) NARM *Shame and Guilt* trainings in Germany. She began experiencing anxiety in reaction to the information presented in the training and volunteered to do a therapy session with me in front of the group. The teachings in this course had made her more aware of her pervasive experience of lifelong shame. She was confused and uncertain about the source and nature of her shame.

In this session with Carla, I work with the nervous system dysregulation that drives the low self-esteem, shame, guilt, and overall sense of badness that individuals with the Connection Survival Style experience. It becomes obvious in the course of the session why it is important to address the nervous system dysregulation before addressing the shame. If you have tried in vain to convince a depressed friend or loved one that they are not as "bad" as they think they are, you have direct experience that painful issues of self-esteem do not generally respond to neocortical logic.

As soon as the session begins, Carla's eyes lock onto my eyes with a glassy, unfocused quality. I have the impression that she is looking beyond me rather than at me. This forced eye contact immediately comes to the foreground for me. Carla's eye contact might give the impression that she is connecting with me, but I do not feel the connection. What I observe is not only the fixity of her gaze, but tension and stiffness in her whole body, which I have come to see as reflective of a highly anxious and sometimes dissociative response. When clients dissociate, they do so because of intolerably high arousal and the related nervous system dysregulation. In general, locked-on eye contact is a way of *limiting* contact and is just as limiting of contact as clients who stare out of the window to avoid any eye contact at all. Many therapists do not know how to respond to this type of forced contact, fearing that they will hurt their client's feelings if they themselves break off the contact. However, not addressing this locked-on eye contact can actually reinforce a client's dissociation. My purpose is not to get Carla to make more eye contact, but rather to bring awareness to her process of contact and contact interruption. The first step in addressing Carla's nervous system dysregulation is to bring her awareness to her fixed eye contact with me. This session demonstrates working with the role of eye contact in the regulation-dysregulation process and the related contact and contact interruption cycle.

LARRY: I want you to experiment with not forcing eye contact with me. Let yourself look at the floor, around the room, anywhere you want.... *Pause as Carla looks around....* What do you experience as you let yourself break off eye contact with me? ... (Ellipses are used throughout the session to indicate pauses and slow pacing. No dialogue has been left out.)

CARLA: *Pointing to her chest and the base of her skull....* It's coming more alive in that region....

My first intervention encourages her not to force eye contact. The paradox is that by forcing eye contact, she is less connected with me and with herself. Each time I notice her forcing eye contact, I encourage her to let herself look away and to come back into eye contact with me only when she can maintain connection to herself at the same time. I am trying to help her build more capacity for connection to her internal experience with the overall goal of helping her "hold" both internal and external connection without losing one or the other.

In working with the Connection Survival Style, understanding how eye contact is a window into a client's capacity for internal regulation is critical. Disconnection in the eyes is a reaction to trauma and is always present in varying degrees with this survival style. In the course of this session, it will become clear that as Carla experiences more connection both with herself and with me, she will experience healing cycles during which she moves from the chronic freeze-dissociation state that she lives in much of the time. Moving out of freeze-dissociation, she comes into more contact with her underlying high arousal. It is the unmanageable internal distress caused by high sympathetic arousal that drives the responses of freeze and dissociation. As Carla learns how to discharge the sympathetic arousal, she progressively experiences increased regulation, connection, expansion, and capacity for aliveness.

CARLA: Am I allowed to do that?
Meaning break off contact with me.

LARRY: I have a simple answer for that: Yes. Even more than allowing you, I am encouraging you. *She laughs, closes her eyes, takes her time.*

CARLA: *Points to her heart as she says these words ...* I feel it's touching my heart, this realizing I can go away.

There is a dance beginning between us: I communicate permission to listen to and trust her internal experience, and with permission to come in and out of eye contact, she efforts less and some of her tension diminishes. The freeze-dissociation that was in her eyes and entire body at the beginning of the session was an indication of a parasympathetic dorsal-vagal dominance. The increase in positive sensation in the heart, throat, and belly that she reports is an indication that as the ventral vagal parasympathetic aspect of her nervous system and her social engagement system (SES) are coming back online, the sympathetic arousal is discharging. Here, Porges's Polyvagal Theory helps us understand how social engagement (ventral vagal) is a more developed way of managing sympathetic arousal states than dorsal vagal freeze. With early trauma, the only option is to go into freeze. This is important for Connection Survival Style clients whose capacity for interpersonal connection and social engagement have been severely compromised.

> CARLA: *Allows a deep sigh.*

This spontaneous deep sigh is significant in that it indicates continuing discharge of sympathetic arousal. Please note that I do not give clients instructions to breathe deeply, because inducing deep breathing with someone who has experienced significant trauma can trigger regression and re-traumatization.

> CARLA: There is a kind of excitement and contraction.... I feel it here.... *Points to her throat and reengages me with fixed gaze.*

I again notice the fixity of her gaze and respond to it. At this point in our work, I sense that her fear of breaking off eye contact is related to her feeling that if she no longer forces the contact, she will lose the connection with me.

> LARRY: Again ... just let yourself go away ... you don't have to force anything....

I notice that her body is relaxing.
> LARRY: That's right.

This simple comment is designed to mirror her positive autonomic shift and increased regulation.

> LARRY: Your body needs a little time to process the energy being released as you let yourself come and go.... *Pause....* I invite you to allow the coming and going and to track it. If you ground yourself and feel your feet on the floor, that contraction in the throat may take care of itself.

As she breaks off the gaze, she takes another deeper breath and settles. As discharge happens and she experiences more expansion, there naturally follows a counter-reaction to the expansion, in this case, a contraction in her throat. The body can integrate only a limited amount of expansion at any one time. I support her not to unduly focus on this contraction in her throat, but to see it as a normal reaction to the expansion process. When individuals understand their bodily responses, they find it easier to accept them.

> LARRY: Just notice what it's like.... You don't have to open your eyes.... I'm not going anywhere.

I explicitly address her fear of abandonment.

> CARLA: *Takes a deep breath and a big smile comes on her face. An emotional reaction of sadness soon follows.*

Her shift from smile to sadness is a reflection of the expansion/contraction pendulation that is in process.

> LARRY: That's it.

> CARLA: *With tearfulness and emotion....* Saying that you would not go away was very important.

LARRY: I'm not going anywhere.

A profound discharge breath is followed by an overall smoother breathing pattern with the chest and belly more engaged. I reflect the developing expansion and self-regulation.

LARRY: What's happening in your chest, neck, and throat right now?

CARLA: It's opening a lot. *Points to her chest and throat.*

I bring my observation of what is happening to her attention so that she can increase the awareness of her own body. A key element of the NARM approach is to track the physiological process, step by step. Each pendulation of deepening contact brings with it an upsurge of physical sensation and emotion. Whether the sensations and emotions feel pleasant or unpleasant, the intention is, in a mindful way, to support the developing capacity for feeling while not becoming overwhelmed by, lost in, or more identified with those feelings.

CARLA: Pain right here.... *Points to her solar plexus* ... and there's a lot of discharge.... *Points to her eye area with wiggling fingers to describe how the discharge of tension around her eyes is taking place....* Also here.... *She holds her shoulders and upper arms and squeezes them....* Feels like trembling on a deep level. Much deeper than the muscles.... *Long pause....*

LARRY: Let's see what happens if you orient through my voice instead of using your eyes.

At this point, I have a sense that the expansion can become overpowering. If feelings of aliveness increase too rapidly, there is the danger of a rebound reaction in which the person shuts down and returns to the freeze response. I choose to shift her attention to the auditory level, which I anticipate is less threatening to her than eye contact. This technique is related to Porges's use of tones to access the SES with autistic children. When the sensory input from the eyes threatens to become overwhelming, it can be useful to shift the attention to touch, grounding, or hearing. *It is essential to titrate small doses of contact as individuals with the Connection Survival Style experience increased aliveness as a threat.*

> LARRY: Is it okay to allow that trembling?

This is the type of question I ask to assess if the bodily and emotional reactions are manageable and whether or not the client has any judgments or fears attached to the experience. If there are, those judgments and fear reactions should be explored and uncoupled so that the client becomes less threatened by and more accepting of the autonomic re-regulation taking place.

> LARRY: What I'd like you to do is to just listen to my voice and orient to me through your ears and not just your eyes.

> CARLA: *Long period of quiet....* Something is happening with my

ears also. Contracting and opening. Kind of breathing.

LARRY: Give that some time ... contracting and opening ... just like your ears are breathing....

Nervous system re-regulation needs mindfulness and time. Notice how I use the client's own languaging, avoiding interpretation.

CARLA: *Another deep breath....*

LARRY: I'm going to offer you another possibility if you want. With your permission, I will put my foot out, and if you want, you can make contact with it.

CARLA: *Nods yes and after a few moments slowly extends her foot till it makes slight contact with mine.*

LARRY: You don't have to make contact with your eyes. Just explore my foot at your own pace.... Do you notice that little trembling in your head?

CARLA: *Nods yes.*

LARRY: As much as is comfortable for you, you can allow that.

The trembling reflects the nervous system re-regulation which I encourage her to allow.
>LARRY: Can you feel just that little bit of contact with your toe against my foot?

>CARLA: Yes. And at the same time from the feet up to the knees there starts a kind of tingling.

This tingling reflects increased sensation as contact with me and with her own body increases. I give her a great deal of time to be present to, and adjust to the upsurge of feeling. And then I say:
>LARRY: Notice what happens if I move my foot away? ... Pause.... It will be back if you want it.

>CARLA: I feel somewhat disoriented.

> LARRY: It's okay. When you feel that, you can open your eyes and check back in [with me].

She opens her eyes and looks at me. I notice that when she first looks at me, there is a relaxation in her body but quickly, she reverts to the fixed gaze. Addressing this, I say:

> LARRY: And the moment you start to force it [contact with me] close your eyes again. It's okay. I'm going to still be here.
>
> CARLA: I get a lot of coldness in my whole body.

As she experiences increased connection in her body, she senses the frozenness that underlies her dissociation. Being present to the coldness without being overwhelmed is an important element of the reconnection process.

> CARLA: I start to feel some shivering, but I can handle it.

The shivering is an aspect of the nervous system re-regulation process.

Carla's confidence that she can handle the shivering tells me that she still feels within her capacity to effectively manage her experience.

> CARLA: I can still feel the chair.

> LARRY: You can still feel the chair even with all that coldness.

I reflect her capacity to be present to an experience that might previously have triggered another round of dissociation.

> LARRY: If you could have anything in the world to help you with that coldness, what would you want?

It could be regressive or re-traumatizing to have her stay too long in the experience of the coldness. Coldness is the usual reaction associated with early experience of abandonment; feeling left out in the cold is more than just a metaphor. I look for an antidote resource, which is an experience designed to help her manage the painful feeling of coldness. I encourage her to get in touch with what would help her counteract the coldness.

CARLA: *Responds to the question with a great deal of emotion.* ... An embrace.

LARRY: Is there anybody in the group you would like an embrace from?[1]

I invite her to look around and choose someone in the group. It is important for her to touch into the experience of coldness because her dissociation is an attempt to avoid the coldness. It is also important for her

---

[1] In the group setting, I use the resources that are available, which in this case is another group member. I do not recommend that psychotherapists who are not trained in the use of psychotherapeutic touch use physical contact as a resource. On the other hand, individuals with early trauma often find supportive touch an essential part of the process. At the appropriate point in therapy, referral to a therapist trained in psychotherapeutic touch can be essential. An example of the use of psychotherapeutic touch used in a case involving early trauma can be found in Chapter 11.

not to go too deeply into the coldness which might take her back into the disorganization of what I assume to be an early abandonment experience. When a client is ready for appropriate physical contact, this contact is essential to help reconnect with the body.

> CARLA: *Looks around and chooses a training participant.*

> LARRY: How would you like her to embrace you? Can you tell her exactly what you want?

> CARLA: *Asks the person to kneel behind her and gently wrap her arms around her shoulders and chest.*

I want to facilitate the experience of contact and not a cradling regressive embrace. I track her physiological and emotional response to receiving this contact, watching to see if she stiffens against it or relaxes into it. I see that she relaxes into it. I am encouraging the opportunity to feel the effect that contact has on her body and nervous system in present time. To support her integration of this experience, I ask her:

> LARRY: Do you find your body fighting against it [the contact], or are you taking it in?

I offer different possibilities in order not to lead her response.

> LARRY: *Long pause....* Do you know each other?

They acknowledge that they do. I establish that there is already trust between them.

> LARRY: Notice how it is for you to experience the embrace. What does it feel like in your body?

> CARLA: I like it.

> CARLA: *Big smile and a deep discharge breath.* I feel a lot of joy.... *Continues to breathe more deeply....*

> LARRY: Is that the right pressure? Would you like less or more?

I invite her to track her reactions, and I support her to ask for what she wants and communicate what feels good to her. The potential for regression to a state when she had no control over her circumstances and felt abandoned is replaced by an increased sense of possibility for connection.

> LARRY: As you feel the joy, notice what happens in your body.

Many individuals with this survival style are disconnected from and unable to feel their bodies. As I am guiding Carla into more contact with her body, it is important that her initial experience be positive in order to make the entry back into the body pleasurable rather than painful.

> CARLA: From the heart there is radiating relaxation ... and discharge that is going out of the legs and out of the arms. Particularly here.... *Points to her solar plexus.*

Tensing in the diaphragm is one of the important ways that early or severely traumatized individuals dissociate from their experience, so it is a good sign that she is feeling relaxation in that area. We are now shifting into a new phase of the process. As the high arousal and shock energy is discharging, she is able to feel progressively safer in her body and in her capacity for contact.

CARLA: *Referring to the woman holding her....* I can feel and hear her breathing, and that also helps me relax.... *Her torso relaxes allowing a more expansive breath.*

LARRY: When you say how it helps you, notice what you experience in your body.

CARLA: It helps me to breathe. My legs are trembling again and discharging.... *Long pause....*

LARRY: Sometimes I notice you're really there in your eyes, and sometimes not quite so much. There is still coming and going. Listen to your own rhythm of coming and going, and when you feel yourself forcing the contact, let yourself look away.... *Long pause....* As you let yourself close your eyes, what happens in your body?

CARLA: It feels like the discharge is much stronger now.

I remain quiet and give her a great deal of time. The discharge is happening on its own now, and I don't want to distract her with words.
LARRY: Still manageable?

It is a good question to ask a client when there is a strong discharge. Keeping one's attention on a response gives it more energy, which must be closely monitored so as not to become overwhelming. If she were to say that the discharge is too much, I would move her attention away, possibly engaging her in conversation, even distracting her to give her body time to settle.
CARLA: *Opens her eyes....* And I need to check if you are still there.

LARRY: *Long pause....* There is a process that I want to bring your attention to. I notice at some moments when you open your eyes [and look at me], there is a deep connection. You are really here with me ... you can trust that I will still be here when you are ready for those moments again. You don't have to force anything.

CARLA: *Flushes.... Color comes to her face accompanied by a great deal of positive emotion. Laughter and tears.*

LARRY: Notice the impact my words are having on you.

I continue to bring her back to her internal experience.

CARLA: *More tears intertwined with smiling. More color comes to her face.* I want to be seen, and I don't want to be seen. Because it's somehow very shaky.... I can see in your eyes that you are not judging anything, that I'm really allowed to be like this. And I can allow myself just to be in contact. The moment I start to go away, I am checking to see if you are judging. It has much to do with your eyes. I can see you're not judging. And it has to do with these hands.... *Pointing to her friend's hands still holding her.*

Carla is identifying for herself the core dilemma of the Connection Survival Style. She is experiencing her discomfort with contact and her limited capacity to tolerate it. This shifts her from the sense that there is no one available for her to the realization that *she herself is not available for contact.* Her deep desire for connection is experienced side by side with her great fear of contact. She becomes aware of the conflict between her profound desire for contact and the simultaneous fear of it.

CARLA: *Sobbing cry.* I feel very grateful.

LARRY: *Long pause....* Notice how that gratefulness feels in your body.

It is important to anchor positive states in the felt sense.

> CARLA: *Lengthy pause....* At the same time I can realize how really deep this checkup goes. At the same time as the gratefulness there are these waves of numbness, of shivering, of fear.

As she reconnects with her body, it is normal to be feeling more intensely, including the unpleasant states of fear, arousal, and shock that have driven her dissociation. Coming back into contact activates the implicit memory of the original trauma where the connection she needed was not available. To the degree that these negative affects become more manageable, she no longer needs to dissociate.

> CARLA: I can feel all of this even on the levels of the cells.

> LARRY: *Pause....* You are able to be present to these deep shifts, to observe them, to track them.

Whenever a therapist sees an increase in a client's capacity, such as the capacity for self-observation, compassion, or being present to difficult emotions, it is important to reflect it. Notice the response that follows my mirroring.

> CARLA: Somehow I feel proud about this because I know most of my life it was not like this ... being able to stay ... that ... I am here....

For Carla to say *"I am here"* reflects an important step towards the resolution of her chronic dissociation.

> LARRY: Notice what you experience as you say those words.

> CARLA: Maturity. I feel maturity. And the shivering stops when I feel this maturity. Now it's much easier to stay in contact.

> LARRY: And again you don't have to force it. It's okay to come and go with it ... yes ... *She takes a deep breath* ... and as you take a deeper breath, what happens nows?...

CARLA: More landing.

LARRY: More landing ... yes....

CARLA: *Big sigh....*

LARRY: From this place where you are now, as you look back at your life, at the shame that you discussed at the beginning of the session ... for your understanding, for the group's understanding, what words would you use to characterize the shame that you have felt.

Now that she is in a more organized and settled state, I bring up the life theme of shame she had mentioned before the session. When clients experience increasing nervous system organization, they are able to work through larger amount of their personal history more quickly.

LARRY: *Very long pause....* Maybe it's too intellectual a question?

Even though I am aware that working with pre- or nonverbal material has a slow pace and requires a lot of time, there is what seems to me too long of a pause. I begin thinking that perhaps my question is not fitting. However, it turns out that something else is happening in Carla.

> CARLA: I was not able to talk at that point [probably referencing a preverbal experience]. At that place there were no words. If I would try to ... words are not really able to describe this. It's like being erased. Like being killed.
>
> LARRY: *Long pause giving her the time to process what she is saying....* And yet there are words to describe this wordless experience. Right now you are coming up with words.

Moving from right hemisphere to left hemisphere, Carla is putting into words the core Connection theme of compromised existence. With early trauma, there is often no explicit narrative. There is only a felt-sense experience of devastation, shame, and badness, often with no clear story. It is therefore important, with the help of the attuned presence of the therapist, to allow sufficient time for the sensations to surface and to give them sufficient time to organize into a coherent narrative.

> CARLA: The feeling inside my body on this deep level is much, much, much bigger [than words can express] ... erased, having no possibility to escape.

A coherent narrative is taking shape out of the nonverbal fragmented trauma of her early life experience.

> LARRY: For somebody who does not have words, you are describing your experience so perfectly. Really, you are describing what I'm hoping to communicate to the group about early trauma. *Pause....* And I notice again, as you do come up with words, something continues to soften in you.

Again, I mirror the positive change that is happening in her body.

CARLA: This not being able to talk is part of being frozen. Like being in a prison and I've lost the key.

LARRY: As you make this very clear description, this frame, I notice that something in you continues to shift.

My mirroring is general and simply describes that I see something changing without going into the specifics of what is changing. This is important because it maintains a sense of flow without getting lost in the discrete sensations and details of the reentry process.

CARLA: I am stepping out [of the prison].

LARRY: And what happens in your body as you are stepping out?

CARLA: I am stepping out of the freeze.... *Big smile....* much softer now ... less numbness ... still [some numbness] in the right knee and left foot.

LARRY: *I now refer to the woman still holding her....* I think you picked the right person. I notice how she is resonating with your experience. *Carla nods and smiles.* Notice how that resonance feels. *Deeper breathing, smiling.*

CARLA: Wow! ... Wow! All this heat is coming.

She feels more heat as she is coming out of frozen state. Carla can now tolerate more energy which, as it integrates, is experienced as more heat and aliveness.

CARLA: It's coming up from there.... *Points to her belly....*

LARRY: And as you give that heat time....

CARLA: *Large breath ... smile....*

LARRY: That's it. *Long pause ...* and you smile.

CARLA: This very delicate quality between us ... the quality of the contact, and being welcomed.... I feel this deep love and this love without thinking from deep, deep being ... now another wave of heat is coming ... it's important to say but I really need to take time ... on this really delicate level of contact.... On this level of love ... trauma happened. I can feel that this is where the wound started. I can really feel when I let myself fall into it that there is this only being and loving. And when I realize that there might be a possibility of being not welcome, there is this shame and body reactions that I described in the beginning.

From Carla's increasingly organized adult state, she is able to be present to, but not lost in, the old wounding. It is from within this new, safe, and contained adult state that she can identify her early wound and its origin. Carla's capacity to stay organized and present while sensing and identifying the wounding that is at the heart of her survival style is a good illustration of

NARM's mindful, non-regressive perspective.

When children experience early preverbal trauma, they develop a distorted self-image in an attempt to make sense of their ongoing distress. Infants in distress feel bad; when the distress continues, they end up thinking they are bad. In Carla's case, the attempt to make sense of her lifelong internal distress took the form of persistent, enduring shame. To work therapeutically with the chronic shame, fear, and cognitive distortions of the Connection Survival Style, it is essential to understand how children internalize and feel shame and responsibility for the early environmental failures they have experienced.

CARLA: *Big sigh ... smile....*

> LARRY: From this place, as you see and acknowledge that old wound, what do you experience in your body?...

I want to further assist her to be present to the old wound but not to identify with it.

CARLA: My first thing that came up ... it's amazing, it's not as dramatic as I thought it would be. It's not such a big thing ... and on another level there is a kind of resistance against the realization that it's not such a big thing.

She evidences some confusion. It is significant that finally feeling the wounding that she had so feared is not as painful as she had imagined. This is one of the benefits of non-regressive therapy. It is not so painful in this session because she is present to the wounding from an organized adult state.

LARRY: I'd like to suggest to you that from your perspective right now it's not a big thing, but at one point, it was a very big thing.

CARLA: *Big exhale and smile. She nods her head....* Yes, I can feel it resonating in my heart. Very deep down, there is a pain, kind of saying yes to this truth that at a certain point it was really a *very* big thing.

LARRY: And as you acknowledge that ... what is happening in your body right now?

CARLA: There is still a lot of discharge, but more important I am more on the left side of my body, but now, very very slowly, I am shifting. I am going over to the right side.

LARRY: That's right. Give that shift the time that it needs. *Long pause....*

LARRY: What is happening now?

I give her time for renegotiation and integration to take place.

CARLA: I want to try to be in contact.

LARRY: Notice just being in contact ... and not trying to be in contact. You don't have to try.

CARLA: I'm not really understanding the sentence "you don't have to."...

LARRY: You don't have to try ... as impossible as that sounds.... *She laughs....* As a matter of fact, what I'd like you to do is to experiment letting your eyes feel like magnets.

Returning to the focus on her eye contact, I support further release of the forced gaze, which, as we saw early in the session, keeps her out of contact. Not efforting with the eyes affects the whole nervous system.

CARLA: *Takes significant time to experiment with letting her eyes become like magnets and then laughs....* At the very deepest center there is a pain, but on the outside it's softening much more.

LARRY: Let me make an intellectual connection for you. It seems that the less welcome you felt, the more you had to try. *She takes a deep breath....* The more welcome you feel, the less you have to try.

CARLA: *A lot of emotion surfaces....* And also the less I try

> the more I am welcome.... *Laugh ... pause ... multiple sighs.*
>
> LARRY: What do you notice now?
>
> CARLA: *Slight movements of the head occurring spontaneously....* Inside of my head there is something which is unwinding and continuing through my neck....

This unwinding of the head and neck is a sign that Carla is coming out of a longstanding pattern of unresolved trauma and its associated sense of chronic threat. She has spent her life managing the physical and emotional symptoms that resulted from an incomplete defensive-orienting response. As we have seen, when threatened, an organism is hardwired to orient to the threat in order to make the necessary biological decision to fight, flee, or freeze. When fight or flight is successfully completed, the body returns to rest. For individuals who have unresolved experiences of threat, the body and corresponding areas of the brain continue to signal danger even though the actual threat is over. An incomplete defensive-orienting response leads to chronic tension and vigilance in the body, particularly in the eyes, neck, and head. Fear becomes chronic as well. The predictable biological sequence of this hardwired survival mechanism and the related emotional fallout is covered in Chapter 7.

When children experience abandonment or when their family or environment is a chronic source of physical or emotional threat, no completion of the defensive-orienting response is possible. The only possibility for the vulnerable child who cannot fight or flee is to freeze and dissociate. Unless resolved, this chronic freeze and dissociation become the foundation of the Connection Survival Style. The Connection Survival Style then continues into adulthood, with negative effects on the person's capacity for relationship and quality of life.

As Carla feels safer, she begins to experience the exploratory-orienting response. Just as fear and freeze are part of an incomplete defensive-orienting response, curiosity and movement toward social connection are indicators of the exploratory-orienting response. As Carla feels safer, small spontaneous movements appear in her head and neck. These small spontaneous movements are the physiological markers that the exploratory-orienting response is coming back online. This is only possible when an organism no longer feels threatened. As we see with Carla, as the sense of threat and corresponding arousal level in her body decrease, her environment is no longer experienced as dangerous. Her head and neck loosen and she experiences the impulse to move out toward her environment with curiosity.

LARRY: Give that time.

> CARLA: Depending on the twist that I experience in my head, some parts are not there and some parts are coming back. *Long pause....* I am feeling unwinding in my neck; it's not split off ... some pieces are coming back on the left ... some on the right....

As coherency is increasing, Carla describes different fragments that are starting to coalesce.

> CARLA: It has much to do with my eyes and my ears and my jaw.... While I am watching this, I also feel the whole body that is relaxed. It gives me the possibility to be curious to notice what is happening in my head.
>
> LARRY: There is a process that has started that I think is going to go on for you for some time. So we are going to take just a few minutes more ... and close the session, but that doesn't mean that the work that has started in your body has to stop.
>
> LARRY: What happens as you open your eyes?
>
> CARLA: I can really see you.
>
> LARRY: I can really see you too.... *Nods repeatedly while smiling.*
>
> CARLA: Thank you.

LARRY: Thank you, too.

10

Moving Toward Resolution

Connecting with Self and Others

This chapter provides information useful not only to therapists who are working with individuals with the Connection Survival Style but also to anyone struggling with this survival style or elements of this survival style. It provides guidelines for understanding the sometimes complex process of coming back into connection.

Connection with self and others, the deepest human longing, represents for individuals with the Connection Survival Style the most profound fear and greatest challenge. The organizing principle for healing this adaptive survival style relates to increasing the capacity for connection with self and others, feeling the "right to be," and the intrinsic right to one's meaningful place in life and in the world. Connection with self includes the capacity to know what we are feeling emotionally and bodily. Connection with others means having the capacity for consistent relationship and intimacy. An essential part of the NARM therapeutic process is to bring to awareness a person's *relationship to the primary principle of connection,* difficulties with which underlie many symptoms. Since the majority of us have elements of this survival style, individuals who struggle most with this theme have something important to teach all of us.

How to help individuals with the Connection Survival Style come out of dissociation and back into connection is the overarching theme of this chapter. Therapeutically, there is an important distinction between a person who has had limited experience with connection with self and others because of early shock or attachment trauma versus someone who, as a means of coping with trauma later in life, has dissociated and disconnected. When individuals have had early experiences of positive attachment, they have more resources available and more capacity for reconnection than those who have had limited lifelong access to their emotions, body, and positive relationships. Shame, disconnection, attachment difficulties, and unintegrated anger are greater for someone with the Connection Survival Style. Dissociation is more profound if a person has never had the experience of connection in their body. In such cases, therapy is more complex and must proceed more slowly.

Over the past thirty years, I (Larry) have supervised and provided consultations to thousands of experienced therapists with a wide variety of training and backgrounds. I have noticed common patterns in the work of these talented and experienced clinicians that limit the effectiveness of the therapy they provide to clients with this survival style. Without a full understanding of the primary organizing principles of this adaptive survival style, success in treatment is inconsistent, and in some cases, therapy can even be re-traumatizing. Therapeutic problems arise when a therapist places too much focus on the symptoms of despair, loneliness, and fearfulness that are characteristic of this survival style: focusing on symptoms does not address the root causes of this survival style, which, at its core, revolve around issues of disconnection, identity distortions, pathological shame, nervous system dysregulation, distortions of aggression, and the loss of the full capacity for aliveness.

More highly symptomatic individuals with the Connection Survival Style show psychological conditions such as borderline personality disorder; obsessive-compulsive disorder (OCD); dissociative, depressive and anxiety disorders; low self-esteem; and attachment and relational difficulties. The roots of dysregulated conditions such as profound despair, phobias, and addictions, to name only a few, begin in this first developmental stage. Physiological syndromes such as irritable bowel syndrome (IBS), chronic fatigue syndrome, fibromyalgia, and environmental sensitivities also can be the result of the profound systemic dysregulation caused by early trauma. At the less symptomatic end of the spectrum of this survival style, we find people who are shy and uncomfortable socially, individuals who do not have access to their emotions, compulsive loners, seekers, and dreamers.

PRIMARY NARM PRINCIPLES

This chapter presents the organizing principles of NARM therapy and applies them to the Connection Survival Style. In the NARM approach we work *simultaneously* with the physiology and the psychology of individuals who have experienced developmental trauma, focusing on the interplay between issues of identity and the capacity for connection and regulation. NARM uses four primary organizing principles:
1. Support connection and organization
2. Explore identity
3. Work in present time
4. Regulate the nervous system

Although presented sequentially in the above list and in Table 10.1, in reality the primary principles, tools, and techniques weave together organically in the process of therapy. In NARM we track several themes at the same time in a figure-ground process: for example, at any given point we might primarily focus on the theme of identity, while the issues of connection-disconnection and safety are in the background. At other times, the process of connection-disconnection might be in the foreground, while other themes remain in the background.

1. SUPPORT CONNECTION AND ORGANIZATION

Connection to self and others is the compromised core capacity that must be addressed with individuals with the Connection Survival Style. There are two parallel and complementary organizing aspects to the process of connection: (1) connection with self, the body, and emotions, and (2) learning to experience connection with others as an enriching reciprocal experience rather than as a source of threat.

PRIMARY NARM PRINCIPLES	TOOLS AND TECHNIQUES
1. Support Connection and Organization	Inquiry
• Tracking Connection–Disconnection	Curiosity
• Tracking Organization–Disorganization	Resourcing
• Developing Positive Resources	Grounding
• Encouraging Somatic Mindfulness	Orienting
• Engaging the Eyes	Focusing on Here and Now
• Understanding the Challenges of Reconnection	Tracking
• Tending to the Therapeutic Relationship	Mirroring
2. Explore Identity	Containment
• Supporting Expansion and Aliveness	Titration
• Working with Identifications and Counter-Identifications	Pendulation
• Teaching Disidentification	Somatic Mindfulness
3. Work in Present Time	Psychoeducation
• Fostering Agency and Empowerment	Learning to Listen
4. Regulate the Nervous System	Capacity for Self-Reference
• Containment | Grounding | Orienting | Titration | Pendulation	NeuroAffective Touch*

*NeuroAffective Touch is addressed in Chapter 11 and should only be used by therapists trained in the use of touch.

TABLE 10.1: Primary Principles, Tools, and Techniques Used in the NARM Approach

Exploring both the conscious and unconscious ambivalence about the desire for connection is a core orientation informing the therapy for individuals with this survival style. Regardless of the symptoms and surface issues, holding in mind the overarching principle of connection makes the therapeutic process richer and more efficient for those who struggle with the pain of disconnection. For individuals with the Connection Survival Style, whose deepest longing for connection is also their deepest fear, the key is to work with the conflict around connection as it is expressed in their symptoms, in their current lives, and in the relationship with their therapist. To effectively support the possibility of connection, NARM therapy uses a mindful, process-oriented approach that tracks how a client moves in and out of connection-disconnection and organization-disorganization in present time: in the body, in the nervous system, in a client's capacity for relationship, and in the therapeutic relationship itself.

Tracking Connection and Disconnection

From the beginning, NARM pays attention to the client's process on three levels of experience: cognitive, emotional, and physical. To support clients' mindful awareness of connection-disconnection while articulating their experience, a NARM therapist might ask:

"As you are talking about this issue in your life, what you are experiencing right now?"

The word experiencing is used purposefully to keep the initial question as open as possible. Clients are invited to pay attention to their own experience *at whatever level they can access it.* Questions that reference the body, and even the emotions, too quickly, can be overly distressing for people with this survival style. We will see why approaching emotions and sensations slowly is a particularly important aspect of working with the Connection Survival Style. NARM therapists mindfully track and reflect a client's tendency to disconnect and isolate. Challenging habitual patterns of disconnection and finding the correct pace to support reconnection is like lifting weights: too much too quickly can cause injury, whereas with too little, no growth takes place. As the therapy progresses and we learn more about clients' capacity to be in touch with their body and emotions, we attune our interventions and pacing accordingly. Finding the optimal way to track and at times gently challenge survival style patterns supports the growth process.

Evoking Positive Experiences of Connection

The capacity for connection is the fundamental resource; it is important to attune to and build from existing capacities for healthy connection, whatever those might be for a given individual. Some people have been so injured that they have no conscious awareness of any internal movement toward connection. In fact, their conscious awareness is the opposite: their impulse is to move away from connection. Whatever my clients' painful personal history, I always help them remain aware of any internal or external resources that have supported connection in their lives. I may ask what or who in the here and now or in their past has been or is a positive source of connection:

> "I'm getting a sense from what you tell me, how hard this has been for you. So before you continue with the story, I'm curious as to whether or not there has

been somebody who has been helpful to you in dealing with all this."

This simple question is usually the first step in orienting a client toward positive resources. Shifting clients' attention to positive experiences of connection, as opposed to pushing for the re-experiencing of distressing states of disconnection, supports self-soothing and brings more organization to the nervous system. It is necessary to help clients slowly shift their attention from what is not working in their lives and encourage them to focus on any area of experience, external or internal, *where there is or has been, positive connection.* Whatever positive connection an individual has experienced provides an important resource to draw upon in supporting the journey back to increased contact and connection.

Experiencing the psychological and nervous system impact of positive memories, images, and associations in the present moment is useful with all clients, but it is particularly helpful with those with the Connection Survival Style who are the most disconnected from their ongoing present experience. As a client is able to find either an external resource such as an important person, or an internal resource such as the will to survive, I track how identifying the resource impacts his or her current state. When I see softening or relaxation—both indicators of increasing organization—I communicate this observation and invite the client to notice how the relaxation feels.

>LARRY: I notice as you talk about your grandmother who was so helpful to you, you seem to be relaxing. Does that fit with your experience?
>
>CLIENT: Yeah … it does feel like I'm relaxing.
>
>LARRY: Can you say anything more about how you're experiencing that?
>
>CLIENT: I'm feeling lighter all over.

In the NARM healing cycle, increasing relaxation and nervous system organization indicate a developing sense of connection with the body, and as connection with the body develops, there is in turn increasing nervous system regulation.

Primary and Default Emotions

Primary emotions lead toward integration while default emotions keep individuals stuck in a groove that does not lead to increased integration, coherence, or greater connection to their core life force. Most people have a tendency toward a particular default emotion. The more habitual and automatic the emotion, the more likely it is to be a default emotion. It is not that default emotions are "bad," but when they are part of a well-worn groove of automatic responses, these emotions keep the survival style in place and do not facilitate reconnection and growth.

We all know individuals who, regardless of what they may actually be feeling, turn to anger. Their primary emotion may be sadness, hurt, vulnerability, or even a more primary unresolved anger, but what they are aware of in themselves and what they show the world is an ungrounded, disconnected anger, which they tend to act out. For them, anger has become a default emotion. For others, anger may be the primary emotion, but regardless of what they are feeling, they default to sadness.

Holding a broad understanding of primary and default emotions is an essential tool in helping individuals experience more depth and connection within themselves. Many clients do not know that they have alternatives when dealing with difficult emotions other than automatically turning to their default emotion and acting out on others or acting in against themselves. In NARM, we present a middle ground where emotions are experienced and contained, leading to increased connection with the life force and the strength, independence, and capacity for intimate relationship that accompany that increased connection.

Tracking Organization-Disorganization

Organization is experienced as a sense of safety, ease, curiosity, productivity, and creativity. Organization provides an implicit sense of continuity and realistic confidence that are available even in the face of life's challenges. Ultimately, organization is reflected in the capacity to live in the present, whereas disorganization occurs when a person experiences life through the distorted and limiting lens of unfinished past experience. Organization is reflected in a person's resiliency; capacity for emotional depth and connection to self and others; physical health; and in the coherence of his or her life narrative. Chaotic lives and disjointed, fragmented narratives reflect internal disorganization. Organization expresses as coherency at every level of experience: cognitive, emotional, behavioral, and physiological. Clients with early trauma who are highly symptomatic tend to focus primarily on the things that are going wrong or have gone wrong in their lives. This tendency, although understandable, is disorganizing to the nervous system. Focusing on a traumatizing narrative without referencing how the body and nervous system are managing, or failing to manage, the arousal that comes with that narrative can cause more disorganization and even be re-traumatizing. In NARM, when discussing life difficulties or trauma, we track disorganization moment to moment and help clients move their attention away from the trauma narrative when it becomes too activating. For example, the NARM therapist might say:

> "As hard as things have been for you, is there some area of your life that feels like it's working or that brings you pleasure or satisfaction?"

As clients discuss painful experiences, a NARM therapist keeps in mind the importance of the capacity for regulation. Bringing clients' awareness to their experience in the present moment, while they are talking about the past, is an important first step in supporting the re-regulation process. By finding and working with areas of organization in the client's nervous system, body, relationships, and life, NARM supports the development of an increasing capacity for regulation. Instead of focusing primarily on stories of trauma and difficult symptoms, an important organizing principle is to find and work with areas of pleasure, satisfaction, or better functioning. Certainly there are times when naming and sharing distress can bring more organization, and therapists must be available to hear a client's distressful narrative. However, at the same time, NARM therapists ask questions that bring clients' awareness to the state of their nervous system, continually supporting possibilities for improved regulation. For example, as a client shares difficulties, I might say:

> LARRY: I'm going to interrupt you for a moment and invite you to notice what you're experiencing right now as you are talking about your difficulties.

CLIENT: I'm getting tighter and tighter all over, particularly in my stomach.

LARRY: I interrupted you because I could see that you were getting increasingly tense and not paying attention to that tension. Eventually, I want to hear the whole story, but I encourage you to talk about it in such a way that you don't get overwhelmed or disconnected.

CLIENT: I'm relieved that you're slowing me down.

LARRY: *Pause....* Tell me more about the sense of relief you're feeling.

CLIENT: I'm not feeling so tight, and my stomach is starting to settle.

Because clients are often unable to notice or identify their own increasing arousal before it progresses into disorganization and dysregulation, it is important to bring their awareness to it. Many clients, as in the dialogue above, express relief at being slowed down. Therapists can track increasing or decreasing organization by paying attention to clients' physiological markers: muscular bracing or relaxation, breathing patterns, facial expressions, skin color, and movement. It is key to pace clients by monitoring and supporting their capacity for regulation and by paying attention to whether or not what is unfolding overall is bringing increasing organization or more disorganization.

> ### Overview of the Basic Steps to Reconnection
> 1. Explore how clients experience disconnection and what the symptoms of that disconnection are in their current lives. It may be helpful to bring into awareness of where and how the patterns of disconnection first developed, but the purpose is not to focus primarily on the past.
> 2. Recognize and understand the survival value of the coping mechanisms and adaptive survival

> styles clients developed and still use that currently create disconnection.
> 3. Identify how these survival patterns are expressed in the body and held in place by identifications and behavior.
> 4. Bring mindful awareness to and help disidentify from shame- and pride-based identifications. Challenge unhealthy behavioral patterns that limit clients' lives and keep them re-enacting the past.
> 5. Work through the distortions of the life force, reconnect with the missing internal resources, and original core self-expression.
> ***
> **TABLE 10.2: Overview of the Basic Steps to Reconnection**

Positive Resources

Therapeutically, positive resources tap into those elements of a person's life, psyche, and nervous system that are functional, organized, and coherent. Positive resources tap into either positive states in the moment or the memory of positive life experiences as they are brought to awareness. Positive resources support stability in the body, in the nervous system, and in social relations by promoting self-soothing, relaxation, and increased organization. Pain, emptiness, anxiety, and myriad fears are *symptoms* of the real problems—the lack of internal organization and the missing capacity for connection.

A hierarchy of resources supports connection and reorganization. Human resources are the most helpful; any person, such as a loving grandparent, an involved teacher, or a mentor, may have been a positive resource whose image can be called upon in the therapeutic process to support reregulation and reconnection. The more chronic the early trauma, the harder it often is to find human resources, since humans are often experienced as sources of threat. It is not unusual for clients with the Connection Survival Style to feel safer connecting to animals, nature, or God, any of which can function as a positive resource.

Most of us have access to more resources than we realize. It is important for clinicians to remember that if clients are functioning in the world, they are drawing on resources, internal and external. Even in the most chaotic of lives, there are healthy capacities and resources from which to draw. We have all heard about individuals who came from dysfunctional or abusive families who went on to have successful, meaningful lives as adults. When we read their stories, we often see that they remember one or more significant persons in their lives—a grandmother, teacher, aunt—who taught them that, despite their traumatic home life, there was still love and kindness in the world.

The Therapeutic Impact of Positive Resources

We can understand the therapeutic impact of resourcing in relation to three different domains: cognitive, emotional, and physiological. One of the first questions I ask clients who talks about a traumatic childhood is who or what helped them get through those

difficulties. This question is helpful on several levels:
- Cognitively, recognizing positive internal resources helps clients not blame themselves for, and feel shame about, their difficulties. When therapists identify and mirror positive capacities in their clients, they help them shift their thinking away from trauma-based cognitive distortions and negative self-judgments to become more self-accepting.
- On the emotional level, it may never have occurred to clients that there has been, and often still is, support for them. They often do not realize the degree to which they have shown tenacity and courage in managing what have been lifelong difficulties. It is helpful to recognize and appreciate both the external support they might not have realized was there as well as the internal strengths they have not acknowledged in themselves.
- On the level of the nervous system, getting in touch with internal and external resources reinforces and enhances the capacity for regulation.

Recognizing and acknowledging resources has a further calming and regulating effect on the nervous system.
- Resources in the here and now interrupt the brain's predictive process and support the important dynamic of disidentification. Body-based resources are even more powerful than cognitive awareness in disrupting the predictive processes of the brain, helping clients not to identify so strongly with the content of their fears.

When we view ourselves and our world through the lens of developmental trauma, our perspective is blurred by split-off anger, pain, disorientation, and shock. A therapeutic orientation focused on internal and external resources is an antidote that shifts clients' attention to a larger, less distorted picture of themselves and their lives. It brings to the forefront of their awareness the capacities they do have and reminds them that there is love and support in the world.

Working with Positive Resources

Focusing on positive resources and the associated experience of safety establishes and reinforces oases of organization in the nervous system. It cannot be repeated often enough that focusing primarily on dysfunction reinforces dysfunction and that, step by step, it is necessary to help clients shift their attention away from focusing exclusively on what is not working in their lives and encourage them to pay attention to areas of experience where they do feel connected and organized.

It is often easier to find and utilize positive resources when working with shock trauma as opposed to developmental trauma. When clients begin a narrative about a shock trauma event, such as a rape or a car accident, they become visibly anxious or disconnected. I interrupt the escalating arousal and explain that, although I eventually want to hear the whole story, I propose that we begin with a different question:

> "Tell me the first moment when you felt safe after the event."

If they have an experience of safety after the event that they can access, they exhale and relax. With developmental trauma, however, when the experience of lack of safety has been chronic, the process is more complex. It is necessary to look for any life experience in which clients felt at least a sense of relative safety. The exercise in Figure 10.1 can be useful in identifying positive internal and external resources.

EXCERCISE

Identifying Positive Resources
External Resources

Take some time to write down all the external resources you have had in your life. Notice what you feel emotionally and physically as you remember the people, places, activities, pets, or organizations that have supported and helped you. It is not unusual for this exercise to continue over several weeks as you remember more resources and add them to your list.

Internal Resources

> Make a list of all your internal resources (tenacity, capacity for friendship, curiosity, openness, etc.). Track your emotional and physiological responses as you recognize the positive aspects of who you are. Notice how you feel as you acknowledge your strengths.
>
> ***
>
> **FIGURE 10.1:** Exercise to Help Identify Positive Resources

Outline for Working with Positive Resources

The following is a simplified protocol for working with positive resources with individuals who have developmental trauma.

- Inquire about positive supportive relationships or life situations that functioned as resources in their life.

    LARRY: With parents as chaotic and abusive as you describe, I'm wondering how you made it.

    CLIENT: For me, school [church, Scouts, a neighbor, relatives] was the only place I felt safe.

- Encourage clients to elaborate on the resource.

    LARRY: Tell me about how it was for you at school.

As clients go into details about the resource experience, reflect any increasing organization. After this client describes his school experience in general, I evoke awareness of the specific needs that were met in the situation.

    LARRY: What in particular stands out that was so helpful?

    CLIENT: My fifth-grade teacher, Mr. Martin, really liked me and cared about me. He saw a potential in me that no one had ever seen before. Looking back now, I realize that it was because of him that I started to see that I was smart. He was so different from my dad, who always put me down and called me stupid.

- Track how clients respond as they talk about those positive areas of their lives. Look for any indication of relaxation or discharge of arousal, such as a smile or softening in the body, and reflect this change. When a movement toward organization and regulation is noticeable, reflect it and help the client track the relaxation.

LARRY: As you talk about Mr. Martin, I notice you're smiling. I'm wondering what you're experiencing right now?

CLIENT: I'm feeling some emotion, but it feels good.

LARRY: See what happens if you give that feeling a little time.

Obviously, interventions are often more nuanced than the bare-bones outline presented above. Nonetheless, in order to support autonomic regulation, simple language that evokes particularly positive relationships is useful in accessing the affective core that has become frozen in trauma.

Therapists often struggle with how to help clients who are shut down and dissociated. When a client identifies a positive resource, there is discharge of activation or arousal reflecting an increase in nervous system regulation. As clients talk about their positive resources, I track to see what impact the awareness of the resources is having: increased expressiveness, softening in the body, deepening of the voice, smiling, positive shift in the breathing, increased skin color.

As the work with the oases of organization continues, clients experience increasing affect regulation and expansion. In a natural movement of pendulation, areas of disorganization—including painful affects, negative beliefs, shame-based identifications, and other symptoms—inevitably surface. Only when clients are stabilized should the therapist redirect their attention to the original painful narrative. The therapist helps clients learn to manage difficult affects as they surface, teaching them to hold the dual awareness of their emotional pain while helping them see that these painful affects are often relics of the past. *It is important not to push painful affects away, but at the same time, it is equally important not to reinforce identification with them* or get submerged in them. This mindful dual-awareness process supports increasing organization, and the increasing organization in turn supports a greater capacity for mindfulness.

Some clients with particularly difficult histories may have a harder time than others identifying resources. If they cannot find any positive human connection, I encourage them to look for areas of positive connection in other parts of their lives. For example, if they mention they have a dog that is the love of their life, I may say:

> "I notice that as you are talking about your dog, something seems to change for you. What are you aware of?"

When a resource is identified, I encourage them to report associated sensory details, such as colors, smells, and sounds. The sensory details of a positive resource have a powerful organizing and regulating impact on the nervous system. I might continue:

> "Give yourself some time to notice what it's like for you as you talk about your dog. Tell me some

of the things you like to do with your dog."

When remembering or imagining positive resources of any kind, past or present, it is important to direct the client's experience to the present moment:

"As you tell me about playing with your dog, what are you noticing right now?"

Eventually, as the therapy progresses, clients will develop more capacity to experience other humans as possible sources of support rather than as sources of threat, but in the beginning the therapist works with whatever resources are available.

Somatic Mindfulness

NARM adds *somatic mindfulness* to the traditional practice of mindfulness to help individuals increase their capacity for self-regulation and connection. In NARM, somatic mindfulness is a primary principle and is used as a technique to both regulate the nervous system and to support clients' efforts to free themselves from the restrictions of distorted identifications, including pathological shame and guilt. Because of early trauma, clients with the Connection Survival Style have the deepest disorganization in the nervous system and the most distorted identifications. As a result, somatic mindfulness is more difficult for them than for the other survival styles but, as their somatic awareness develops, they experience significant growth.

A core value in NARM is to support clients as they learn to listen on every level of experience. The more we learn to listen to our thoughts, feelings, and sensations, the more we experience an internal flow. When we chronically do not pay attention—do not listen—to our body, it finds ways to get our attention, even if it needs to "scream" at us in the form of symptoms. When we learn to listen to our internal states, it is easier to regulate ourselves, and we become less symptomatic.

Tracking Somatic Connection

In NARM the development of a grounded and stable connection to the body is the physiological base for nervous system reorganization and reregulation as well as a primary source of support for the process of disidentification. The dissociation commonly experienced by individuals with the Connection Survival Style reflects their disconnection from their physical and emotional core. Since every cognition and every emotion has a physiological substrate, it is important to track the somatic connection that underlies thoughts and feelings. In the following dialogue, I help the client develop a deepened awareness of her emerging emotions using mindful emotional tracking:

> LARRY: As you're talking about your situation, I notice some tearfulness. What are you aware of on an emotional level right now?
>
> CLIENT: I feel some sadness.
>
> LARRY: Is it okay to allow that sadness to be there?
>
> CLIENT: It's okay, but it scares me.

Larry: Take your time with it. Take a moment to ground yourself again, and we'll explore the feelings that are coming up at a pace that feels manageable.

CLIENT: *Takes time to ground....* I've always been afraid that if I let myself feel the sadness, it would never end.

LARRY: Are you feeling the sadness right now?

CLIENT: A little bit.

LARRY: Notice what happens in your body if you just allow that little bit of sadness.

CLIENT: Strangely, when I allow it, I start to relax a bit.

LARRY: When you don't struggle against the emotion, you start to relax. We've seen many times before that emotions come and go.

Notice that this is a non-goal-oriented process. It is not focused on getting a person into the feeling. The implicit understanding is that as clients feels safe to allow their emotions, whatever emotions need to be addressed will surface. In the comment that emotions come and go, I am reminding this client to be mindful of, but not identified with, her emotions—to be open to her emotions and at the same time not to take them as ultimate truth.

Here is an example of mindful sensate tracking:

LARRY: What are you feeling in general right now?

CLIENT: *Concerned look....* I thought I was getting more relaxed, but I just started trembling.

LARRY: Trembling often happens when the nervous system is reregulating. Take a moment and see how it is for you to allow it to happen.... *Pause....* Is the trembling pleasant or unpleasant?

CLIENT: It feels weird, but it's really not unpleasant.

LARRY: Okay, then see what happens if you give it time.

Trembling is often an indication of discharge of high arousal, and we support the client to allow it as long as it does not become overwhelming.

When Clients Cannot Track in the Body

Many somatically oriented psychotherapists are confused when they work with clients who are unable to talk about their bodily experience. Individuals with the Connection Survival Style are estranged from their bodies, find bodily experience threatening, and have difficulty sensing their bodies. These clients feel anxious and disorganized when asked to focus on sensations too early in the therapeutic process; even if they look affectless and shut down, their bodies and nervous systems carry such a high sympathetic charge that until they are able to discharge some of this high arousal, they cannot access their internal states. It is not advisable to push them to feel their bodies or emotions prematurely because it can be disorganizing to do so. In the long term, however, it is essential to help these clients develop access to their emotions and bodily sensations. Individuals with the Connection Survival Style discover, slowly and over time, that grounding in their biological and emotional selves can become a source of pleasure and comfort.

Individuals who are dealing with significant fragmentation tend to focus on discrete and distressing internal experience even when overall, there is organization and increasing coherency taking place. In such cases the NARM therapist references the overall experience rather than focusing on discrete bodily sensations. Addressing a client who is clearly settling and relaxing, I might say:

> "I'm wondering what you are experiencing right now...."

Individuals with the Connection Survival Style tend to focus their attention on what feels wrong even when overall, they are actually becoming more regulated. Such a client might say:

> "I feel tension in my throat, and my belly feels tight."

This tendency to focus on distress has a disorganizing result and needs gentle redirection.

> LARRY: It's fine to notice the tension in your throat, but see if you can bring your attention to your overall experience right now.
>
> CLIENT: Overall, I'm actually feeling better.

As the painful levels of arousal and unresolved emotions that keep clients out of their body diminish, they naturally begin to have access to awareness of their body.

Relationship to Internal States

In NARM, we explore clients' internal states as well as their *relationship* to their internal states—what they are feeling and how they relate to what they are feeling. Are the emotions and sensations they are experiencing manageable, or do they have judgments or fears about allowing them to surface? If they are aware of fears or judgments about their internal state, those are explored. We never push clients to feel an emotion; we want to help them notice internal states as they arise and expose any internal conflict they have about experiencing them. Because Connection clients often present with little affect, some therapies and some therapists may prematurely push them to feel emotions and sensations in the body. It is a failure of attunement to push clients to feel before they are ready. This lack of attunement is experienced as rejection and can reinforce these clients' shame about their difficulty connecting with their internal experience.

Engaging the Eyes

Trauma, and particularly early trauma, has a profound impact on the eyes. Hans Selye's research confirmed what Wilhelm Reich knew fifty years earlier: that under stress there is a narrowing of the visual field and other visual distortions. The unbearable, acute stress of early developmental and shock trauma is managed by chronic contraction, tension, and freeze in the musculature around the eyes. This contraction in the eye segment is part of a larger dynamic of tension and immobilization in the face, neck, and shoulders, all elements of an incomplete defensive-orienting response.

The Eyes and the Defensive-Orienting Response

For individuals with the Connection Survival Style, who have had early shock, attachment, and/or developmental trauma, the early environment has been experienced as dangerous or threatening. This experience of early threat is held as high levels of arousal, freeze, and an incomplete defensive-orienting response that expresses as hyper- or hypovigilance. For most clinicians, the darting eyes of the hypervigilant client are more familiar and easier to recognize; the hypotonic responses can be subtler and harder to track but have an even greater disconnective impact on the client.

Individuals with the Connection Survival Style have difficulty making eye contact. Typically, there are two ways in which therapists encounter this difficulty. Some clients find it uncomfortable or frightening to engage visually, and in therapy they avert their gaze, looking anywhere but at the therapist. Others, as we saw with Carla in Chapter 9, lock on with a fixed, contactless gaze, trying to hold on to a sense of connection. Encouraging clients to engage their eyes by finding non-threatening objects or colors to explore visually functions as an antidote to projection; successfully engaging the eyes can disrupt panic attacks and support reregulation. Table 10.3 summarizes the characteristics of hypertonic and hypotonic eyes.

Attachment Dynamics and the Eyes

When I teach NARM's psychobiological approach to attachment dynamics, I give participants in my training groups the exercise described in Figure 10.2.

This exercise gives participants an insight into their own early attachment dynamics. As is well known, the gaze interaction is part of the larger attachment dynamic that functions as a template for later relationships. Attachment researchers have explored how a mother's gaze, particularly when it conveys chronic anger, depression, or dissociation, impacts the developing child. Some participants, in reporting their experience, mention that they were unable to bring up any image of their mother's eyes, which in itself is telling. Other participants, for whom the mother's eyes were a source of trauma, report strong emotional and physical reactions, including fear, sadness, dissociation, and tightness in the chest or belly, to mention but a few. Finally, for others, the exercise is a positive experience and brings up a sense of closeness and appreciation.

HYPERTONIC EYES	HYPOTONIC EYES
Chronically angry eyes	Contactlessness
Chronic squinting	Each eye tracking in a different direction
Whites of eyes visible all around	Lights on but no one home: indication of dissociation
Darting eyes	Looking without seeing

Exophthalmic "bug" eyes	The "long distance" gaze; diffuse focus
Frightened eyes	Disengaged
Frightening eyes	Impaired capacity to orient
Excessive blinking	Waxy, frozen quality to the eyes and face
Tics	Fixed gaze
Hypervigilant eyes	Sleepy eyes
Predatory eyes	Difficulty making eye contact

TABLE 10.3: Impact of Trauma on the Eyes

> ***Your Mother's Eyes***
> *Ideally, this exercise is done with a partner with whom you can share your experience, but it can also be done alone or with a therapist. It can be quite evocative, so if at any point, it becomes too challenging or painful, please do not continue with it alone.*
> • Take a moment to center and ground yourself.
> • From this centered, grounded place, bring up an image of your mother's face and eyes.
> • Take a few minutes to be with the image and at the same time track both your emotional and physical experience.

> - Share your experience with a partner, or if you are doing this alone, write it down.
>
> ***
>
> **FIGURE 10.2:** Exercise to Explore Early Gaze Dynamics

Working Clinically with the Gaze and the Eyes

The eyes are a good diagnostic marker to gauge a client's coherency, connection, and organization. As we saw with Carla, paying attention to a client's gaze is an extremely useful way of tracking the connection-disconnection process. The first step in working with the eyes is to bring mindful awareness to the gaze and gaze-aversion process. Therapists reflect to their clients what they observe while encouraging clients not to force contact. In NARM the overall orientation is to help clients stay in contact with their internal experience and make eye contact only when they feel able to maintain internal connection with themselves.

Therapists need to modulate their own gaze with clients who have this survival style. Very direct gaze is threatening. It is helpful if the therapist looks away periodically to give these clients sufficient space. The challenge is to be present for the contact when the client wants it but not to push for it, holding the space without coming too strongly into the client's field. For these clients, too direct a gaze on the part of the therapist can be experienced as judgment and attack.

Eye contact should not be forced. When clients attempt to force themselves to make more contact than they can manage, other areas in their body will tighten up or shut down. It is relieving for most clients to track their gaze and gaze-aversion process with a clear understanding of not forcing contact, uncoupling shame responses that surface when they are not able to tolerate much eye contact, and simply bringing curiosity and inquiry into the dynamic. In this non-pathologizing atmosphere, in which clients become mindful of their process of connection and disconnection, possibilities for connection become increasingly available. After NARM sessions clients often report sharper vision, brighter colors, and a broader visual field.

The Challenges of Reconnection

Individuals with the Connection Survival Style have retreated into frozen and dissociated states, a certain kind of non-being that has helped them survive. These clients know, at a deep level, that their survival strategy is no longer serving them, but it is frightening for them to live without it. In the beginning of treatment, many of these clients have little capacity to tolerate either positive or negative affects and sensations. Since too much feeling of any kind threatens to overwhelm them, therapists must be able to anticipate the challenges that these clients face as they slowly confront the vulnerability of moving beyond their survival strategy.

The Tenuous Homeostasis of the Connection Survival Style

Despite their dissociated, depleted, and undercharged appearance, clients with the Connection Survival Style are energetically highly overcharged at the core; their entire nervous system has been flooded with shock energy. Their dissociation and disconnected lifestyle are attempts to manage this intense activation. Their ability to sense their body can be slow and initially difficult, because feeling the body initially brings a greater sense of threat than the non-feeling state.

Even a gradually titrated process of reconnection presents distinct challenges. As clients increasingly feel their bodily sensations and emotions, every increase in connection brings with it an upsurge of bodily sensations and emotion. As self-awareness increases, awareness of distress states also increases. Clients need to be educated about how this upsurge is part of a natural growth process, otherwise they can become frightened by the welling up of feeling and will tend to retreat into the non-feeling state. Since freeze and dissociation are driven by unmanageable levels of high arousal, the focus of the therapy is to find ways to help the client discharge these unbearably high levels of arousal. Some body-centered therapies, and even relaxation exercises that encourage deep breathing or use techniques that increase charge in the body, are often destabilizing for individuals with this survival style. Since they are already in a hyper-aroused state, adding more charge to their system is harmful. Because it is frightening to come out of dissociation and to feel again, the process of returning to feeling and to the body must be carefully titrated.

Working with Dissociation and Supporting Reconnection

The following techniques are useful in managing the challenges of reconnection. Several of the techniques discussed here are explained in more detail in the section on regulating the nervous system later in this chapter.

Mirroring
In guiding clients to connect to their experience, the NARM therapist is careful not to ask too many questions.

Rather than asking questions, it is useful to mirror or reflect. When there is settling in a client, the therapist reflects it. When positive reorganization is occurring, it is useful to reflect it in a general way, to point out any positive shifts, such as relaxation, softening, and increased connection or regulation. It is important to observe and note visible behaviors, being careful not to interpret. The therapist might say:

> "I notice when you're talking about your grandmother, you are smiling. What are you feeling right now?"

It is more helpful to be descriptive than prescriptive, to reflect the client's internal conflicts rather than try to resolve them. The therapist might say:

> "From what you are saying, there seems to be both anger and fear of your anger coming up right now.

Open Questions

At the beginning of the process, questions are as open as possible:

> "What are you aware of?"

Or:

"What do you notice in your experience right now?"

Only after the therapy has progressed and a client is ready would the NARM therapist ask:

"What do you notice in your body?"

Paying attention to whether referencing the body is organizing or disorganizing

Early in the therapeutic process, we reference the body when:
- The reference is to a positive, not a painful, state.
- The client is in touch with a resource or is in the process of discharging shock energy.
- There is sufficient capacity for containment.

Once clients begin to experience their body sensations again, the NARM therapist:
- Pendulates between negative and positive states, emphasizing positive states.
- Anchors positive states in the felt sense.

As reconnection occurs, negative affects will, of necessity, emerge, and the NARM therapist is careful to support mindful awareness of negative states while encouraging clients not to let themselves get overwhelmed by these painful states.

Titration

For individuals with the Connection Survival Style any shift in arousal can feel like too much. At first we work with the subtlest shifts, helping clients stay at the edge of what they can tolerate without being overwhelmed.

Containment

In NARM, we encourage containment of affects, not catharsis. Over time we help clients develop the capacity for depth in feeling both positive and negative emotions. We encourage clients not to act emotions out against others nor in against the self.

Mindful Inquiry

There is a seeming paradox between having a clear understanding of the organizing principles specific to this and other survival styles and, at the same time, coming to each moment of the therapeutic encounter with curiosity and without preconceived ideas. Organizing principles only constitute a working hypothesis which is always subject to change based on what unfolds, moment by moment, in therapy. Open curiosity informs the NARM process; this means coming to each moment fresh and supporting clients to be curious about their own situation and difficulties. Curiosity is an openness and a "not knowing" that functions as an antidote to our judgments, fixed ideas, and rigid, distorted identifications.

Working with the Fear of Feeling

The NARM therapist educates clients to know what powerful emotions and tremendous charge they hold inside without pushing for too much expression. *It is as important to work with a client's fear of feeling as it is to get to the feelings themselves.* When an individual is finally able to track his or her experience in the body, it indicates that a major milestone has been reached in the therapy; the client has developed enough organization to feel the sensations in his or her body.

LARRY: It seems that you're recognizing there's anger there, and at the same time it's frightening to you.

CLIENT: That's right.... It scares me, and I don't like it.

LARRY: Do you feel in a place to explore the fear and the judgments you have about anger?

The Therapeutic Relationship

The therapist is the representative of attachment and social engagement. The role of the therapeutic relationship is particularly important in working with early shock trauma, attachment wounds, and themes of abuse that are present with individuals who have the Connection Survival Style. Since these individuals tend to see other human beings as a threat, there are specific difficulties, challenges, and complications that surface in the dynamics of the transference. The following describes some of the key issues that arise in the therapeutic relationship with Connection Style individuals.

> ***Managing the Therapeutic Process of Connection***
> • Pointing out and reflecting positive shifts
> • Being invitational, not directive
> • Not focusing solely on what has gone wrong
> • Titrating small oscillations in sensation and emotion
> • Offering unconditional kindness, compassion, and acceptance
> • Pendulating between distress states and positive resources
> • Not pushing for trust or connection before the client is ready
> • Not pushing for sensation or emotion before the client is ready
> • Mindful awareness of negative states without becoming identified with them
> • Keeping one foot in the here-and-now, discouraging regression
> ***

> **TABLE 10.4:** Techniques Useful in Managing the Therapeutic Process of Connection

The Dangers of Inauthenticity

These highly sensitive clients are extremely attuned to the therapist in both positive and negative ways. They are particularly attuned to inauthenticity. The quality of therapists' presence and their ability to authentically *be* with these clients is of greater importance than any technique. If the therapist's approach is "techniquey," these clients will experience it as a misattunement. Since Connection Survival Style individuals tend to believe that no one will understand them, they do not respond well when the therapist *does to* them rather than *is with* them.

The NARM approach to working with this survival style offers mindful, nonjudgmental ways of being that can help therapists avoid approaching these clients in a mechanical manner. It is important to let these clients decide how much of themselves they are ready to reveal and at what pace. Individuals with the Connection Survival Style already see their lives as problems to be solved, so that if a therapist holds a primarily problem-solving focus, these clients' vulnerable inner world can be missed.

The Challenge of the Transference

It is important to attune to the natural connection-disconnection cycles of the Connection Survival Style. Because of their frozenness, individuals with this survival style are challenged by human warmth. When these individuals allow themselves to feel connected, the feeling is quickly followed by fears and suspicions. For them, small oscillations in feelings, positive or negative, represent a major risk, and the therapist should be prepared for powerful positive and negative transference reactions.

In NARM we:
- Explore clients' attachment dynamics and the various ways they turn away from connection. A NARM therapist keeps in mind how much contact clients can tolerate before becoming disorganized and how much

expansion is possible before contraction is triggered.
- Support both autonomic and affective regulation by carefully titrating and working with clients' rhythm of connection and withdrawal.
- Support clients' slow but progressive mindful attunement to their emotional and somatic states.

Clients with the Connection Survival Style will, at some point, be disappointed because their therapist cannot always live up to their expectations. It is important to communicate to these clients that they have a right to their needs even if their needs cannot be met. With these clients in particular, the process of rupture and repair in the therapeutic relationship is ongoing. Underneath the surface disconnection are needy, angry, and demanding parts, which of necessity must emerge and be explored. Therapists should not work with these clients unless they are willing to address the disappointments, suspicions, anger, and resentments that will inevitably surface toward them.

The importance of understanding attachment dynamics and the need for affective attunement between therapist and client has been addressed by many researchers and clinicians, but the critical role of somatic attunement—knowing how to clinically address the functional unity between disorganized attachment and a disorganized physiology and how to work with the disorganized physiology—is less well understood. Understanding regulation on a somatic level is key to implementing effective clinical interventions that can help clients in the process of moving from what Attachment Theory calls disorganized and avoidant attachment to what is called earned secure attachment.

Contact and Contact Rupture

Being mindful of the moment-to-moment process of contact and contact rupture is extremely important in working with individuals with the Connection Survival Style. For these clients, sharing distress in a compassionate relationship is in itself a new form of connection. While the therapist's warmth and acceptance are absolutely necessary for these individuals, these qualities can, at the same time, evoke high arousal along with fear and suspicion. This high arousal can quickly lead to a freeze response, leaving the therapist confused as to what happened. Moment by moment in the therapeutic process, NARM therapists work with the experience of contact and contact interruption. As the therapeutic alliance develops, the NARM therapist tracks and reflects the client's coming in and out of connection without pushing for more connection than the client is able to manage. For example, a NARM therapist might say:

> "I notice that as you're talking right now, you seem distracted and are going away. What are you noticing right now?"

The mindful inquiry into the process of contact and contact rupture is gently repeated many times over the course of therapy. With these clients, it is important not only to point out when they go away but also to reflect moments when they are more present. It is important to reflect any increase in a capacity for connection as it becomes evident in a session or in the client's life. The therapist might say:

> "I notice that today, even though we're dealing with some difficult material, you seem to be staying more connected. Does that fit with your experience?"

If it fits with the client's experience, the therapist might then offer the following invitation:

> "See what it's like if you take a moment to notice how it feels to be more present here today."

Presence and Safety

In the long term, experiencing the presence of a caring other has a calming effect. For some, a caring therapist may be the first truly kind person in their lives. The therapist's quality of contact offers a corrective experience of connection that allows clients to feel heard, understood, and appreciated, giving them the opportunity to feel received and valued.

Individuals with the Connection Survival Style tend to be harsh with themselves and are filled with self-hatred. Their self-hatred and self-judgment can be so automatic and reflexive (ego syntonic) that they are not aware of how harsh they are with themselves. It is important to consistently point out to clients when they are directing their anger and rage against themselves and to encourage them not to be so harsh with themselves. In psychodynamic terms, the therapist's consistent, kind presence allows the client the opportunity, sometimes for the first time, to introject an empathic other. A client who has begun the therapeutic process of introjection might report:

> "The other day at work I was struggling and getting really upset with myself. Then I thought about you and how you encourage me to be kinder with myself.... I just let go of it [the judgments]. It was really helpful."

Pacing

It is important for clients to know that they are in charge of how fast or slow the therapeutic process will unfold. Many clients have been pathologized as "resistant" when they are simply trying to keep their internal experience manageable. We explain to clients the importance of proceeding slowly and at their own pace. The therapist's pacing and rhythm are as important as the quality of his or her presence; a therapist can be generally empathic yet not be sensitive to clients' need to move at their own pace.

2. EXPLORE IDENTITY

In order to make sense of early trauma and distress states, individuals with the Connection Survival Style have taken their experience of environmental failure to be their own personal failure. This often implicit sense of personal failure shapes and distorts their developing sense of self. In addition to creating dysregulation, contraction, and freeze responses, trauma-based identifications also distort an individual's identity.

Supporting Expansion and Aliveness

Individuals with the Connection Survival Style learned to shut down their aliveness by withdrawing from their own bodies and emotions as well as from engagement with others. As a result, aliveness and expansion are threatening to both the vulnerable physiology and to the identity of a person who has adapted to a dangerous environment early in life. It is important to track how both the fear of and desire for connection and aliveness compete with each other and are expressed in the moment-by-moment process of a session and in everyday life.

The Dynamic of Expansion and Contraction

It is essential to help clients understand that there is a natural process of expansion and contraction in life that becomes even more evident in the therapeutic process. As psychological difficulties are resolved, increased regulation and embodiment are experienced as a sense of expansion. Toward the end of a session during which important experiences of resolution occurred, a client may say:

> CLIENT: Wow! Everything seems brighter.
>
> LARRY: Take a moment and explore that.
>
> CLIENT: All the colors in your room seem more intense.
>
> LARRY: And what do you notice in your body as you look around?
>
> CLIENT: I feel lighter and bigger.

In the nervous system and elsewhere in the body, every expansion and uptick in aliveness will naturally be followed by contraction. NARM has specific interventions to help clients manage the contraction phase. There is a tendency for clients to assume that when they experience the contraction phase, something is wrong. At this point a cycle of self-judgment is often triggered. It is important to let clients know that this expansion-contraction dynamic is a normal part of the therapeutic process and help them release any fears and judgments they have about it.

Sometimes psychological material that emerges in the contraction phase needs to be explored, but at other times, it is sufficient merely to be present to, and mindful of, the expansion-contraction dynamic. After a powerful session the previous week during which the client reported feeling more in his body that ever before, this interaction took place:

> LARRY: I'm wondering how it was for you after our last session.
>
> CLIENT: I had two days where I felt really good, and then my boss pointed out a mistake I made, and I got really tense and anxious.
>
> LARRY: How are you feeling right now?

CLIENT: I'm not feeling so anxious right now.

LARRY: As you look back on those first two days when you felt really good, what do you see?

CLIENT: *Pause....* It felt nice, but as I look back, I see it was also a little vulnerable and scary.

LARRY: So feeling good was scary and vulnerable, and then your boss said something to you.

CLIENT: He said I was late on my project. I felt really criticized, even though I sort of knew I was overreacting.

LARRY: Take a moment and ground yourself.

CLIENT: *Takes a deeper breath and sighs.*

LARRY: And from this perspective now, where you're feeling more grounded, what do you see about your reaction to your boss?

CLIENT: *Chuckling to himself....* Feeling so good those first two days seemed too good to be true.

LARRY: It sounds like you were expecting something bad to happen.

CLIENT: It's true.... In a way, I was.

LARRY: What do you see about your reaction to your boss from your perspective right now?

CLIENT: I see that I really was overreacting. He just pointed out that I was late with the project—he wasn't being critical.

LARRY: And what are you experiencing right now as you see your reactions to what you took to be your boss's criticism.

CLIENT: My body is relaxing again. I'm starting to feel better.

LARRY: *After giving the client time to re-regulate....* This seems to fit with the expansion-contraction dynamic we've been exploring.

CLIENT: It does.

This client was in an expanded state after the previous session; it was only a matter of time before contraction set in. In the contraction phase old shame-based identifications and sensitivities inevitably surface; sometimes they need to be explored, but at other times they are simply a way to make sense of the contraction; in either case, the trap is that when clients attach content to the contraction and identify with that content, they lose sight of the overarching dynamic of expansion-contraction and get stuck in the contraction phase.

Fear of Life
Individuals with the Connection Survival Style often come into therapy

with fears and even obsessions about death and disease. For example, one client, a young man, came in wanting to talk about his continual fear of dying, which had been a central subject in three previous therapies that were, according to him, "not very helpful." My comment to him was:

> "I think we may get more mileage out of exploring your fear of living than your fear of dying."

For such clients, expansion and aliveness are more frightening than the half-alive state in which they live. For every uptick in aliveness, the therapist should be prepared to help the client manage the corresponding contraction and increase in symptoms that often follow the expansion. Table 10.5 provides a summary of the therapeutic themes pertinent to clients with a Connection Survival Style.

Mindful Awareness of Increasing Aliveness

NARM therapists explore the psychological and physiological patterns that limit expansion and aliveness. Helping clients understand their fear of aliveness as well as exploring the ways they disconnect from themselves and others helps them learn to mindfully tolerate the increasing aliveness they experience as they learn to reconnect. Intellectual insights alone are rarely enough to alter the deep-seated psychological and physiological patterns that foreclose aliveness. Key to successful personal development for Connection Survival Style individuals is supporting the feelings of expansion that arise as their conflicts about connection move toward resolution. It is necessary to help them tolerate and manage the upsurge of energy that comes when they move into greater organization. For example, the therapist might say:

> "We've seen, time and again, that when you start feeling more alive, these symptoms come up. Let's see today if you can notice them and let them move through without focusing all your attention on them."

Identifications and Counter-Identifications

As with all the adaptive survival styles, the Connection Survival Style has underlying shame-based identifications that develop in order to make sense of the distress of early environmental failure. Later in life, in reaction to the underlying distress and shame, these clients develop pride-based counter-identifications. A large part of what we take to be our identity consists of these shame-based identifications as well as the pride-based counter-identifications. Shame-based identifications, which we often believe to be the truth about ourselves, can be conscious or unconscious. The more energy individuals invest in the pride-based counter-identifications, the more strongly the underlying shame-based identifications are reinforced. Table 10.6 provides examples of both types of identifications.

> **NARM therapists keep the following therapeutic themes in**

mind when working with clients with the Connection Survival Style:
- What is their capacity for connection?
- How do they disrupt the connection?
- What is their emotional range?
- Can they feel their body?
- Can they ground?
- Can they find and utilize resources?
- What is their relationship to anger and aggression?
- Do they tend to act their aggression in or out?
- What is their capacity for self-soothing and self-regulation?
- What is incomplete on both emotional and physiological levels?
- How do they manage the expansion-contraction dynamics?
- Is the overall trajectory of the therapy over time toward more regulation?

***

TABLE 10.5: Therapeutic Themes to Keep in Mind When Working with

the Connection Survival Style Connection Survival Style	
SHAME-BASED IDENTIFICATIONS	**PRIDE-BASED COUNTER-IDENTIFICATIONS**
Shame at existing	Disdain for humanity
Feeling like a burden	Pride in not needing others
Feeling of not belonging	Pride in being a loner
Shame at not being able to feel	Pride in being rational/disdain for emotions
Undeserving	Demanding neediness and entitlement
Feeling unlovable	Spiritual superiority (spiritualizing subtype) Intellectual superiority (thinking subtype)

TABLE 10.6: Shame-Based Identifications and Pride-Based Counter-Identifications (partial list)

In NARM, regardless of how a client presents, we keep in mind that both identifications and counter-identifications are always present. It is particularly important when working with Connection types not to expose the fiction of the pride-based counter-identifications without, at the same time, addressing the equally false, shame-based identifications. Therapies that focus on dismantling the pride-based identifications—the so-called defenses—can leave Connection clients feeling more identified with their shame. NARM emphasizes, in many different ways, that the shame-based identifications result from the attempt to come to terms with early environmental failures, being careful not to leave clients more identified with feeling like a helpless child, a burden, undeserving, or unlovable. A dialogue on this topic might go as follows:

> LARRY: As you're seeing through this image of yourself as superior for not feeling, it's also important to understand how life-saving it was to be able to turn off your feelings the way you did.

> CLIENT: I've always felt so out of step ... it's always seemed weird that other people had so many emotions about things and I never did.

> LARRY: From your perspective right now [adult consciousness], what are you able to see about these patterns of shame with which you've struggled your whole life?

In this example, the client is seeing through the pride-based image he has tried to maintain in not feeling and in not needing anyone. As his feelings and needs surface, they are accompanied by shame that he was not as self-sufficient as he wanted to believe. It is important when working with the Connection Survival Style, not to focus solely on working through the pride-based counter-identifications. Though on the surface this client presents as a prideful loner who is without feelings, underneath he feels shame, seeing himself as an outsider and wondering why he does not feel emotions like other people. As I challenge this client's pride-based counter-identifications, I also help him see that the shame he feels about himself is just as unreal as the prideful self-image he has tried to maintain.

With clients who present as more identified with the shame-based elements of their personality, there is usually a hidden and unconscious grandiosity that surfaces in the course of therapy: "My suffering is greater than anyone else's" or "I'm so wounded—my needs are much more important than anyone else's. I need more attention than everyone else." In the course of therapy these clients can swing from the pride-based "I have no needs" to "I have so many needs, and I need them met now, and I need you to take care of them." Rejecting their needs and feelings would constitute a repetition of the early environmental failure, but the demand that all needs be met merely acts out the needy "inner child" without leading to resolution. It is important that these clients have the corrective experience in which their needs are validated; at the same time, the therapist must avoid the trap of infantalizing them by attempting to meet all their needs. It is important to attune to, but over time to gently challenge, the demanding neediness. As the neediness surfaces, the NARM therapist communicates acceptance of the infantile needs while at the same time, supporting the development of an "inner adult" who can understand and manage the tension that comes with not having needs immediately met. In the NARM healing cycle, we find that as the nervous system regulates bottom-up, there is increasing physiological support for the development of the executive functions; as executive functions develop, there is top-down support for increasing self-regulation.

Disidentification

The principle of disidentification is a core element of the NARM approach. Disidentification helps clients see through the fiction of both the shame- and pride-based identifications of their survival style. As they progressively disidentify from the limiting elements of what they have come to believe is their identity, clients consistently report feeling more at ease and more connected. Since every distorted identification is reflected in the body in the form of tension and collapse, when identifications dissolve, clients consistently describe themselves as feeling lighter, as having a sense of more internal space.

Identifying Fixed and Rigid Beliefs

One component of the disidentification process involves developing mindful awareness of the fixed and rigid beliefs we hold about ourselves and about the world. As part of the disidentification process, NARM encourages clients to hold lightly, and to be curious about, the fixed beliefs they have about themselves or the world. Curiosity and inquiry are part of the disidentification process. Curiosity implies a not knowing; through a mindful disidentification process NARM helps clients move from the frozenness of fixed beliefs to flow, from narrowness and contraction to expansion. We challenge fixed beliefs and identifications by encouraging clients to look at themselves from a fresh perspective.

The following are typical fixed beliefs about self and the world found in individuals with the Connection Survival Style:
- "Life is meaningless."
- "I'm a failure."
- "Everybody has love but me."
- "The world is a cold, empty place."
- "People are dangerous."

- "I'm better off being by myself."
- "Emotions are weak and stupid."
- "I can work everything out rationally."
- "As long as I stay in my head, I'm safe."
- "I'm a horrible person."
- "Other people are angry. Not me, I'm gentle and nice."

To the degree that clients label themselves, or put themselves in rigid categories—"I am a person who always..." or "I am a person who never..."—they narrow their life and block their capacity for open inquiry.

Addressing Shame

Clients are often not aware of the element of judgment that is implicit in their shame, so it is important to identify patterns of self-judgment. It is also true that as the nervous system regulates and internal distress diminishes, shame will also diminish. But to work effectively with pathological shame, therapists need to work both top-down and bottom-up.

In NARM, we address these clients' identifications with shame and badness without trying to convince them that they are good; they "know" they are not.

> CLIENT: I'm a loner. I've never been good at relationships. I've always felt that there is something basically wrong with me.

> LARRY: I understand that you have various explanations for why relationships are so hard for you and that you blame yourself for what you see as your failures. But maybe the reality of why relationships have been difficult for you is more complicated than that.

NARM therapists explore the broad patterns of self-judgment by identifying toxic self-criticism and sometimes even using paradox to highlight the foolishness of toxic self-judgments. After listening to a client's monologue for several minutes on how bad they are, we might say:

> LARRY: You've convinced me—you really are bad!

> CLIENT: *Laughs.*

This client's laughing at herself is part of the process of disidentification, not taking her self-judgments so seriously.

The Designated Issue

Because early trauma is held implicitly in the body, causing significant systemic disorganization, identity distortion, and shame, it is often impossible for clients with the Connection Survival Style to identify the actual source of their distress. What these individuals identify as primary issues often can only serve as general landmarks for the therapy. Their narrative often centers around what in NARM is called *the designated issue*—what they *believe* to be the source of their pain. Although their pain is real, the narrative with which they explain their pain may not be accurate. As described more fully on pages 143–144, the designated issue involves a real or perceived personal or physical deficiency or defect, such as a dissatisfaction about the body, shyness, not feeling smart enough, not feeling tall enough, or a persistent health problem.

Individuals with the Connection Survival Style believe that if their particular designated issue were resolved, their life would then be great. The therapeutic challenge is that although there may be a real problem, these clients do not realize that the designated issue is a symptom of deeper difficulties.

Therapeutically, it is important not to fall into the trap of problem solving or over-focusing on the designated issue without addressing the fundamental theme of disconnection. For example, we might say to a client who is focusing on the pain she feels about a perceived personal shortcoming:

> "I know that you believe that you understand what your pain is about ... but let's see if we can stay open to the possibility that it may more involved than that."

Here we are introducing a bit of space between the client and her explanation for her difficulties. This is part of the disidentification process.

Self-Acceptance

Self-acceptance is an important part of the healing process. We invite the possibility of including or even embracing those parts of the self that have been condemned, expelled, and rejected. We might say:

> "You've said several times during the course of our therapy how much you hate this scared part of yourself, but maybe you could be curious about this scared part rather than hating or rejecting it."

We support clients to accept themselves even when they have a problem. We want to help clients separate their self-esteem from whatever has become their designated issue. In the case of a client who is truly overweight and has hated herself her whole life for her weight problem, we would say:

> "I wonder if it's possible for you to see yourself as a good person who at the same time has a weight problem."

This pattern of self-rejection will not change overnight, but we are planting a seed of possibility, a different way for this client to relate to herself. When real-life problems such as difficulty with weight are approached from a perspective of self-rejection rather than self-acceptance, self-hatred can be reinforced.

3. WORK IN PRESENT TIME

NARM moves a person's attention away from past history to the moment-by-moment process of therapy. As we saw in the session with Carla in Chapter 9, attending to the process in the present moment is fundamental when working with early shock and developmental trauma. The following clinical vignette illustrates NARM's orientation toward process rather than content and to the here and now rather than personal history.

Linda came to my office following the breakup of a relationship. Feeling betrayed by her ex-partner, she was bitter and cynical about ever finding love with men she described as "commitment phobic." From previous therapies, she was aware of her dysfunctional personal patterns and she explained how she picked men who were like her father. She berated herself for "doing it again," for perpetuating her "dysfunctional relationship patterns" by choosing a man who was intellectual, emotionally cold, and who, in the course of the relationship, became increasingly withdrawn. She was concerned that since the breakup, she was overeating, not sleeping well, and fighting the impulse to smoke, although she had given up the habit ten years earlier. When I asked her at different times during the session, "What are you experiencing right now as you're talking about this?" she answered are you experiencing right now as you're talking about this?" she answered by telling me what she was thinking: "I think this has to do with my father. He could never be there for me either." Although I could see that she was visibly upset, when I asked her directly what she was experiencing emotionally, she drew a blank.

As Linda sat with her arms tightly wrapped around her thin torso, I noticed that her voice sounded strained, that she avoided eye contact, and that she seemed quite disconnected. The content of her narrative revealed consistent difficulties with relationship, and I noticed that these same difficulties were present in the therapeutic relationship with me. Her insights about her difficult relationship with her father did not address the here-and-now difficulty she was having in knowing her current emotional and sensate experience and being present with me.

Linda's cognitive understanding of the sources of her problems did not address her ambivalent and compromised capacity for connection. From a NARM perspective, it is less important to focus on the theme of her father than on her own current ambivalence with contact. As much as Linda longed for connection, she did not realize until later in therapy how frightened she was of it. She also did not learn until later that choosing men who were unavailable was her way of limiting connection in her current life.

Distortions in Time

Developmental and shock trauma trap our consciousness and our life force, effectively keeping part of us stuck in past time. In cases of developmental trauma, we continue to see the world through the eyes of a child. When we filter the present moment through past experience, we live through our memories, identifications, and old object relations.

Because of their early trauma, individuals with the Connection Survival Style are the most stuck in past time and most identified with their trauma. Bringing clients' attention to what is happening in the here and now starts in the first session and is ongoing throughout therapy. NARM explores, on the level of both body and identity, how individuals have incorporated the environmental failures that they have experienced, and over time, helps them to see how they continue to recreate their history in the here and now. The focus is less on *why* clients are the way they are and more on what they are experiencing in the moment and *how* they disconnect from themselves in present time. Exploring personal history is part of the therapeutic process *to the degree that it helps clients see the bigger picture of their survival style.* Seeing the survival value of old patterns that are now dysfunctional as adults helps them be less critical of themselves.

It is possible to come home to oneself only in the present moment. In our minds we can anticipate the future or remember the past, but the body exists only in the present moment. Even when working with personal history, NARM maintains a present-moment focus, always supporting the dual awareness of what was then and what is now. A NARM therapist might say:

> "As you're talking about your relationship with your father, what are you noticing in your body right now?"

Over time, as therapy continued with Linda, I repeatedly brought her awareness back to her experience in the present moment; by separating how things were for her as a child from who she was in the moment, her beliefs that there were no good men out there and that she herself was a failure greatly diminished. By learning to listen to what she was feeling, both on an emotional and on a sensate level in the present moment, she reconnected to her emotions and her body.

As clients learn to listen to themselves, their nervous systems become more regulated. As their nervous systems become more regulated, it is easier to listen to themselves. As the nervous system regulates and as painful identifications resolve, clients move progressively into the here and now. The reverse is also true: as clients move progressively into the here and now, the nervous system re-regulates and old identifications become more obvious and resolve. In this process, Linda's impulse to overeat diminished, her sleeping returned to normal, and she no longer experienced the impulse to smoke. As she shifted her focus away from what had happened to her in the past, blaming her father and blaming herself, and as she was able to identify and own her current fears about intimacy, her agency and sense of empowerment increased, and she came to see herself less as a victim of circumstances.

The Paradox of Change

In NARM, it is maintained that the more we try to change ourselves, the more we prevent change from occurring. On the other hand, the more we allow ourselves to fully experience who we are, the greater the possibility of change. This understanding is core to NARM. The orientation is one of working with what is, rather than with how we want things to be. This perspective is consistent with a present-moment focus because it is only in the present moment that we are able to fully experience ourselves.

Agency and Empowerment

NARM uses the term *agency* rather than the term *responsibility,* which is commonly used in other therapies, because for many people, responsibility carries overtones of blame. *Agency* comes from the Latin *to act* and conveys more neutrality. As human beings, we are constantly organizing and reorganizing our experience. It is the agency inherent in this organizing capacity that the NARM approach addresses and supports. For example, a client who responds fearfully to other people's anger might say:

> "Anger is really frightening to me because my dad was such a rageaholic."

The fact that this client's father was a "rageaholic" is only part of the picture. This client's fear of anger is more complex than this statement implies. Based on the belief that the past determines the present, many therapists would take this statement at face value and accept the premise that what happened in childhood determines this client's fear of anger as an adult. This paradigm of the past, however, may lead a person to feel like a victim of childhood experiences and can reinforce a sense of helplessness.

Usually, it is clients' disowned and unrecognized anger that is more germane to their fear of anger. After exploring what it was like for this client to be around a rageaholic, I would inquire into his current relationship to anger:

> LARRY: I wonder what your relationship to your own anger is.
>
> CLIENT: Anger.... I don't have any anger ... except maybe at myself.

Consistent with the Distortions of the Life Force model (Figure i.2), working through the splitting, judgments, and fears about their own anger is usually a multilayered process: "Only bad people like my father have anger. I'm a good person; I don't have anger." As clients work through the internal fears and identifications that have foreclosed for them the experience of anger, they progressively integrate their own anger and aggression. As they experience how they have split off and turned their anger against themselves in the form of self-rejection, self-loathing, and self-judgment, the energies that have been turned against the self become available for life. It is tremendously empowering to integrate the survival energies inherent in anger and aggression. In every case, when clients can integrate their own aggression, they feel stronger, less afraid, and more connected.

As part of our survival patterns, we have all adapted to, aligned ourselves with, and literally incorporated the life-denying elements of our early environment. Unless we can identify and own our adaptations to early childhood experience, including how we have adapted to and internalized the life-denying elements of our early environment, we continue to suffer. It is, of course, a given that many of the patterns addressed in therapy began in early childhood. However, NARM makes a critical distinction: clients perpetuate dysfunctional patterns because they do not know how to do it differently. A NARM therapist might comment:

> "It's clear that you didn't start this process, but it's important that you see how you continue it."

Agency is seeing what we do to ourselves as adults, how we have internalized and continue to re-create the environmental failures we have experienced. We choose people in our lives who resonate with our dysfunctional survival patterns. Unless we can see how we turn against and abandon ourselves by rejecting our core needs and emotions, we have a tendency to feel like victims. Addressing the issue of agency with a client who had been in a series of abusive relationships, I might say:

> "If you, on some level, think you are bad and deserve to be punished, it's not hard to find people in the world who will agree with you and find ways to punish you."

Helping clients experience how they maintain dysfunctional patterns requires tact and sensitivity to each individual's vulnerability as well as, when necessary, an element of confrontation. It is important that clients do not feel blamed or shamed for perpetuating patterns that were once life-saving; at the same time it is important for them to see that they are "actors" re-creating and acting out old survival patterns. It is implicit in this understanding that until clients develop a sense of agency in regard to their survival patterns, they will feel like helpless victims of others or of circumstances. There are, of course, times when a person truly is a victim, but here we are addressing the effects of adaptive survival styles on adult life. Agency involves owning the split-off aspects of oneself and is a here-and-now process. The dynamic of progressively experiencing more agency feels liberating and empowering.

In summary, to reestablish agency, a NARM therapist explores with clients how they are contributing to their own suffering—how they may be consciously or unconsciously instrumental in creating their own distress as adults. Individuals with the Connection Survival Style are certainly not responsible for the early trauma or attachment difficulties they have experienced. Over time these clients come to see that although in early life they were victims of circumstance—family patterns, parental abuse, neglect, etc.—as adults it is important that they come to see how they continue to perpetuate their victimization.

4. REGULATE THE NERVOUS SYSTEM

In the NARM healing cycle, nervous system regulation can be addressed from both top-down and bottom-up vantage points. From a top-down perspective, nervous system regulation increases as the distorted identifications of adaptive survival styles are resolved and as disavowed emotions become integrated. From a bottom-up perspective, which is the focus of this section, the principle techniques used to support nervous system regulation are containment, grounding, orienting, titration, and pendulation.

Containment

Working within a client's range of resiliency supports containment. It is essential that clients be able to work with their difficulties while, at the same time, remaining grounded in their bodies and in the present moment. We regularly ask clients questions whose answers clarify for us how they relate to their various internal states. For example:

> CLIENT: Now I'm starting to feel upset.
>
> LARRY: Is it okay for you to allow that upset to come up, or does it feel like it is too much?

It is important not to push painful affects away but rather, over time, to learn how to become less submerged and less identified with them. As long as difficult emotions feel manageable to clients, we continue to explore them. If the emotions feel overpowering or if clients start to dissociate, then we have them slow down (titrate), ground, pendulate to a resource, or focus on their experience in the present moment (ground and orient).

Focusing on positive resources and the experience of safety that comes with them establishes and reinforces oases of organization in the body and in the psyche. As the work with these oases of organization continues, areas of disorganization, which include painful responses such as shame, self-judgments, and identity distortions, as well as painful affects such as grief and loss, will likely surface and temporarily increase the disorganization. In a contained therapeutic process, therapy overall brings increasing systemic organization. This mindful process of containment supports increasing organization, which in turn supports a greater capacity for connection (see Figure 12.1).

Working with painful experiences from childhood becomes overwhelming when a client loses the capacity to hold a dual awareness and is no longer mindful of what was then and what is now. In abreaction, the traumatic memories become more real than present reality. In such cases, we ask questions designed to reinforce the distinction between past and present. It is useful to explore the past only as long as the client is able to remain anchored in the present. When clients act as though a past situation is still in the present, such as with powerful intrusive imagery about an abusive father who is long dead, we may intervene:

LARRY: How long ago did these beatings take place?

CLIENT: A long time ago.

LARRY: How long has your father has been dead?

CLIENT: Fifteen years.

LARRY: What are you experiencing as you remind yourself that he's been dead for fifteen years?

CLIENT: I'm starting to calm down.

LARRY: Take your time. Notice how you experience that calming.

CLIENT: *Long pause.... The client is visibly settling and his breathing is becoming more regular.*

LARRY: From this calmer place right now, what do you see about this situation that you weren't able to see as a child?

CLIENT: I can see that part of me really wanted to fight back, maybe even kill him.

LARRY: And what do you notice in your body as you acknowledge those impulses?

CLIENT: It actually feels good. Stronger.

LARRY: Give yourself some time to feel that "good, stronger" feeling.

Grounding

Grounding is a basic technique widely used in body-centered psychotherapies. In NARM, grounding is used to support an increasing capacity for somatic mindfulness, connection, and nervous system regulation. Grounding functions as an antidote to disconnection, helping to literally bring awareness back into the body, supporting reconnection on all levels of experience. To the degree that clients can feel their feet on the floor and their body in the chair, they are mindfully present in the here and now. Like all therapeutic processes, grounding should not be pushed; it needs to be done slowly, in a way that is manageable and does not overwhelm. In the initial stages of therapy some dissociated clients find it difficult, if not impossible, to ground themselves. Therapists support the processes of connection and organization by bringing their clients' attention to the process of grounding:

> "As you are talking about the challenges you are facing, take a moment to see if you can get a sense of yourself in the chair. Can you feel your feet on the floor ... your seat in the chair ... the support of the backreast?

As we attend to clients' capacity for self-awareness, we support their awareness not just cognitively and emotionally, but also in their physiological experience. Many clients will find grounding to be organizing and settling, whereas some will find it anxiety provoking. When clients become more anxious when attempting to ground, or when they are unable to do it, it is an indication that there is too much activation in their body to allow them to ground at that moment. When grounding is not possible, facilitating discharge of activation can be supported by other regulating techniques such as pendulating, resourcing, and orienting. As activation is discharged, grounding becomes more possible. From a NARM perspective, grounding in the body provides an anchor to reality. From an increasingly more grounded and embodied place, the truths and fictions of our shame- and pride-based identifications become clearer. Attuning to the body gives us a stable platform on which to work with the adaptive survival styles that are often mistaken for our true self.

Orienting

Grounding and orienting are seemingly simple but valuable tools. As clients ground and orient to their surroundings, they come into the present moment and simultaneously begin to emerge from dissociation. Orienting techniques are useful with all clients, but they are particularly useful for clients with the Connection Survival Style for whom dissociation is the primary coping mechanism. Clinically, NARM therapists encourage orienting as a simple yet powerful technique to help clients "come down" into their bodies, out of their fantasies, and be more present in the here and now. Consider this orienting exchange:

> LARRY: Check out the room and see if there's anything that attracts your attention.
>
> CLIENT: That painting on your wall is interesting.
>
> LARRY: Tell me what you find interesting in the painting.
>
> CLIENT: The colors, for one thing.
>
> LARRY: What colors in particular attract your attention?
>
> CLIENT: The blues and the reds.

LARRY: As you're paying attention to the colors, what's happening in your body right now?

CLIENT: I feel a little more here, a little more relaxed.

LARRY: Notice how you experience physically being "a little more here" and "a little more relaxed."

As seen in this dialogue, when clients are panicky or begin to dissociate, it is useful to encourage them to orient to an object or a color in the room. As soon as clients engage their eyes, both panic and dissociation diminish.

Titration

NARM does not focus on painful or traumatizing experiences until there is a capacity to settle, ground, and regulate. Over time, NARM uses grounding and containment to support an increasingly organized and organizing adult consciousness. It is only when some capacity to self-regulate is possible that we can begin to focus on a client's trauma narrative. By approaching traumatic experiences slowly and obliquely, we are using a technique from Somatic Experiencing called titration.

Titration is a word borrowed from chemistry. In chemistry, when two containers, one with an acid and one with a base, are poured one into the other all at once, it produces an explosion. But if the two substances are combined drop by drop, the discharge is very small and gradually, the two substances neutralize each other. This analogy communicates the importance of taking highly charged emotional material one manageable piece at a time. This measured approach helps avoid catharsis—the explosion—and facilitates the integration of the highly charged affect.

It is important to carefully titrate disorganizing experiences such as extreme fear. In developmental work, extreme fear is often an indication that disowned and disavowed anger and rage are moving toward awareness. Trauma narratives that are not titrated effectively can be overwhelming and disorganizing. Knowing when and how to titrate effectively—going fast enough but not too fast—is an art that requires continually adjusting the pacing to the client's developing capacity. To titrate effectively, we track observable cues, pay attention to our own resonant responses, and ask clients directly how the pace is working for them, remembering that traumatized clients do not always know when they are becoming overwhelmed and dissociated. We often have to use various techniques to manage the pace of the session, particularly at first, because clients are often unable to do so. The following examples highlight some important points:

- Slowing the process down and shifting focus.

    "I notice that as you're talking about your father, you start to get agitated and go away. So let's slow things down a bit ... take a moment and give yourself time to settle."

- Psychoeducation.

"It's important that you don't go into the painful memories all at once."
- Reinforcing clients' capacity to pay attention to and titrate their own pace.

    "It's important for you to listen to your own capacity to manage the feelings that are coming up and find the pace that is right for you."
- Freeze frame.

    "When you talk about your father's abusiveness, the memories come rushing back. See what happens if you bring up a static, single-frame image of him and put it at any distance that feels right for you."
- Finding a pace where the client remains connected.

    "In our work together, control isn't a bad word. It's important to go at a pace where you are able to stay connected and in control."

Pendulation

Pendulation is a natural pulsatory phenomenon of expansion and contraction. It is also a clinical intervention that can be consciously utilized by the therapist as part of the overall containment process.

Natural Pendulation

As clients experience more aliveness, there is an accompanying expansion. At some point, this expansion will be followed by contraction. It is important for therapists to explain to their clients that growth is a process of expansion and contraction and that the contraction phase is natural and inevitable. This understanding of the natural pendulation process helps clients navigate the contraction phase without becoming overly concerned that something is wrong.

In NARM, we attend to the natural pendulation process within a session and between sessions. Particularly following a session in which clients have a strong experience of expansion, it is important to inquire into how they managed the inevitable contraction that can be expected to follow. If a client responds with unmanageable contraction, evidenced by regression, strong anxiety, depression, or increased physical symptoms, this indicates what in NARM is called a boomerang effect and is an indication to the therapist to titrate more carefully and go forward at a slower pace.

Clinical Pendulation

In clinical pendulation, the therapist consciously shifts the focus from difficult memories to resources that bring soothing and settling. Observing that a client is beginning to dissociate while addressing a new element of their abuse history, this exchange took place:

> LARRY: Let me interrupt you for just a moment. I notice that you're starting to go away. I want to direct your attention back to feeling your body in the chair and your feet on the floor. *Long pause....* How is that for you?
>
> CLIENT: *Deep exhale.* That feels better.

In slowing down the process, we are titrating. In consciously encouraging clients to shift attention back to the body and away from the narrative, we are pendulating. Pendulation is used simultaneously with titration to support the nervous system's capacity to integrate highly charged affects in a way that brings increasing self-regulation.

When addressing painful elements of personal history, NARM therapists pay mindful attention to their clients' changing states. When a client is becoming overly activated, it is useful to pendulate to resource-oriented questions. For example:

"I'm wondering what or who helped you get through all this?"

Both shock and developmental trauma trap our consciousness in the past. The question above reinforces the fact that the client is here, in the present moment, and safe; it is intended to evoke an external resource such as a loving grandmother or an internal resource such as the will to live. The ultimate resource that clients have when working with any trauma is that they have survived. Working in the present moment helps clients progressively integrate the reality that they survived. In this way, we pendulate between the reality of the present moment wherein the client is safe and the painful, frightening memories while reminding the client of resources that have been and are available.

Safety

In teaching therapists how to address the issue of safety with clients who have the Connection Survival Style, I use the analogy of befriending a feral animal that has been living on its own as best it can. We see that the animal both wants to come in out of the cold—meaning, wants to connect—but, at the same time, is fearful. If we attempt to approach the feral cat or dog, it will run away, but if we hold an invitational space, over time the animal will increasingly trust and approach us.

It is similar with clients who have experienced early trauma. They want to trust but are scared and angry. As with a feral animal, the therapist communicates that it is safe to come in out of the cold. At the same time, the therapist respects their fearfulness and does not push them to trust prematurely or try to force connection. These clients desire closeness but are not always aware of how frightened they are of it. Pushing them to trust before they are ready ignores how frightened they are of connection. As with the feral animal, the therapist addresses the ambivalence of clients with the Connection Survival Style by holding a space in which they can slowly experience and take in that there is no threat and that the situation could actually be safe. Initially, therapists will find that when they move toward clients with the Connection Survival Style, these clients will freeze or run away. Over time, as the therapeutic alliance strengthens, these clients will discover that not only will the therapist not hurt them, but that the therapy can be a haven of safety.

Even though many readers have not experienced such extreme ambivalence about connection, most of us know the feeling of both wanting and fearing closeness in relationship. Many individuals have reached a certain comfort level with their own tendency toward disconnection, not consciously aware of how frightened they are of feeling close connection. For those clients who identify with wanting close connection in relationship but feel like they can't find partners with whom to connect, the road to growth and healing lies in owning their own ambivalence about closeness and seeing how they pick partners who act out their own need for distance in the relationship.

CONCLUSION

The dance between connection and disconnection is a core organizing theme for all five adaptive survival styles. For individuals with the Connection Survival Style, however, who have experienced early shock and developmental trauma, the resulting dissociation, nervous system dysregulation, and identity distortions are the most severe. It is easy to become confused by the complex and painful symptomatology that these clients present, losing sight of what drives their painful symptoms.

In this chapter we have presented principles, tools, and techniques that address the major issues that weave together in self-reinforcing loops and drive this survival style.
- We have presented how to work with the global high-arousal states as well and the frozen and dissociative states that are associated with the nervous system dysregulation and the lack of social engagement that clients with the Connection Survival Style experience.
- We have detailed how to work with identity distortions such as low self-esteem and self-hatred that result from early trauma.
- We have illustrated how to work with the continuous interplay and self-reinforcing loops between nervous system dysregulation and identity distortions.

Primary NARM Principles
Being available to clients' inner world without pushing for connection
Tracking and reflecting the connection-disconnection process

Tracking organization-disorganization

Helping clients navigate the challenges of reconnection

Understanding and tracking the dynamics of expansion-contraction

Working with the fear of aliveness and supporting increasing aliveness

Exploring clients' relationship to anger and aggression

Helping clients to disidentify from shame and pride-based identifications

Understanding the function of the designated issue

Encouraging self acceptance

Supporting clients' capacity for self-reference, self-reflection, and mindfulness

Using somatic mindfulness to work with the nervous system and identity

Supporting increasing self-regulation

Tracking and supporting somatic connection

Helping clients resolve identity distortions including shame and self-hatred

Tools and Techniques

Creating safety and containment

Working in the here-and-now even with personal history

Establishing resources

Evoking positive experiences of connection

Tracking clients' range of resiliency

Titrating to help clients come out of dissociation in a manageable way

Working with the difficulties that emerge with increasing connection and expansion

Working with clients who cannot feel their bodies

Working with the eyes, the gaze, and projective processes

Compassionate feedback and confrontation of clients' acting in of aggression

Maintaining a dual awareness of past and present

Avoiding regression

***

TABLE 10.7: Summary of Principles and Techniques that Inform the NARM Therapeutic Process with the Connection Survival Style

Therapeutic Process with the Connection Survival Style

- We have discussed how to work with clients' simultaneous desire for and deep fear of connection and how to create an environment that supports increasing connection while also exploring how clients disrupt their connection with self and others.
- We have explained the functional unity that exists between being in the body and being in the present moment and how to help clients become more embodied and more present. We have offered therapists and clients tools for working with difficult early survival patterns as they express in the therapeutic process and in a client's life.

11

Healing the Relational Matrix

NARM™ and NeuroAffective Touch™ in the Long-Term Treatment of Early Developmental/Relational Trauma

The process of separation/individuation can take place only when connection has been fully established on all levels of experience.

This chapter presents excerpts from the long-term treatment of a woman whose trauma and life struggles encapsulate the earliest issues of the Connection Survival Style. These excerpts illustrate how the specialized use of connection through NeuroAffective Touch, an aspect of the NARM approach, can be transformative when working with preverbal developmental/relational deficits.

Emma was referred to Aline by a colleague who, after eight months of therapy with her, had come to a therapeutic impasse. This colleague thought that Emma's issues would benefit from an approach that specifically addressed early attachment and developmental deficits. As we have seen, because early trauma can interrupt the development of the capacity for affect regulation, it requires specific interventions that take into account the somatic dimension of the formation of self.

Withdrawal and Isolation

As Emma sat down in my office, she was nervous and uncomfortable. Choosing her words carefully, she avoided direct eye contact, keeping track of me with a periodic glance. She was almost forty years old and felt hopeless about her enduring, overwhelming fear of people, her need to withdraw and isolate herself, and the profound loneliness she experienced. Emma was, by her own account, extremely sensitive to people's judgments of her and found them to be an ongoing source of pain and disappointment. She referred to people as *"the humans,"* a designation that conveyed the hopelessness of her feelings of disconnection and of not belonging.

Emma's had difficulty with social interactions. She did not know how to read people's behavior or what was expected of her. She experienced almost all interpersonal human contact as intrusive disruptions to her daily routine that readily escalated into intense, chaotic emotion. Living in a constant state of fear, Emma felt she had no choice but to disengage from her environment in order to attend to her confusing and exhausting internal states. The only way she knew to stabilize her internal sense of overwhelm was to limit contact with people, minimize stimulation, restrict her life, and retreat into the quasi-security of isolation. She could neither participate in life because she felt she did not belong, nor could she turn her back on it. Although she worried that she might be opening herself to another traumatic disappointment, her presence in my office showed that she still had some hope.

Relational Attunement

Emma experienced herself as trapped in a living hell. To hide her high level of internal activation, and in an attempt to meet social expectations, she had developed a smiling façade that thinly masked her extreme discomfort. Experience had taught her to expect rejection and she reacted painfully to any indication of misattunement. When opportunities for connection presented themselves, she vacillated between excitement and withdrawal into a heart-wrenching fear of disappointment. Afraid to express anger that could lead to rejection, not able to carry out a defiant "I don't need you," she felt condemned to feeling shame, self-hatred, helpless frustration, and despair. Nevertheless, Emma had not entirely lost the desire to actively participate in social life. In spite of her lifelong pain, she wanted to be loved and continued to yearn for connection. She began to cry as she described how she so often felt unseen and misunderstood.

Establishing Trust

I quickly became aware of Emma's highly intuitive capacity to sense my emotional states. She carefully tracked my responses and reacted to any misattunement on my part with despair and shame. I was repeatedly reminded how, moment by moment, mother and infant co-regulate their emotional arousal, influencing and being influenced by each other's changing behavior. Neurologically, signals between a mother and child pass back and forth at amazing speeds, as fast as 1/300th of a second, and it has been shown that mother and infant, in response to each other's facial expressions, show sympathetic cardiac acceleration and parasympathetic deceleration. With Emma, who, like a baby, sensed every affective nuance of relational attunement or misattunement *implicitly in her body,* I had to be emotionally present and genuine. She needed a consistent demonstration of my trustworthiness and capacity for empathic attunement.

It took a few months for us to develop a common language. In the beginning, she frequently expressed how important it was to her that I *"take her seriously,"* meaning that I not pathologize her. She felt that a diagnosis would strip her of dignity and show *"one-upmanship"* on my part, proving that I discounted her experience on a fundamental level. She wanted to be seen as a person of value and was both terrified and infuriated by the possibility of being put in a diagnostic box. To connect with Emma, I initially needed to join her on her terms—I needed to enter *her* world with the utmost respect. She would accept nothing less.

> EMMA: How do I know if you care about anything I say?

> ALINE: When you talk about your pain, I sense it as a contraction in the pit of my stomach. What you say resonates inside me, right here ... *pointing to my solar plexus and heart.* My gut responds to what

you say and feels in ways similar to how you describe your body responding to me.

EMMA: You mean that what I say has an effect in your body? I never really thought about that before....

Emma was surprised to hear that her words and internal states could impact mine. Because she had so often been told that she was too sensitive, she had foreclosed the possibility that another person could *"get her."*

Recognizing Emma's Developmental Challenge

Tears came easily to Emma, and she often experienced herself falling into a void, a great bottomless emptiness—a marker of developmental trauma and neglect. Seen through the lens of early trauma, I could imagine her sensation of falling into the void as a primal disorganization rooted in the absence of attuned caregivers.

It is through attuned relationship that a mother co-regulates her infant's developing nervous system and capacity for connection. A baby's essential developmental task in the first year of life centers around developing a secure emotional bond with mother (or whoever is the primary caregiver). A mother's essential job is to support her baby's developing capacity to self-regulate by attuning to her own and her infant's internal states. The communication between mother and baby is largely nonverbal, consisting of body-to-body signals moving through the nervous systems of both parties. The communications between mother and infant directly influence the maturation of the infant's brain and nervous system, regulate social and emotional stimuli, generate the somatic aspects of emotion used to guide behavior, and allow the brain to adapt to changing environments and integrate new information and learning. It is through these communications that infants internalize the regulatory capacities that shape their capacity to cope with stress.

Emma's moment-to-moment tracking of my internal fluctuations was as sensitive as that of a baby and required a reciprocal high level of emotional engagement, attunement, and resonance, fully calling upon my embodied intuitive capacities—she needed a regulatory parenting process. Emma lacked the experience of securely resting in the loving arms and under the watchful eye of a caring presence. She needed a supportive approach that provided highly attuned physical, emotional, and energetic presence *from the bottom-up.* Seen through the lens of early developmental trauma, it is easy to understand why a top-down cognitive therapeutic approach could be unbearably painful and had been re-traumatizing for her.

Birth Trauma, Early Neglect, and Emotional Abuse

Emma's gestation and birth had been traumatic. Her mother, an aspiring actress who was obsessed with maintaining the "perfection" of her 18-inch waist, had unsuccessfully tried to abort her. Labor had been difficult, and Emma had almost died. In addition, she was born prematurely and put in an incubator.

From birth, Emma had been the victim of neglect and emotional abuse. Emma's mother immediately resumed her acting career, leaving her in the care of her sister who was unmarried and bitter about her own situation. Emma's father showed little interest in his baby daughter and was almost never home. Her early memories were of a cold, uncaring aunt, of a mother who was obsessed with her own appearance and success, and of a father who flew into a rage if she disturbed him in any way. She had spent much of her childhood years in her bedroom, alone, seeking safety in imaginary games, all the while wondering if anyone would ever come to find her.

The long-term impact of neglect and emotional abuse includes chronic feelings of worthlessness, guilt, self-blame, self-hatred, vulnerability, generalized mistrust of others, and a pervasive sense of powerlessness, hopelessness, and despair. Emma suffered from all these symptoms. She was haunted by many of the deficits and much of the emotional suffering that result from developmental/relational trauma in the Connection phase.

Naming the Body's Nonverbal Experiences

Emma experienced a great deal of confusion about her sensations and feelings: mostly she was unclear about why they were so intense, and she was afraid of them. She found it difficult to share her internal experiences verbally; she often reminded me of a young child who is learning to speak.

> EMMA: My parents never talked to me. They never talked to each other either. Our house was silent. They only paid attention to me to feed me and clean me.

Giving Emma the time and support to find words to express the neglected parts of herself—the child who had faced a self-absorbed mother, an absent, "rageaholic" father, and an uncaring, embittered aunt—was an ongoing learning experience. It is widely held in both somatic and psychoanalytic theory that without words to mentalize physical experience, unnamed, overwhelming emotions and sensations remain lodged in the body and its organs and are expressed as psychosomatic symptoms—a somatic encapsulation of unarticulated states. An attuned parent or caregiver begins the work of emotional and mental differentiation by naming aspects of experience in a way that modulates the unformed urgency of an infant's emotional storms. Naming an experience brings sensations and emotions into consciousness. Since Emma lived in a largely nonverbal state, she felt great relief when I could accurately bring words to her internal experience. If Emma and I were to succeed in our therapeutic endeavor, the nonverbal communication moving at lightning speed between us would need to be slowed down and brought to awareness; we would need to describe in words and in the present moment what happened inside her and what passed energetically between us. She needed words to know and reflect upon her internal states.

Sensory-motor functions develop simultaneously with emotional, relational, and social capacities, and all build on each other. From this perspective, I believe it is important to view the body as *having its own reality* and its own struggle to come into being. When children miss their developmental markers *at the sensory-motor level,* the physiological foundation is not in place to support the emergence of their emotional and relational capacities, and they have no alternative but to compensate and work around the compromised capacities. Without the necessary sensory-motor skills, children have a diminished capacity to respond, the demands of the environment cause greater stress, and they cannot keep up with other children. More importantly, they often lack the key defensive reflexes that would allow them to adequately protect themselves, and they are therefore more vulnerable. As a result, other children who sense their vulnerability will scapegoat and attack them. In response, children who suffer from early developmental trauma avoid situations that demand capacities that are not developed in them, leading to a life strategy of withdrawal and isolation.

In my experience, when neurological development has been compromised, it is necessary to support the emergence of the body's own impulses and movements. For Emma to feel secure and learn how to relate to another "human," both of us had to openly communicate our internal reality in an interactive process. We made an agreement that, when appropriate, we would share our internal states: I would share my sensations and my emotional reactions with her, and she, in turn would express hers. She appreciated the structure and could relax when inner reality, mine and hers, was painted in clear, stark colors. It was reassuring for her to have a verbal interpersonal context for her experience. Emma's fear abated whenever I expressed heartfelt feedback that made emotional sense to her. Slowing down and taking the time to break down key experiences into small present-moment increments, much like playing a movie in slow motion, frame by frame when necessary, helped her find words to describe her sensations and emotions and thus begin to make sense of her internal states. We were developing a first tier of language for her largely nonverbal experience. Finding words allowed her to share and match her internal reality and her external perceptions against my feedback. This meant that she was no longer alone in her struggle to know if her perception was accurate.

Psychoeducation

Emma was intellectually gifted and had in her twenties begun a medical degree but had abandoned the program because she found the social pressures unbearable. To engage the scholar part of her, I asked her if she would like to learn about the new theories of attachment, child development, affective neuroscience, and the impact of trauma on behavior. My intention was for us to develop a broader common reflective vocabulary. Her eyes lit up. She expressed great interest in the knowledge I shared with her about affect regulation, the effects of the mother-child relationship on the nervous system, the dysregulation caused by developmental trauma, and the fight-flight-freeze response that accompany threat and curtail an infant's exploratory responses. She particularly resonated with the importance of dyadic attunement and its impact on attachment styles and began to do her own research on the subject.

Our psychoeducational conversations and her own readings had the effect of empowering her and normalizing her vulnerability and sensitivities. Emma was able to relate the information to her own childhood experiences. In essence, by identifying the developmental, neurological, and emotional bases of her difficulties, she created her own "diagnosis." The understanding Emma gained about attachment and trauma gave her top-down descriptive concepts she could use to talk about the pain, fears, and social limitations she experienced. The knowledge she now had about the impact of developmental trauma initiated a process of disidentification from the experience of the helpless child and the deep shame she had felt about her social awkwardness and her dysregulated emotional states.

The NeuroAffective Touch Connection

Having set a foundation for our work by establishing bottom-up sensory and emotional guidelines and attending to top-down cognitive understanding, I proposed an exercise used by somatic psychotherapists to engage a client's capacity for attachment and help develop a felt sense of boundaries. The exercise is as follows:

1. The therapist leaves the room and stands just outside the door.
2. The client, now alone in the room, pays attention to her internal experience. If she feels activated by the therapist's leaving the room, she takes the time to calm herself and only when stabilized does she invite the therapist to reenter the room. As the therapist reenters, the client notices any shifts in internal experience.

3. Having reentered the room and closed the door behind her, the therapist waits by the door for instructions from the client: for example, the client can tell the therapist to remain still, to face away from her, to slowly come closer step by step, to go back out, etc.
4. With each request, the client tracks and shares any change she notices in her internal experience and the therapist supports her to wait until any activation has abated before giving her next instruction.

This exercise often continues until the client can bring the therapist into her subjective field. It is intended to support the experience of agency through the implied message that clients are in charge, that the therapist will follow their lead and their pacing. It is also intended to give clients the experience of tracking and giving words to the sensory fluctuations that signal the state of their energetic boundary and relational capacity. We began the exercise with Emma sitting on cushions at the farthest end of the room, some twenty feet from the door. I left the room and after approximately five minutes, she called me in. I came in, closed the door behind me, and stood facing her with my back to the door. Her response was immediate and intense.

> EMMA: I couldn't calm myself when I was alone in the room, so I decided to tell you to come in anyway. My anxiety started to rise as soon as I saw the door handle turn.... Now I can barely stand to be in the room with you.... I'm so embarrassed.... I feel like I shouldn't be here ... that I'm such a burden to you. I can't take in that another person exists separate from me. I'm really numb right now.

As she described her anxiety and dissociation, I realized that this exercise required more resources than Emma had at her disposal.

> ALINE: Emma, can I share with you what I'm experiencing right now?
>
> EMMA: *Nods.*

ALINE: I'm finding it quite painful to see you struggle with this exercise that I set up. I didn't realize that it would create such difficulty for you. Right now, you feel so alone and so far away over there across the room that I want to go and sit close to you and put my arm around you. But I'm conflicted because I also don't want to impose more discomfort on you by invading your space.

EMMA: If you were closer, it would be easier.

ALINE: Is it all right then if I come to sit by you?

EMMA: *Nods.*

ALINE: I'll come over slowly, and you can tell me if you need me to do anything differently.

As I crossed the room to sit next to her, I asked her to tell me where she wanted me to sit. She asked me to sit next to her, on her left side.

EMMA: Now I can feel myself calming down.

ALINE: Take as much time as you need ... go at your own pace ... there is no need to force anything to be other than the way it is. *Pause for several minutes....* I notice that it seems to be an effort for you to sit up. Is that right?

EMMA: Yes. I like you here, but I just want to curl up into myself. My back hurts.

ALINE: I would like to support your back. Would it be all right if I put my hand on your back? You can tell me if it doesn't feel right, and I'll stop right away.

She agreed and I placed the flat of my right hand behind her diaphragm to support the apex of the collapse.
ALINE: How does that feel?

EMMA: It's a relief. It's calming me even more. *Sighs....* It's easier to have you touch me than to have you all the way across the room.

ALINE: That's important for us to know. *Pause for several minutes....* I would like to experiment a little with the position of my hand on your back and with the amount of pressure. Tell me what feels better for you.

EMMA: *Nods.*

ALINE: First, does my hand feel like it's in the right place to give you the support you need?

EMMA: Could you move your hand down a little lower? *Directs me to the area on her back, just below her diaphragm....* Right there. That feels better.

ALINE: Now, let's experiment with the pressure.

EMMA: I think I'd like more pressure.

I gradually increased the pressure of my hand against her back until my pressure matched the internal pressure she was exerting in her own spine.

EMMA: Like that ... that feels right.

ALINE: Remember, you can always tell me to stop if it no longer feels right. Or you can tell me to do something different.... *Quiet for a few minutes....* What are you experiencing now?

EMMA: I don't feel I have the right to be here. I must be such a burden to you, and I feel so embarrassed at my reaction ... but I like you there too. Don't stop.

We explored what she meant by *"the right to be here."* Talking about not having the *right to be* gave words to the feeling that she was not wanted, that she had always been a burden and annoyance to her mother and particularly to her father. We explored how it felt to have me next to her, supporting her. The caring intention she could feel in my touch was a new experience. She giggled and squirmed and found it hard to believe. She had never felt that she had a right to exist, let alone that someone would actually want to be with her and respond to her need.

Some weeks later, she told me how pivotal this session had been in giving birth to her feeling of being wanted, seen, and understood.

> EMMA: It started that day when you went out, then came back in the room, then came over and touched my spine, and I felt the support. I had spine hunger and didn't know it.

Although the initial exercise was never completed, it served as an important catalyst. It opened our work to the use of touch and helped Emma realize that her despairing responses, *when shared,* could elicit empathy in a way that led to a positive response to her needs.

> EMMA: No amount of talk about my problems seems to make much difference in the way I feel about myself. Mostly, just talking makes

it worse. It's hard to explain, but when you touch me I start to feel real. Like I exist.

Building Bonds of Attachment

From this session on, Emma wanted to be touched. Extensive training and experience in working with touch has taught me to allow touch interventions to evolve out of the client's need. I approach the use of touch slowly, always asking for permission and direction, and inviting the client to give feedback, to guide or stop the interaction.

Being touched helped Emma feel the surface of her skin and literally locate herself in time and space—*an antidote to her dissociation.* We discovered that Emma had no integrated image of her body and its boundary—of where she stopped and another started. Consequently, she lived in symbiotic confusion. She reported feeling as though she did not inhabit her body and more often than not, felt herself spinning *"somewhere above my head,"* a common description of dissociated states.

Touch is a valuable tool with which to address breaches in the development of the relational matrix that cannot be reached by verbal means alone. There is now documented evidence for the critical role of touch in human psychology and biology. Basic research conducted by Tiffany Field, PhD, director of the Touch Research Institute at the University of Miami School of Medicine, shows that touch is at the foundation of relational experience. It is a fundamental mode of interaction in the infant-caregiver relationship. When we consider the somatic reality of an infant for whom language is not yet formed and the neuronal and biochemical processes that underlie verbal thought, we can understand how paying attention to the body and to the relationship between bodily experience and mental states is critical to support the developmental progression and integration of the capacity to relate to self and others.

> EMMA: I can feel your hands, but I don't have a sense of anyone attached to them. It's enough to just feel your hands. It would be too much to have a person attached to them. This way, I can just feel myself as not alone.

Emma perceived my touch as a source of comfort even though she could not yet experience me *as a separate person.*

> EMMA: I trust your touch. When I get a massage, I have to force myself to like it ... but your touch comes right in. It's as if you're touching my emotions. Sometimes, during a massage, I actually feel something good, but it only lasts a second, then I shut down and I'm numb to the rest of it. It doesn't happen with you. They [mother, father, aunt] all had an agenda for me. It was never about me. It was about me being a certain way to please them. That's what humans do.

Typically, I began sessions by asking Emma to identify an area of her body that she perceived as wanting attention. Usually, she led me to her belly, mid-back behind the respiratory diaphragm, or to her right hip or jaw. My touch was quiet and consistent, my intent to nurture, and my movements deliberate and slow, trying to offer a quality of presence that her body could receive. After silently holding a chosen area for a while, I usually opened a verbal dialogue by describing my experience—the emotional valence, the density, the wave pattern I felt in her tissues.

> ALINE: Today, I sense you suspended and sort of pulling in ... my belly is getting tighter. I sense your belly as very still, a little frozen even, as if you're holding your breath and waiting for something bad to happen....
>
> EMMA: Yes ... there was a message from my aunt.... I haven't called her back. I'm afraid she's going to invite me to a family

reunion, and I won't know how to say no.

ALINE: I see ... that makes sense then: your body isn't sure if things are safe.

EMMA: Things aren't safe. I know I'm going to lose myself. I always do when I talk to my family. *Her belly visibly contracts.*

ALINE: Emma, I'm going to place my hand over your belly. Take a moment to see if that feels right or not.

EMMA: *After some time....* The more I think about my aunt, the tighter I get there. I had no idea until you touched me.

ALINE: Let's take a moment to allow your belly to settle before continuing to talk about your family.

EMMA: *Pause....* I'm really scared. No ... actually, I'm scaring myself into that horrible state where I feel totally worthless and incapable.... I was building up to an anxiety attack.

ALINE: And now?

EMMA: No more words. I just want to be quiet and feel my body quiet down. I don't have to go just because she invites me.

Touch helped Emma build a conscious connection to her felt sense and became an essential aspect of the dialogue evolving between us. Tracking sensation in my own body as well as in hers was an important source of relational information. While I made physical contact with her, I used words and metaphors to link sensations with feelings and thoughts in order to strengthen the feedback loops between her nervous system, viscera, and cortical functions. My touch was intended to awaken and support a sensory exploration of her internal states, and my words were an invitation for her to verbalize her experience.

Knowing that I was sharing my own experience as an invitation for her to share hers, she in turn compared her experience to mine and we explored the similarities and differences—when we were in alignment and resonance and when we were not. Emma learned that when she paid attention and made connections between her sensations, feelings, and thoughts, her internal world became more manageable, and new insights and solutions could emerge.

The Void

The empathic and nurturing intention of my touch was deeply regulating for Emma's nervous system, and the resulting direct and implicit connection to a caring other contrasted with her memories of childhood neglect and with the fear and disconnection she still experienced as an adult.

> EMMA: I'm not fighting to get something that I wasn't getting anymore. I can see that I'm getting something real, that I'm not making it up. It's very sweet,

and soft, and satisfying.... I didn't know that before, but now I do. I can really feel the difference when I'm not getting anything and when I am. It's such a relief. After every session I realize that my trust is growing, but when I go home I feel the emptiness. I got held and then I'm alone and I want more.

The contrast between the contact during our sessions and the contact hunger she experienced when alone at home brought up the grief of years of neglect and lonely yearning. She was realizing, on a conscious as well as on a visceral level, how painful the absence of connection had been and how much she had yearned for it even without knowing what it was she had been yearning for. Emma could now put words to her early experience. She described a frightening inner void, a painful emptiness that is one of the far-reaching effects of early developmental trauma, particularly neglect.

> EMMA: It's like there was a cold, dark, bottomless, never-ending

void. It was always there, and it never stopped. Now I have moments when I feel that it's good to be alive. And I can feel that it isn't my fault. I'm not empty because I'm defective. It's because I never got what I needed.

Becoming Attached

Without the comforting touch connection, Emma's overwhelmingly painful emptiness had been unspeakable. We used our growing relational matrix to explore the adaptive survival strategies she had developed to insulate herself from the unbearable pain of neglect and isolation. Emma expressed the fear that if she opened herself to relationship, her pain would be even more unbearable.

> EMMA: I feel really embarrassed that I might like you more than you like me. It feels dangerous that I'm letting myself need you. Isn't that dependency? Isn't that wrong? I'm afraid you're going to

"drop the baby," and I don't think I could survive that one more time.

She began to regularly use the expression "drop the baby" when she talked about past experiences of misattunement and neglect. She was terrified that I too would drop her if she let herself trust our connection. Emma wanted reassurance that it was safe to allow herself to become attached to me.

> ALINE: Emma, let's look at this together. We know that your body and nervous system are hungry to be touched ... and that you experience relief when I attune to you and give you the attention you need and never had. And we also know how painful it was for you to grow up so isolated without anyone caring for you. I understand how vulnerable this must feel ... there's a lot riding on our relationship. So let's see if we can create safeguards so that the baby is protected. The last thing I want is to drop the baby or for

you to experience being let down or abandoned yet again.

We explored how to proceed in a titrated way that would allow her to manage the new experiences of expansion that come with feeling connected. Emma realized that the fear of being dropped was particularly strong on days when I touched areas close to her heart. We made a concerted effort to fine-tune our interactions; the more specifically my touch could meet her body's needs and emotional yearning, the better she became at giving me directions and regulating her own affect. We identified areas where touch felt safe, calming, and brought comfort, and others that triggered emotional pain. We found that she did better when I changed my holding position often rather than when I held one position for a long time. We also explored the resources she had with which to comfort herself at home between sessions. She found that the longer she could be on the massage table and in contact during a session, the easier it was to hold onto what felt good when she went home.

She realized that what was most resourcing was to remember, in her body, how it felt to be held during sessions.

> EMMA: I know from the reading that being touched is bringing up my baby experience ... the part that really needed a mother. They all dropped me ... my mother, my aunt ... and my father.
>
> ALINE: And what happens when you connect with the part of you that knows?
>
> EMMA: Well ... I'm telling myself that you're not them, and that it's okay to remember how it feels when we're together in a session. That it isn't me being too needy but more that it's about healing something I needed and didn't get.

I took this to mean that she was developing some object constancy and capacity for self-soothing and self-regulation. After several sessions, during which I held one hand under her spine and very lightly massaged her belly with my other hand, creating a "sandwich" with her digestive track as its center, she had the following clarity:

> EMMA: The touch puts me in touch with my pain ... but in a good way. There's something crying in me, crying as it lets go. The touch is filling me, and it's going into the pain in a good way. I'm getting there, cell by cell. It's like when I cut my finger. It takes time to heal, and there will be a time when I'll be full. I need to be touched. I'm not feeling so guilty about needing to be touched anymore.

Emma was learning to receive. Slowly, she was learning to take in and integrate the experience of connection.

Repairing Lost Connection

The work was moving forward smoothly, too smoothly perhaps, when an unfortunate scheduling confusion tested Emma's developing trust.

> EMMA: I was feeling so good, so open. I was trusting you ...

crying.... Now I'm closed and alone again. I know consciously that you haven't done anything wrong, but my body doesn't know it. It's closed, and I'm afraid I've lost my only opportunity to heal.

She angrily wondered how she could have let herself open as much as she did, felt shame that she had allowed herself to care for me, and berated herself for being a burden.

EMMA: I must be a bad person because you haven't done anything wrong. I'm the one fucking it up. I knew it! Nobody can ever be there for me. I'm a burden, and you don't really want to see me anymore.

Dysregulation and fragmentation resurfaced. She reported that she was again crying at home, crying her feelings of intense loneliness and loss that were now back. She had had a few months of feeling hopeful, and now, after just a little taste of how good it felt, it was gone again. Perhaps forever. I was also concerned. What if the lost connection could not be repaired? I anchored myself in the process of mindful presence.

She huddled in the armchair, curled up, pulled in, and withdrawn. I then realized that she had had many experiences of loss, but none of *finding* again. Emma had never had the opportunity to move through an experience of reconnection once contact had been lost. The excerpts that follow detail the exploration and repair of her experience of broken connection.

> ALINE: Do you know what happened in the past when you lost your sense of connection?
>
> EMMA: People freaked out, and I ended up taking care of their upset.
>
> ALINE: Do you know what was missing that didn't allow you to find your way back?
>
> EMMA: They said it was my fault and that I was too sensitive. They never listened to me.

When in the past Emma had tried to talk about her loss of connection, she had been attacked for being overly sensitive and demanding. Or she was berated for being wrong and for misperceiving the situation. I understood that she had not been received in a way that allowed her to express her feelings of disconnection and remain in contact with the other.

Working with Contraction

As she sat huddled in the corner of the armchair, knees up to her shoulders to cover her belly, arms wrapped tightly around her chest, eyes staring blankly, I suggested covering her with a shawl so that she did not have to protect herself using body tension. She made no motion to stop me as I lay a light shawl over her.

> ALINE: Emma, I have a sense that there's too much going on right now. Let's see what happens if I put a protective cover over you.
>
> ALINE: *Addressing her need for boundary....* Feel the shawl act as

a shield and see if your body can feel safer under its protection. See what happens if you close your eyes so that you don't have too much stimulus coming in from the outside.

Her body slightly released its constricted and retracted position. She reported being numb from the waist down, with little awareness of her feet.
ALINE: Take your time.... I'm going to sit on the floor by the chair. I want to stay close to you, because in the past you've always been alone when you've been in this state. *Several silent moments passed during which her breath slowed down....* I'd like to put my hand lightly on your foot. *I put my fingers on the top of her foot, near her toes....* Tell me if that feels good, or if it feels intrusive. You don't have to answer right away. Let your body pull away from my touch if the contact doesn't feel right. *She did not pull away. After a little while of silent contact, I offered to remove my hand.*

EMMA: No. I like your hand there. Somehow, it's helping me to slow down and come back.

We spent the next thirty minutes in quiet contact. Periodically, I would reassure her that there was no pressure to make anything happen, that we had no way of knowing what the outcome would be or if we would ever find our way back. We would just practice being in the moment with what was.

ALINE: All we can do is be quiet together and see what happens in its own time, like we have done many times in the past months.

I knew that Emma struggled with the intensity of her feelings. I reassured her that her feelings had their own course, their own rhythm, and that if there was an inkling of a chance to make it through, we both had to honor what was going on inside her, without any time pressure, without any judgment, without any preconceived idea of outcome. The contact of my hand on her foot allowed me to track the responses in her nervous system: I could feel the retraction in her legs softening, and concurrently, I could sense my own visceral turmoil calm down. As we neared the end of the session, I let her know that our time was coming to an end, that there was no pressure to have accomplished anything, because we had many more sessions to continue exploring this break.

> ALINE: We don't know what will happen, but I want you to know that I trust your sense of what you need. I trust that you know what is right for yourself, and that I am open to what you might need from me. I want to remind you that we have an agreement with each other to be truthful about our inner experience.

In the session that followed, she announced:

> EMMA: I'm not back yet, but I do feel more hopeful. I lost it, and you didn't freak out. You didn't make me wrong.

She had "lost it," and I did not punish her, berate her, blame her, get scared, or give up on her. I did not pull away, abandon her, or deem her hopeless. In her words, I did not "drop the baby." She could retract and peek out of the corner of her eye to see that I was still there. I had urged her to stay with her feelings, even if those feelings were of mistrust and disconnection. She needed to feel them and not be rejected for having them. In these vulnerable moments of interactive repair, I was the representative of the "good-enough" mother, and my capacity for attunement was called upon to act as the external organizer of Emma's internal dysregulation.

> EMMA: I didn't have to take care of you. I didn't have to worry about hurting your feelings. You didn't make it about you.

Though she was more present, I noticed that she was still retracted in the chair, holding her hands tightly closed in little fists.

ALINE: Emma, as we talk I notice that your body is still needing to protect itself and that your hands are tightly closed ... it reminds me somehow of a frightened baby who has no one to hold on to.

EMMA: Yes. I just can't let go. And I can't trust you yet either.

ALINE: If you will allow it, I would like to spend some special time with the frightened one who is here today. I feel like making a cradle for her. How does that sound?

EMMA: *Giggled as a little spark shot through her eyes....* A cradle?

ALINE: Are you wondering how a cradle could happen in this room?

EMMA: Well, yes!

    I took the flat cushions from the two large armchairs, which when laid flat on the floor made a little bed. Then I gathered all the other pillows in the room and built them up around the flat cushions. And there it was—a cradle, just her size. She giggled even more as she crawled in to nestle in the middle of the pillows. I covered her with the shawl.

>ALINE: Just as I did last week, I would like to stay in contact with you.

>EMMA: Yes. The touch connection was the most important part of the session. I didn't have to say anything, and I knew that you were there.

This time, I asked her to hold two of my fingers in one of her clutched fists. I chose this intervention based on the knowledge that babies are born with a grasp reflex that allows them to securely hold on to the mother should there be a need to flee danger. It seemed to me that her tightly squeezed hands were an indication of that early reflexive position. She decided to lie on her back and curled her right hand tightly around my fingers. She closed her eyes and after about ten minutes began to talk about how devastating it had been to lose the connection with her previous therapist and not find her way back. She cried as she continued to describe the pain of her mother not connecting to her. At the end of the session, she reported:

> EMMA: I'm feeling better. I'm not all the way back ... but some of the way.

In the following session, we went back to the cradle but found that it had mutated into a nest. She grabbed a heavy blanket and lay down in it. I sat by her head.

> EMMA: The resistance to open to you is almost gone.

> ALINE: I'm glad to hear that. Let's see what happens today.

I sat silently beside her, with presence and intent. After about five minutes, she found words.

> EMMA: I'm starting to feel now.... *Tearful....* It's the loneliness. There just is no one in my life I enjoy

being with.... I don't know what to do about it.

ALINE: Emma, I have an impulse to hold your head. Is that all right with you?

She nodded, and I moved to sit above her head. As soon as I touched her head, she began to cry harder. I intuitively followed an impulse to put very gentle pressure on the top of her head.

EMMA: There just isn't anything to hold on to....

Her hands were above her head with her fingers again curled tightly. As I had done before, I offered my index and middle fingers, and this time she grabbed on with her left hand and held on tightly.

EMMA: I have no idea how tightly I'm holding. Am I crushing you?

For the next hour, she alternated between tears and silence, while I internally cycled through anxiety, fear, heart pain, and confusion.

EMMA: I've gotten rid of everybody who upsets me in my life. I'm glad about it, but it leaves me so alone. Thank God for my animals. I don't know what I would do without them.

I remained quiet as she naturally resourced herself with stories about her animals. When the session ended, she simply said:

EMMA: That helped.

We continued nesting for several sessions. Often during these sessions Emma could not tell me what she needed, and I had to trust my sense of attunement. During one of these sessions, I rested the flat of my fingers on her temples, imperceptibly contacting the temporal part of the masseter muscle, thus addressing the tightness of her jaw and the frozenness of her face.

EMMA: I feel a wall, and you are outside of me ... *clenching her fist to express her experience of the wall.*

ALINE: I feel a wall too. As I came close, I felt myself coming up onto the surface of you, and it feels impenetrable.

EMMA: There's no opening, and I can't make one happen even if I want to.

ALINE: It's fine to hang out here. It's the way it is. There's no need to make something happen. Energy moves in its own time. Let's be curious about the wall.

My hands remained on her temples and slightly over her cheekbones. While I held her temples, our breath synchronized. Five minutes passed.

ALINE: I can feel little stirrings.

EMMA: Yes. It's moving like that ... *makes little fluttery movements with her fingers.*

ALINE: Yes, just like that. Like the density of the wall is breaking up, and I have the impulse to make those same little fluttery movements with my fingers.... *I let my fingers move lightly and randomly over her temples.*

EMMA: Yes, that feels good.

Within a few moments, the random flutters suddenly organized into a multi directional pulsing pattern that radiated outwards from her temples. We had found a common rhythmic pulse and were able to allow that pulse to move both of us together—in somatic terms, we had entered a state of vibrational resonance.

EMMA: I felt that move!

ALINE: Yes! We both felt it at the same time. Now I feel drawn to put my hands on your upper chest, just below your collarbone. Tell me if that doesn't feel right, because we know that your heart area is very sensitive.

EMMA: It's good.... In a way, describing what is happening with words doesn't allow me to go as deep, but it's good to know how it works.

More silent holding followed. I applied a light pressure on the manubrium, mirroring and following the expansive and retractive pulls as I sensed them. The area of the manubrium seems particularly sensitive to issues of bonding. Feelings of sadness surfaced.

> EMMA: I'm grieving again. I'm grieving the untouched, unseen baby. When you do that, it makes me realize that you're giving me what I didn't get.

A tightness in my throat suddenly released, and I felt myself dropping into my body, now able to breathe more deeply. I had not been aware that my breath had become tight and shallow until I felt it release. At that same moment, Emma sighed in relief.

> EMMA: There, it opened!

An apt naming of the experience. What was the *it* that opened in both of us at the same time, I wondered. The *it* that cannot be forced, that cannot be made to open except in its own time, that knows when the right sequence of subtle movements has unfolded, when the progression has reached its culmination, and suddenly, as a key turns in a lock, opens a door, dissolves a wall, sends an impulse moving through what had been rigid and immovable.

> ALINE: What just happened?
>
> EMMA: It feels so good. If I follow the good feeling, it seems to open me. We had lost it, and now we are finding it again.
>
> ALINE: I also felt it. A tension let go in my belly, and a sense of relief flooded my body.

She tracked the good feeling as it moved though her body, a feeling of letting go that connected her to herself and to me, and me to her. In attachment terms, I believe that the "it" that had opened was a result of the specifically fitted touch interaction that replicated the psychobiologically attuned attention a mother gives her baby. The fact that my frequency coincided with Emma's own internal rhythms was key. This was not something we could have planned; it was pure grace.

Our nervous systems recognized and responded to the state of attuned synchrony we had found, and we discovered what appears to be a fundamental building block of nervous system regulation: a synchrony of attunement that brings with it soothing sensations and emotions—a positive state of implicit relational knowing that recognizes genuine connection.

The Fear of Life

Emma opened the following session in a joyful state.

> EMMA: I'm almost back to normal with you. I'm not all the way back with trusting you, and I want a lot of time on the massage table today.

She was back in an adult state, able to reflect on the journey she had taken into the frozen and dissociated feelings of her infancy.

> ALINE: Let's listen to what your body needs today. Are there any sensations you would like to report, or areas you would like to bring to attention?

EMMA: Tension around my whole left eye and face.

Emma lay on the table, on her back, and I cupped my hand around her eye and eyebrow where she had indicated the tension. After a while, her left shoulder made a quick but strong spastic movement upward and inward toward her neck.

> ALINE: Emma, did you notice that movement in your shoulder?

EMMA: Now that you mention it, yes.

> ALINE: Do you remember it well enough to repeat it?

She repeated it exactly. I asked her to repeat it very slowly several times while I held different areas of the shoulder girdle. Finally, as my hand lay flat under her mid-back, a little above the insertion of the trapezius, she told me that it seemed to be the area from which the spastic movement was originating.

>ALINE: If that movement had a message, what might it be?

>EMMA: This might sound silly, but the first words that came to mind were "I don't want to be born." Right after that I thought "I know life hurts," and I felt that I didn't want to participate in life because of the pain that comes with it.

This statement triggered a flurry of spastic movement in her shoulder. The movement, which at first was incoherent with spastic repetition, organized into a retraction, and she curled her whole body into a tight ball. I was reminded of playing in tide pools, trying to touch an open sea anemone and witnessing its protective reflex to close. As she slowly relaxed back to a normal position, her left hand remained tightly closed.

> ALINE: I notice that your left hand is closed in a tight fist.

> EMMA: I know. It just won't let go, and I can't make it.

> ALINE: I'd like to try something, if you will let me.

> EMMA: Okay.

As I had in previous sessions, I put my left index and middle fingers into the palm of her tightly closed left hand. This time I sensed a different intent in the grip; it no longer felt like that of an infant needing to hold on, but I could not discern exactly what had changed. After a while, I found my fingers microscopically pushing against the palm of her hand and curled fingers with the implicit message to soften her grip. At first there was no force to my push; it was an intent flowing through, energy expressing through my fingers into her hand. She received the message, and her hand relaxed a little.

We continued back and forth for some fifteen minutes, my fingers gradually pushing more strongly against the palm of her hand, her hand slowly letting go. No words were exchanged. At the end of the session she shared:

> EMMA: I had new sensations that I've never had. I had to keep reminding myself that no harm was going to come to me. Your pressure was so subtle that I was able to override the reflex to close down and follow the new direction.
>
> ALINE: I didn't want to impose anything, but I had a clear desire to let your nervous system know that it could release the clutching.
>
> EMMA: My experience with people has been so bad, no wonder I'm not willing to trust anyone. Images of my aunt came up. She was so rough with me. It's important for me to be handled in a gentle way. My experience was that touch always hurt. It's really good to be handled in a gentle way.

Emma was developing a felt sense understanding of the defensive measures her body had taken to protect itself against inexpressible intrusions and rough handling. I remembered the baby pictures with her aunt and mother in which she was twisting away. This tiny infant had never been embraced, her fearful grasp could never release into safe holding.

ALINE: Emma, what do you need now?

EMMA: Something in my upper chest and throat.

I slid my hand under her back, just above her heart, and placed the other on her chest, creating a line of energy between my two hands through the manubrium, esophagus, upper lobes of the lungs, and upper vertebrae. I could feel that the tissues in that area were energetically frozen: the bone lacked vibration, the muscles were rigid, and there was no breath in the upper lobes of her lungs. Moving my hand along her spine, I found a hard, knotted area between her shoulder blades. I supported that area, and it began to soften as she reported waves of fear coming up. She spontaneously began to breathe slowly and evenly as the waves of fear moved through.

> EMMA: I never let down. I was born in fear. No one comforted me, and it has just continued ever since. I've never known anything but fear, until a few moments on this table.

In the following sessions Emma continued to release her fear. She could tolerate more concentrated holding as I steadily held, sandwiched between my hands, different areas of her torso and organs—her navel, solar plexus, stomach, liver, digestive track, and for increasingly longer periods, her heart. She allowed herself to enjoy the sensations of being cared for, essentially "feeding" her nervous system. In this process of psychobiological attunement, she felt understood. During one session, we focused our attention on her navel, bringing special attention to this fetal "mouth," the original in utero feeding channel. The next time we met, she said:

> EMMA: Well, the last session was really useful ... the part when you held my navel with your hand underneath. It's really hard to put into words, and I was looking for words to explain the feeling when I went home. I came up with the word *entitled.* Being held like that, sandwiched between your hands, was telling me exactly where I was and what my shape was. And I could feel myself inside, between your hands. Like I *was,* and I had a right to be. It reminded me of what you had talked about months ago about existing. Most of the time, I don't feel like I exist, and I hate being around people because I feel like a big fake. But now I really get it, what it feels like to exist. I can't tell you what a relief it is.

Coming Back

I now felt that we had enough common understanding and trust to directly focus on her tendency toward dissociation.

EMMA: ... when I leave my body....

ALINE: Leave your body ... how do you do that?

EMMA: I pull in and up.... *Points to an area about three feet above her head, to the right.*

ALINE: If I follow where you are pointing, you go to a place above your head and to the right.

EMMA: *Stops, looks surprised....* You're right! I feel like I'm right there.... *Points more specifically to the area above her head....* and when I'm there, my face freezes in a fake kind of expression ... like I have to pretend to be happy. That's why the touch is so important. It brings me back down into my body.

ALINE: Can you describe how you do that—how you come back down into your body?

EMMA: Typically, I come down into my body and then I pull right back out.... *Points to her body and then above her head....* I do this over and over until finally, I drop in. It feels so good to be in. It's such a relief. All those years that I felt so crazy, I didn't know I wasn't in my body. That's why I was so upset when the break happened. I thought, here is my chance to find my way in, and I've lost it. I've lost it, and I'll never find it again. After a session, I can hold it for a day or two, and I feel so great, then I lose it again. But it's not so scary when I lose it because I know I can find it again.

Knowing that she left her body through the top right side of her head, I included some holding of her head during each session. Her craniosacral rhythm pulled to the right, and she described the right side of her head and face as *"bigger"* than the left. We experimented and found that putting my hands over her skull, with the slightest pressure downward on the right side, accelerated her *"coming back in."* When she was back in, the cranial symmetry was restored.

Connection

Her confusion about attachment, which we had touched upon before the disconnection incident, came up for review.

> EMMA: You know that whole thing I was beginning to feel before the phone incident ... about attachment ... about not knowing what's right and what's wrong. I'm really confused. When I try to attach, I get slammed. I get told I'm being needy. If I let myself feel attached to you, I think I'm doing something wrong. I don't want to be needy, so I keep pulling myself back.
>
> ALINE: So often, when you feel comfortable with me, I see joy bubbling up into your eyes, and

something comes alive in you. It's very strong.

EMMA: I feel a lot of sadness now. I was slammed so many times. My parents always used to say, "You're too sensitive" and "Why do you care so much?" They were right, I do care too much. I wish I didn't.

ALINE: I've noticed that when your feelings emerge, you feel deeply and passionately. That can be both a gift and a curse. Feeling deeply is a good thing, but managing all the energy that arises from feeling passionately is a challenge.

EMMA: Sometimes, I don't know what to do when I come here. I'm excited to be coming, but I don't know how to make contact with you, so lately, I've been talking ... otherwise it gets too intense.

ALINE: Yes, I did notice that you've been reporting more on the events of your week. What are you experiencing right now as you tell me this?

EMMA: I feel all pulled in and scared.

Emma pulled up in a ball to show me how she felt, pulling her legs into her stomach and wrapping her arms around her torso. It was a familiar position, yet there was something different in its quality: Emma did not feel as "young" to me.

EMMA: It's like I want to be in a cocoon. Protected.

A *cocoon* rather than a cradle or a nest. I offered her a heavy blanket, with which she covered herself. I sat on the floor in my usual place with my hand lightly on her foot. She closed her eyes and began to cry.

EMMA: I don't know why, but here are the tears. I'm grieving again. All those years of isolation ... it makes me cry.

Her tears were gentle, and I sensed a softening around her heart. Her urge to shut down was counterbalanced by the desire to stay open, even as she was experiencing sadness. We allowed the grief to be.

Growing Up

The therapeutic process described above covers a period of about twenty months of twice-a-week sessions. Emma continued to move through processes that alternated between excitement and despair, connection and distance, expansion and contraction, between stable states of regulated affect and unstable states of dysregulation. On an expansive day she might say:

> EMMA: I feel it in my chest, under the breastbone: a warm, full feeling moving upward. There used to be only pain there. It's really different.

On another day, she might be in contraction, again plunged in the fear of life and people:

> EMMA: I lost it again. Yesterday I didn't get out of bed ... and I still don't like people. The craving for

contact is always there in spite of what I say about not liking people.

Emma often brought up the fact that our time-limited sessions were not enough to fill her deficits. She yearned for a haven where she could immerse herself in a nurturing environment—not a clinic, hospital, ashram, or retreat center, but a special place where nurturing resources were available whenever needed. I would remind her that since she could imagine it, this nurturing place existed in her as an internal resource.

Overall, through the ups and downs, Emma continued to grow.

>EMMA: I'm not a baby anymore. I'm reading all kinds of books now, and I'm really enjoying them. The reading stimulates my brain in a completely new way. I'm making pictures in my mind as I'm reading, and I've never done that before.

>ALINE: And since you are no longer a baby, how old are you?

EMMA: I'm about five years old.

Discussion

Creating a narrative for Emma's primarily nonverbal experience was a multi-leveled developmental journey. She needed to learn how to observe and be present to her internal experience and to develop a language to describe it. As she did, her capacity to contain negative emotions without fear and positive emotions without overstimulation, face disappointment without collapsing, and bring up memories without blurring past and present consistently improved.

Symptoms of the Connection Survival Style Addressed in Therapy with Emma

Active and unfulfilled within Emma was a deep longing for connection, yet the idea of connection aroused terror about her very survival. Her ability to

feel connected went through cycles of hope-expansion and despair-contraction. As she cycled through varying states and degrees of fragmentation to coherence, from numbness to vitality, from chaos to functional harmony, different elements of the Connection Survival Style could be clearly observed:
- Lifelong patterns of withdrawal and isolation
- Awkward social interactions
- Fear of life and people
- Narrowing and limiting her life to manage over-stimulation
- Feeling herself to be alien, nonhuman
- Longing for connection while expecting rejection
- Shame about her symptoms
- Exquisite but often painful sensitivity to others
- The after-effects of birth trauma, early neglect, and emotional abuse
- Sensory-motor disorganization
- Internal experience of a void

NARM Principles, Tools, and Techniques Used in Therapy with Emma

While NeuroAffective Touch was a particularly important factor in the work with Emma, all of NARM's principles, tools, and techniques were brought into play. In order to facilitate new strategies for self-regulation and internal organization, I used the following NARM principles to engage Emma in a process that nurtured her positive sense of self, reduced hyper-activation, elicited undeveloped impulses, and encouraged new neurological connections:

- Emotional authenticity on the part of the therapist
- A non-pathologizing approach
- Therapist's self-disclosure to normalize and resource the client's experience
- Moment-by-moment mindfulness and sharing of emotional and physiological processes
- Working bottom-up as well as top-down
- Learning to track the felt sense

- Finding words for the body's nonverbal experiences
- Tracking the cycles of connection and disconnection
- Psychoeducation
- Supporting adult consciousness and avoiding regression
- Working with the fixed beliefs about self, the world, and the therapeutic process
- Disidentification from shame-based identifications and pride-based counter-identifications
- Renegotiating the experience of shame
- Working with the undifferentiated sense of self to support separation/individuation
- Helping develop clear energetic boundaries
- Using NeuroAffective Touch to access the felt sense and support attachment
- Using NeuroAffective Touch as an antidote to dissociation
- Active repair of lost connection; working with the difficulties of reconnection

- Working with expansion and contraction cycles
- Supporting necessary grieving while avoiding regression
- Integrating aggression, self-expression, separation/individuation
- Integrating the therapeutic interactive regulation into the capacity for self-regulation

From Felt Sense to Felt Self

According to Eugene Gendlin, PhD, who coined the term, *the felt sense* emerges at the intersection of the psychological and the physiological and allows us to *"form meaning from bodily experience."*[2] The felt sense becomes known at the intersection of top-down and bottom-up processes; felt sense perceptions bring together the awareness of our body's reactions concurrently with emotional responses and thoughts, and the combined experiences, each belonging to a different order of being, allow us to

---

[2] Eugene Gendlin, Focusing, 1981.

make meaning of our internal world. The felt sense is not a mental experience, nor is it only a bodily awareness; it is the coming together of (1) the body's direct sensory and emotional responses to internal and external events, (2) the mind's attention to and synthesis of the information gathered by the senses, and (3) the level of congruence between these channels of experience and their integration to form the awareness of a particular state of being, a situation, or a problem. On the somatic level, to access the felt sense is to retrieve the knowledge and wisdom implicit in bodily experience. On the level of the mind, it is a process of developing a capacity for sustained, focused attention that supports relaxed, nonjudgmental awareness so that internal processes, both psychological and physiological, can truly be heard and tended to. The capacity to accurately assess whether the signals between body and mind are congruent or disjointed is critical to stabilizing internal chaos and making sense of one's world.

The felt sense is usually not "just there": it forms as we pay attention to our internal experience, moment to moment. When the felt sense is given time to emerge and form, we discover that our often-intangible bodily states progress from silent existence at the periphery of our awareness to a vivid presence on the map of our consciousness. The more we bring our focus to perceiving our sensations—skin sensitivity, body heat, involuntary and voluntary muscular contractions, organ vibrations, body positions, and so on—the more vivid the awareness of our internal visceral-affective experience becomes. Sensory qualities unfold according to the body's flow, much as in free association, thoughts are noticed as they float to the surface of the mind. By finding words to describe the qualities of pulsation, movement, texture, color, or temperature that make up the information we receive from our senses, nonverbal experiences are brought into a verbal narrative. Sensory attributes can then be shared and processed and their implicit information translated into explicit personal meaning. In this way, new awareness is drawn from and given back to the biological realm, strengthening the links between body and mind.

Emma had never learned to notice and name the shifting rhythms and oscillations of the felt sense that are the language of the nervous system and that underlie the formation of self. Antonio Damasio, MD, PhD, has shown that developing an expanded vocabulary to increasingly differentiate the awareness of the bodily self is the foundation upon which the entire structure of consciousness is built.[3] When Emma found accurate descriptions for her sensate experience and when she was able to objectively describe it without regression, interpretation, or premature ascription of meaning, her bodily self felt mirrored, confirmed, and accepted on its own terms. As she mindfully refined her capacity for sensory attention, verbally connecting sensations and cognitions, her capacity

---

[3] Antonio Damasio, The Feeling of What Happens, 1999

for agency over her internal world increased.

Ethical Considerations

Touch became an essential element in Emma's healing process. There are important considerations to keep in mind when using touch as a therapeutic intervention. Not all clients respond positively to touch, nor is it appropriate to use with everyone. We must be aware that touch is a complex therapeutic intervention imbued with cultural conventions, gender-sensitive issues, and veiled power games. It can sometimes trigger deep-seated emotional experiences that can quickly become overly activating. It is therefore essential that a psychotherapist be trained in the use of touch before using it as a therapeutic intervention.

The ethical fears, prohibitions, and even taboos that surround the therapeutic use of touch reveal an overall lack of knowledge about its use as an important *implicit healing language.* In truth, few of us have been well touched. Our fear about the use of touch as a therapeutic modality speaks to the pervasive dysfunctions of touch that many have experienced. It speaks to the untold suffering that physical and sexual abuse, both dysfunctions of touch, have inflicted upon so many. Fear about touch also speaks to the deep yearnings and disappointments that the lack of loving touch leaves in our lives. For a client such as Emma, who requires a reparative experience to rework the effects of early trauma and neglect and the resulting dissociative responses, it could be argued that avoiding touch reenacts the initial missing connection she experienced as an infant. From this perspective, the use of touch can greatly expand our psychotherapeutic horizons and add effective, perhaps critical, forms of clinical reparative interventions, particularly with issues of early developmental and relational trauma.

Healing the Relational Matrix

NeuroAffective Touch is a sensory dialogue that engages the language of the body on its own terms, at the deepest biological level, and invites the mind as an active partner. By placing my attention on specific layers of Emma's body—skin, connective tissue, muscle, nervous system—and by following existing rhythms and lines of force and suggesting new ones, I could attune to Emma and assist her in defining her felt sense experience. As Emma learned to be present to her visceral-affective experience, touch supported her in maintaining the focus inward on her interoceptive sensations—body heat, involuntary and voluntary muscular contractions, organ vibrations, skin sensitivity—and in bringing awareness to these invisible, usually unconscious, internal activities.

By specifically addressing the ways in which Emma had never been met or understood at the most fundamental level, my intention to nurture and support her initiated in her experiences of connection and trust. The unconditional acceptance inherent in a mindful, nurturing presence and touch reached through the traumatized layers of neglect, invisibility, unworthiness, and numbness and validated the foundation of self that is anchored in the body. My attuned attention to the rhythms of her breath, inner sensations, and movements enhanced her ability to stay connected to herself and to me, to attune to her own needs, and to regulate her strong emotions. In the direct containment of touch, Emma could increasingly feel and be present to her own body and mind and find relief in the congruence of her felt sense experience. Her growing capacity to be mindful gave her support to live in a world that had never welcomed her and to which she found it painful to relate.

12

Healing the Distortions of the Life Force

A Systemic Approach

In NARM, we use the mindful awareness of the life force and its distortions as an orientation to the healing and growth process. Figure 12.1 provides principles for NARM's psychobiological approach and offers guidelines to help individuals work toward increasing connection and aliveness.

In the Introduction and in Part A, we presented the process of how the life force becomes progressively distorted in adapting to developmental trauma and environmental failure. In Chapter 10, we developed a clinical understanding of the NARM principles, tools, and techniques needed to work therapeutically. In this chapter, we focus on tracking the life force, reading the chart from top to bottom—from the most symptomatic parasympathetic distortions, through sympathetically dominant symptoms, and ultimately to core expression and health. Figure 12.1 was initially presented in the Introduction (as Figure i.2) and is repeated here as we focus on the process of reconnection and the healing of the distortions moving from top to bottom.

Developmental versus Shock Trauma

Working therapeutically with developmental trauma as opposed to working with shock trauma requires overlapping but different sets of skills. On the surface, a person who has experienced shock trauma can present similarly to someone who is struggling with developmental trauma. Both individuals may be anxious, depressed, dissociated, self-isolating, and suffer from diverse physical symptoms. The process for working with developmental trauma, however, is quite different from working with shock trauma.

In cases of shock trauma we work primarily from the bottom up, focusing on the completion of the fight-flight response in a process called *biological completion.* As clients experience biological completion and the survival energies of fight-flight are integrated, anxiety decreases, the nervous system re-regulates, and autonomic symptoms recede. Clients often say, "I feel like I've gotten my life back"—which is to say, as can be seen by following the shock trauma branch of the chart from the top to the bottom, that these clients have successfully moved from freeze, fear, and helplessness, through completion of the fight-flight responses, to reconnection with their core energy and life force.

From a practical clinical perspective, we are making an important distinction between shock trauma and developmental/relational trauma, but it should be noted that shock trauma experienced as an adult commonly brings earlier developmental traumas to the surface. It is rare that we are able simply to address shock trauma without encountering developmental issues. As a result, it is often necessary to work with both shock and developmental trauma at the same time.

For a person whose symptoms are primarily the result of developmental/relational trauma, a new paradigm is necessary. The sources, causes, and resolution of this kind of trauma are more complex. In cases of developmental trauma, although individuals are reintegrating survival energies, they are also dealing with more than the completion of fight-flight responses; they are struggling with intrapsychic conflict. With developmental trauma, NARM works concurrently with both top-down and bottom-up dynamics that are fundamental to the healing process. Top-down, we address identity distortions resulting from shame-based identifications and pride-based counter-identifications. Bottom-up, we work with nervous system dysregulation. We continually keep in mind the distress cycle, which involves the interplay of top-down and bottom-up dynamics (Figure i.4). As described in the distress cycle, when there has been developmental trauma, we incorporate the environmental failure both in a bottom-up process of disturbed regulation and in a top-down process of distorted identifications. NARM developmental work, addressing clients' cognitive, emotional, and sensate world, addresses nervous system dysregulation, the distortion of identity, and the interplay between the two.

Developmental Trauma and the Life Force

When working with developmental trauma, the goal of the NARM approach is to help clients connect to and live their original core expression and thereby recover their right to life and aliveness. To illustrate working with the life force as it has been distorted through environmental failure and developmental/relational trauma, we will track the progress of Paul, who reflects the experience of many clients with the Connection Survival Style. Although Figure 12.1 is relevant for all the survival styles, we chose a client with the Connection Survival Style because it is with these individuals who have experienced the earliest developmental/relational trauma that the life force has been most distorted and is most bound in symptoms. Following Paul's progress allows us to follow the process of healing from the top of the chart to the reintegration of core expression and aliveness at the bottom of the chart through the three stages of healing the resolution of (1) parasympathetically dominant symptoms, (2) sympathetically dominant symptoms, and then (3) healthy connection and re-regulation. For clarity and to illustrate how to work with the life force from its most distorted symptomatic form to its core expression, we are conflating Paul's process that developed over the course of long-term therapy. The focus here is specifically on the expression and distortions of the life force and less on the therapeutic techniques that were presented in Chapter 10.

Paul was symptomatic in a number of ways. Early in therapy, the symptoms he described were predominantly parasympathetic in nature. He described himself as lonely and isolated, with strong self-judgments about his inability to sustain a close relationship. Additionally, he had a number of physical symptoms, including stomach problems, various muscle pains, and environmental sensitivities. He reported often feeling phobic and fearful and periodically quite depressed. It also became clear, as I (Larry) got to know him, that he was significantly dissociated; he had little capacity to reference either his emotions or his bodily experience.

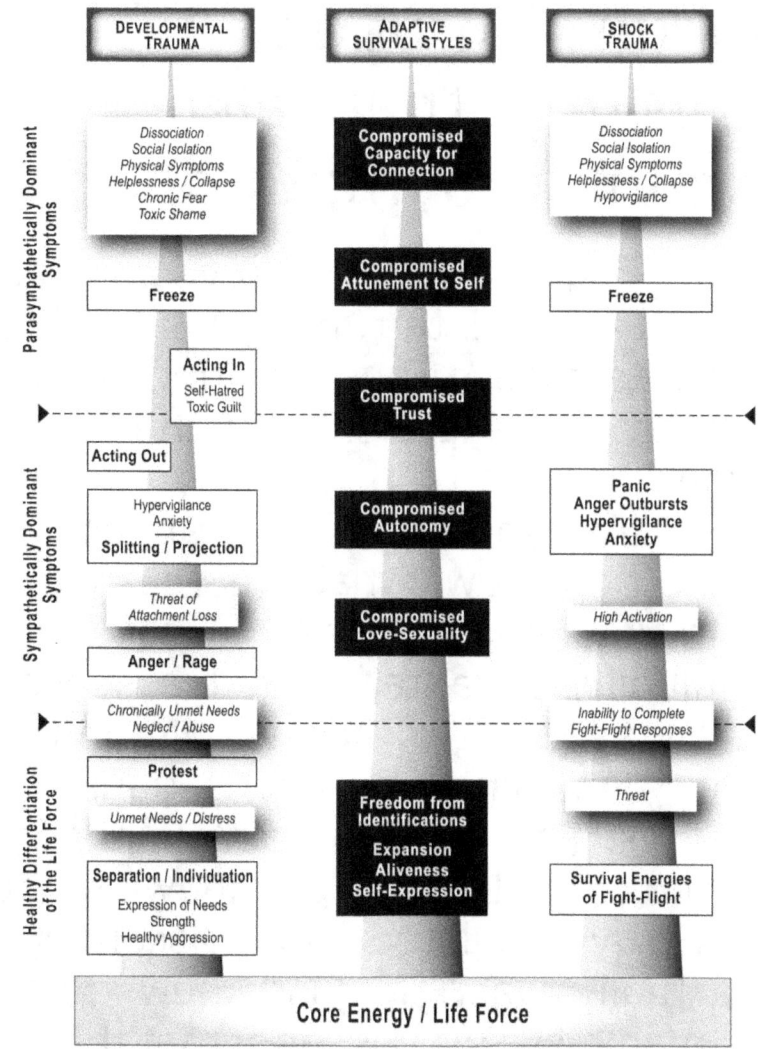

FIGURE 12.1: Distortions of the Life Force. To understand the therapeutic process described in this chapter, read the chart from the top down.

Working Through Parasympathetically Dominant Symptoms

I began to address Paul's dissociation by interrupting his tendency to intellectualize and inviting him to reference his experience in the present moment:

> "As you're talking about your life right now, what are you noticing in your experience?"

Initially, I wanted to get a sense of Paul's capacity to access his internal world, including his sensations and emotions. Paul at this point in therapy, had no direct way of knowing how frozen, dysregulated, and disconnected he actually was. He just knew that he had many symptoms and that he was hurting. The parasympathetic response of dissociation is driven by underlying sympathetic global high arousal. Paul's global arousal was partly the result of bottom-up processes that most likely began with his premature birth and the inadequate physical contact he experienced during his month in the incubator. In addition to this early trauma, both of his parents were profoundly unattuned to his needs and sometimes abusive; his father was physically and emotionally abusive, and his mother was highly anxious and emotionally invasive.

At the same time as I tracked Paul's capacity to access his internal world, I also paid attention to his capacity for personal connection with me. As awareness of his internal experience developed and he became more comfortable with me, on the level of the nervous system the ventral vagus and social engagement system slowly came online, helping him to come out of dissociation and giving him more effective possibilities with which to manage his high sympathetic arousal other than through dissociation and social isolation.

Acting In

Unintegrated aggression can be *acted in* against the self or *acted out* against others. Acting in involves turning aggression toward the self. In Figure

12.1, we placed this dynamic in the transitional area between parasympathetic and sympathetic symptomatology because the aggression itself is sympathetically dominant, but when it is turned against the self, it leads to parasympathetic symptoms.

On Paul's journey toward reintegrating the life force, he followed the very common pattern of clients who act in their aggression against themselves, which leads them to a sense of helplessness and hopelessness. At this point in therapy, Paul did not know he was angry, except at himself or in a vague or generalized sense when he felt bitter and "hated the world." Referencing the sequence of distortions in Figure 12.1, the unacknowledged anger that Paul experienced as self-hatred was the result of his earlier splitting off of aggression, which was then turned inward and which now reinforced his nervous system dysregulation. Although it was clear to me that Paul was very angry, at no time did I push him to feel the anger. Instead, I explored his fear of anger, at first of others' anger and later his own.

With Paul, I used elements of the exercise in Figure 12.2 by inquiring into his relationship with anger, both his own anger and other people's. His first response was "What anger?" Like many individuals who have experienced relational trauma, Paul was unaware of his own anger and frightened of other people's anger.

Splitting

For Paul, who as a child experienced abuse and neglect, the initial responses of anger and rage toward his parents were profoundly threatening. It was too frightening to feel anger and rage toward the parents he loved and upon whom he was completely dependent. Unable to tolerate the negative feelings toward his parents, Paul tried to protect the attachment relationship and his loving feelings for them by splitting off his negative feelings into a "bad self" that became the container for the aggression he experienced as dangerous. There is a vicious cycle at work here:

early environmental failure naturally provokes aggressive feelings, which in turn are experienced as too dangerous to be felt and as a result are split off; this split-off aggression becomes the source of increasing dysregulation and distress. The capacity to split off dangerous emotion is, particularly for children, a life-saving mechanism. Splitting is a dissociative process leading to parasympathetic symptoms, as seen in Paul's self-hatred, freeze, and dissociation.

EXPLORING YOUR RELATIONSHIP TO ANGER

Do you tend to act your anger in against yourself or act it out against others?

If you are easily angry, then anger is probably a default emotion and in this case, it is useful to do a personal exploration into what you are really feeling when you automatically default to anger.

If you are self-critical, self-judging, self-hating, then you are acting anger in against yourself. If this is your pattern, then you undoubtedly have many fears about anger. An exercise that can be useful for you is to write down as many fears about anger as you can find. Write down why it is not safe to feel or express anger.

If you have strong internal inhibitions against anger, see if you can find a situation in your life when you uncharacteristically expressed protest that had a positive result.

Explore your family of origin's relationship to anger. In some families, no one is allowed to be angry, or everyone is angry all the time. In other families only one or both of the parents can be angry, but not the children.

***

FIGURE 12.2: Exercise to Support the Exploration of One's Relationship to Anger

Paul's father was a rageaholic who was both emotionally and physically abusive—behavior that only further reinforced his son's splitting. Paul eventually had this insight into his lifelong sense of "badness":

"Because I felt that the badness was inside me, I felt I had more control. I could figure out how to be 'good' so I wouldn't get hurt anymore."

For Paul, being angry meant that he was like his father and therefore "bad." Splitting off his anger and rage reinforced a sense of powerlessness but also meant he was unlike his father and therefore "good." This is often the compromise that people who grow up with early relational trauma or abuse work out for themselves: foreclosing a part of themselves to preserve the attachment relationship with the parent.

Splitting takes different forms depending on circumstances, but the common component is to feel that aggression, anger, and rage are "bad," whereas powerlessness and gentleness are "good." The tendency is to project the split-off anger onto other people and be frightened of *their* aggression. The end result of this common process left Paul imagining judgment and rejection coming from others that was for the most part not there. Paul's "bad" self became the object of his hatred.

Paul hated himself for needing, for feeling, for his many symptoms, and ultimately even for existing. By splitting off and redirecting his negative emotions, he protected his love for his parents, though at great cost in terms of his sense of self and his capacity for engagement and aliveness. When his aggression was split off, his aliveness and strength were split off as well, and his connection to his core life force was diminished.

Splitting cannot be resolved simply on the level of the nervous system or from the perspective of the "inner child" or child consciousness. Unlike working with an incomplete fight response against a stranger, when there has been relational trauma, children develop many internal inhibitions against their anger at the parents in order to protect the attachment relationship and their feelings of love. Since only the adult consciousness can hold both love and hate, tenderness and anger simultaneously, I explained this dynamic of splitting to Paul's "inner adult" at an appropriate point in therapy. This understanding became a reference point to which I returned whenever he slipped back into patterns of self-hatred and self-rejection. An unexpected side effect for Paul, as with so many people, is that as his splitting resolved, and as he owned and integrated his aggression his chronic fearfulness greatly diminished. Disowned and disavowed aggression and anger are often a significant hidden source of chronic fear. In general, it is useful when working with chronic anxiety to look for split-off anger. On the journey toward reconnection with core expression and the life force, anxiety and anger are ultimately transformed into healthy self-expression, strength, and the capacity for separation/individuation.

Threat of Attachment Loss

As described above, splitting is fueled by the need of abused and neglected children to keep their attachment system intact. Children use splitting to manage the experience that their parents, who can sometimes be loving and upon whom they are completely dependent, are the same parents who are manipulating, neglecting, and abusive. Splitting results from the biological imperative that children experience to keep their attachment with their parents as secure as possible.

It was easier for Paul to recognize his rage about his father's physical and emotional abuse. Less obvious to him was his anger toward his mother for her clinginess, chronic anxiety, and invasiveness. He was able to recognize and begin to integrate his anger toward his father earlier in his therapy, but it was not until later that he could recognize and acknowledge anger at his mother. In his mind, she had been the good parent, and as he acknowledged his anger at her he at first felt guilt and then the fear of losing the sense of close connection he had with her. Each step that children take toward individuation is ultimately a psychological step away from their parents. Unfortunately, Paul's mother experienced his healthy drive to individuate as his abandoning of her. Lacking emotional maturity, she reacted by undermining and covertly threatening him rather than by supporting his developing autonomy.

We can speculate that some of Paul's chronic resignation came from his early incubation experience. It was also true that Paul's attempts to establish his autonomy, particularly with his mother, were met with what he came to understand as his mother's own abandonment reactions. She used fear and guilt to bind Paul to her. She would threaten him by saying or implying, "Okay, you can go off on your own, but I may not be here when you come back."

Because at an early age protest had been so unsuccessful, Paul had a hard time standing up for himself as an adult. This meant that co-workers would often foist unpleasant tasks on him, knowing that he would not protest. When served a bad meal at a restaurant, he could not speak up for himself and communicate his displeasure. In Paul's inner world protest was experienced as dangerous and futile. He rationalized his lack of protest with "What's the use? It's not going to change anything anyway."

Self-Hatred

When aggression and anger are split off and *acted in,* they are turned against the self in the form of self-hatred. Paul was filled with self-hatred but did not recognize it in his self-rejection for "never fitting in," never feeling "smart enough," or "worthy of relationship." He had always felt like an outsider and hated and blamed himself for feeling that way. Paul felt shame and judged himself for his many symptoms; he was so used to feeling this shame and self-judgment that he did not recognize it as self-hatred. He also did not understand the original secondary gain of his self-hatred, which was to protect the attachment relationship with his parents.

Addressing his adult consciousness, I contextualized the bigger theme of self-hatred by explaining how it was an attempt to come to terms with and manage both his early trauma and his anger. It was useful to repeatedly name his self-hatred as it emerged and to support him to become more compassionate and accepting toward himself. I regularly pointed out the different forms his self-hatred took because it was so automatic and reflexive that at first, he did not recognize it for what it was; it had become part of his identity. I helped him see that he, like all children who experience trauma, abandonment, or rejection, had developed a pattern of blaming himself. Helping him to see that when he was a child he could not experience himself as a "good person in a bad situation" had a relieving impact on his negative sense of self. He came to see that he would never direct at anyone else the vicious messages that he routinely directed toward himself.

Acting Out

Paul primarily tended to act in, but some children, and later adults, identify with the "bad" aspect of the splitting and the seeming power it gives them, becoming abusers themselves. Until the splitting is resolved, the terrible choice is to identify as either victim or victimizer, prey or predator.

It is useful here to mention the narcissistic and borderline dilemmas. Though individuals with narcissistic and borderline personality disorders have seemingly easy access to their anger, their anger is a default emotion and not in service of separation/individuation. Their acting out of aggression is in sharp contrast to the integration of the healthy aggression that leads to individuation. Their acting out of aggression keeps them psychologically merged with, and re-enacting patterns learned with abusive/neglectful parents.

Challenging Isolation

Paul, though in his late thirties, had had few friendships and no lasting intimate relationship. When not at work he liked to spend his time surfing the web and playing computer games. For years he had isolated himself, reflexively withdrawing from social contact. This lifestyle supported and reinforced his dissociation. Over time I gently encouraged Paul to challenge his withdrawn lifestyle. As he experimented with social connection, more sympathetic arousal inevitably surfaces. At first it took the form of increased anxiety, but as he became more in touch with his emotions, he became more aware of the anger he had not realized was there.

Working Through Sympathetically Dominant Symptoms

As can be seen in Figure 12.1, freeze, dissociation, and social isolation are the strategies of last resort when internal experience has become unmanageable and overwhelming. Paul came to see that underneath his frozen façade and cynicism was sympathetic high arousal that initially expressed as anxiety and later as anger—anger at the abuse from his father and the invasiveness of his mother as well as primitive survival responses related to his early incubation. Paul's anxiety signaled that he was moving away from the known territory of his adaptive survival style to something new and unknown. Anxiety is often a signal of unrecognized and disowned emotions coming to the surface, particularly aggression and anger. As Paul's sympathetic charge was freed from the depression and dissociation that bound it, he became progressively more aware of his anger. Having foreclosed anger for so long, he was afraid that if he allowed himself to feel it, he might become destructive. Anger becomes integrated on a psychological level by recognizing and owning it as one's own rather than splitting it off and turning it against the self or projecting it. Physiologically, anger becomes integrated not by acting it out, as in beating pillows and screaming, but by identifying, containing, and tracking the energetic experience of anger in the body.

I helped him uncouple the fears he had about his anger from the experience of anger itself:

> PAUL: All this anger that's coming up is scary, and I don't like it.

> LARRY: I know you have a lot of fears and judgments about the anger that is starting to bubble up,

but I'd like you to notice what the anger feels like in your body, separate from the ideas and reactions you have to it. See if you can just notice the energy of it.

PAUL: *Long pause as he checks into his experience....* It's not as scary as I thought. It kind of feels strong and expanded in my body.

LARRY: Are there any other words you can use to describe "strong and expanded"?

PAUL: *Pause....* I feel warm, tingly, and ... *with surprise in his voice* ... big.

LARRY: "Warm, tingly, and big." *Pause....* What happens if you give that warm, tingly, and big feeling more time?

PAUL: *Long pause; expressing surprise, and with a stronger and deeper voice....* It feels good and, strangely, my vision seems clearer.

Integrating Rage and Anger

One of the differences between traditional psychodynamic and NARM's psychobiological working through of aggression is that in NARM, anger is tracked in the felt sense with nervous system regulation being continually addressed. It is difficult to integrate and embody the powerful energies of aggression and anger without a body-centered orientation. Anger, and the aggression inherent in it, is a bodily and energetic dynamic that, when integrated, is empowering. It is important, whenever possible, to explore the implicit intention driving the anger. There is always an implicit communication within anger: a communication to an environment that has failed to respond appropriately. Uncovering the implicit intention helps an individual understand what is needed for completion. It is also important to distinguish anger from blame. Though blame often has elements of anger within it, it is primarily a mental state and is ultimately disempowering.

As therapy progressed Paul became better at recognizing not only his anger but also the telltale signs that he was avoiding it. As Paul reconnected with his anger, I used techniques such as pendulation and resourcing to help him manage the anxiety that inevitably surfaced as disowned feelings and impulses emerged. In essence, for Paul, the perspective of the child consciousness could be summarized as follows: "My life emerged and met a rejecting and threatening environment. I used whatever strategies I could as a child to shut down my body and my emotions to survive. It was too painful and too frightening to feel. If I start to feel my body and my emotions, it will be too much. My needs and my rage will come out, and I might hurt myself or someone else."

As I further explored Paul's relationship with his father, he began to recognize his impulse to fight back against his father's physical and emotional abuse. Over time, as Paul recognized and integrated his anger toward his father, he was able to connect with other feelings that he had also split off: his desire for his father's love and approval and the sadness and grief he had about never having felt loved by him. Dissociation, apparent indifference, and unresolved anger had disconnected him from the unfulfilled desire for connection with his father.

Paul's increasing awareness of and connection to his *healthy* aggressive impulses also served the process of psychological separation/individuation from his mother. He used his developing connection to healthy aggression in service of setting clearer boundaries with her, becoming emotionally and psychologically more independent. As his anger became integrated, Paul's dissociation diminished, and he found himself progressively more able not only to identify what he was feeling physically and emotionally but also to feel more comfortable with interpersonal connection in general.

Integrating Grief about Broken Connection

Though grief is not presented in Figure 12.1, grieving is an important element in the reconnection process. Grief is how human beings come to terms with irrevocable loss. It was normal and healthy that Paul would grieve the relationship he never had with his father. As he became increasingly present and connected, Paul also experienced short periods of grief about the lost years during which he was so disconnected from himself and others. This grieving is a normal reaction in the reconnection process, but it is important that it not lead to hopelessness and collapse. Becoming submerged in and too identified with grief can disrupt the reconnection process and reinforce the identification as the helpless child who needed a loving, attuned parent, as opposed to the adult who has the capacity to create healthy connections. Healthy grieving leads to reconnection; it has vitality and aliveness that contrast with the frozen, collapsed grief states that individuals with early trauma present at the beginning of therapy.

Healthy Differentiation of the Life Force

Initially, the life force expresses as healthy aggression. To review what we have already addressed earlier, the aggressive impulse is the biological expression of the basic needs for attachment, safety, and attunement. When the environment is misattuned, unresponsive, or threatening, infants experience distress. When the environment continues to be unresponsive, infants' distress increases and escalates into protest. This initial protest is simply the infant's way to get the environment to respond to his or her needs. Infants are hardwired to respond with protest when their needs are not being met. If protest does not bring about the needed response, the child's distress escalates into anger and finally rage. The escalation continues until the need is met or until the child collapses into resignation. In some cases, the escalation of aggression on the child's part is met with anger by the caregivers. This increase in threat will trigger instinctive responses involving collapse, freeze, and shut down. On an instinctive level children understand that to continue to protest is to risk encountering even more danger.

The Separation/Individuation Process

The life force energy described in Figure 12.1 is the same energy that fuels the separation/individuation process in the child. It is an energy that exists from the very beginning of life. It is the life energy that fuels the chick's push to break out of the egg and propels babies to be born. It is the physiological energy that later fuels psychological processes. Developmentally, it is healthy aggression and self-expression that lead children to want to feed themselves, tie their own shoelaces, and progressively explore the world on their own. When this healthy, natural aggression and self-expression are short-circuited through lack of attunement, abuse, and neglect, it becomes coupled with fear, shame, and guilt. When this happens, the separation/individuation process is disrupted and children fail to psychologically individuate.

The core energy that is accessed in the healing process supports the psychological individuation that did not take place to an adequate degree in earlier years. It is a psychological axiom that true intimacy is impossible without adequate autonomy. Increasing connection to the life force allows individuals to experience themselves as progressively independent of the shame- and pride-based identifications that developed out of their personal histories, helping them to become more autonomous and in turn to have a greater capacity for attachment and intimacy.

In the course of therapy, as Paul integrates his aggression, he begins to speak out more at work, in personal relationships, and even in impersonal situations such as dining in a restaurant. As he becomes more comfortable with his healthy self-assertion, the original fears that he might act out inappropriately and that protest is futile and even dangerous lessen considerably. Paul begins to wean himself from his obsession with computer games and becomes less self-isolating. Toward the end of therapy, he starts having his first ongoing relationship with a woman.

Healthy Integration of Core Energy and the Life Force

The growth process is not complete until clients learn how they have incorporated and perpetuated the original environmental failure into their bodies, identities, and behaviors. As we experience the development of personal agency, we come to see that the rejection we fear from the world has already happened. As children it was devastating. For adults, however, as the core life force is integrated, we experience ourselves as increasingly less dependent on our environment in order to express our core or more authentic self.

Nelson Mandela addressed the fear of living life to its full potential when he quoted Marianne Williamson in his 1994 inaugural speech:

> "Our deepest fear is not that we are inadequate. Our deepest fear is that we are powerful beyond measure. It is our light, not our darkness, that most frightens us."

It may come as a surprise that living life in a full and expanded way is one of the most difficult challenges we face as human beings. Growth and change happen as connection to the five core capacities of connection, attunement, trust, autonomy, and love-sexuality is established or strengthened. Identity distortions dissolve and self-regulation is reestablished. In a healing cycle, connection to our body, emotions, and life force allows for greater connection with others, and in turn, connection with others supports greater connection to ourselves. The connection that has always been our deepest desire is now no longer our greatest fear.

FURTHER READING

Aposhyan, S. (2004). *Body-Mind Psychotherapy.* New York: W.W. Norton.

Aron, L., Sommer Anderson, F. Eds. (1998). *Relational Perspectives on the Body.* Hillsdale: The Analytic Press.

Bainbridge Cohen, B. (1993). *Sensing, Feeling, and Action.* Northampton: Contact Editions.

Balint, M. (1968). *The Basic Fault: Therapeutic Aspects of Regression.* Evanston: Northwestern University Press.

Beebe, B., Lachman, F. (2002). *Infant Research and Adult Treatment.* New York: The Analytic Press.

Bowlby, J. (1988). *A Secure Base: Parent-Child Attachment and Healthy Human Development.* London: Routledge.

Damasio, A. (1999). *The Feeling of What Happens.* New York: Harcourt.

Damasio, A. (2003). *Looking for Spinoza.* New York: Harcourt.

Gendlin, E.T. (1981). *Focusing.* New York: Bantam Books.

Hedges, L.E. (1994). *Working the Organizing Experience.* Northvale, NJ: Jason Aronson.

Hedges, L.E. (2000). *Terrifying Transferences.* Northvale, NJ: Jason Aronson.

Kornfield, J. (2011). *Bringing Home the Dharma: Awakening Right Where You Are.* Boston: Shambala.

LeDoux, J. (1998). *The Emotional Brain.* New York: Touchstone.

Levine, P. (1997). *Waking the Tiger: Healing Trauma.* Berkeley: North Atlantic Books.

Levine, P. (2010). *In an Unspoken Voice.* Berkeley: North Atlantic Books.

Lewis, T., Amini, F., Lannon, R. (2000). *A General Theory of Love.* New York: Vintage Books.

Lillas, C., Turnbull, J. (2009). *Infant/Child Mental Health, Early Intervention, and Relationship-Based Therapies.* New York: W.W. Norton.

Lowen, A. (1975). *Bioenergetics: The Revolutionary Therapy That Uses the Language of the Body to Heal Problems of the Mind.* New York: Penguin Compass.

Mahler, M.S., Pine, F., Bergman, Anni. (1975). *The Psychological Birth of the Human Infant.* New York: Basic Books.

Montague, A. (1971). *Touching: The Human Significance of the Skin.* New York: Harper and Row.

Ogden, P., Minton, K., Pain, C. (2006). *Trauma and the Body.* New York: W.W. Norton.

Ogden, T.H. (1989). *The Primitive Edge of Experience.* Northvale: Jason Aronson.

Pally, R. (2000). *The Mind-Brain Relationship.* New York: Karnac Books.

Panksepp, J. (1998). *Affective Neuroscience.* New York: Oxford University Press.

Porges, S.W. (2011). *The Polyvagal Theory.* New York: W.W. Norton.

Reich, W. (1973). *The Function of the Orgasm.* New York: Farrar, Straus and Giroux.

Schore, A. (2003). *Affect Dysregulation and the Disorders of the Self.* New York: W.W. Norton.

Schore, A. (2003). *Affect Regulation and the Repair of the Self.* New York: W.W. Norton.

Siegel, D.J. (1999). *The Developing Mind: Toward a Neurobiology of*

Interpersonal Experience. New York: Guilford Press.

Siegel, D.J., Hartzell, M. (2003). *Parenting from the Inside Out.* New York: Jeremy P. Tarcher/Putnam.

Tatkin, S. (2011). *Wired for Love.* Oakland: New Harbinger Publications.

Tolle, E. (2009). *The Power of Now.* Novato: New World Library and Vancouver: Namaste Publishing.

Wilber, K. (2000). *Integral Psychology: Consciousness, Spirit, Psychology, Therapy.* Boston: Shambhala Publications.

Winnicott, D, W. (1964/1987). *The Child, the Family, and the Outside World.* New York: Perseus.

ABOUT THE AUTHORS

LAURENCE HELLER, PHD, is the originator of the Neuro- Affective Relational Model™ (NARM), a unified system to work with developmental, attachment, and shock trauma. His work integrates psychodynamic approaches, Somatic Experiencing®, as well as a non-traditional orientation to working with identity. He was the cofounder of the Gestalt Institute of Denver, has been on the faculty of several large universities, and is a senior faculty member for the nonprofit Somatic Experiencing® Training Institute (SETI). Dr. Heller coauthored *Crash Course,* a book about auto accident trauma published in four languages. He is fluent in several languages and currently teaches NARM and Somatic Experiencing throughout Europe and the United

States. For further information on the NARM approach, visit www.DrLaurenceHeller.com.

ALINE LAPIERRE, PSYD, is the developer of NeuroAffective Touch™, a component of the NeuroAffective Relational Model™ and has developed an extensive series of experiential exercises that support the practice of embodied mindfulness. She was a faculty member at the Somatic Psychology doctoral program at Santa Barbara Graduate Institute for ten years and is a psychoanalytic associate at the New Center for Psychoanalysis in Los Angeles. She is trained in a number of body-centered modalities including Body-Mind Centering, Somatic Experiencing®, Continuum, and acupressure, as well as craniosacral, deep tissue, and neuromuscular bodywork. In private practice in Los Angeles since 1990, she specializes in the integration of psychodynamic, developmental, and somatic approaches. For further information, visit www.AlineLaPierre.com.

Carl Studna

BACK COVER MATERIAL

The spontaneous movement in all of us is toward connection, health, and aliveness. No matter how withdrawn and isolated we have become, or how serious the trauma we have experienced, on the deepest level, just as a plant spontaneously moves toward sunlight, there is in each of us an impulse moving toward connection and healing. is organismic impulse is the fuel of the NARM approach.

***

Although it may seem that people suffer from an endless number of emotional problems and challenges, Laurence Heller and Aline LaPierre maintain that most of these can be traced to five biologically based organizing principles: the need for connection, attunement, trust, autonomy, and love-sexuality. They describe how early trauma impairs the capacity for connection to self and others and how the ensuing diminished aliveness is the hidden dimension that underlies most psychological and many physiological problems.

Heller and LaPierre introduce the NeuroAffective Relational Model™ (NARM), a method that integrates bottom-up and top-down approaches to regulate the nervous system and resolve distortions of identity such as low self-esteem, shame, and chronic self-judgment that are the outcome of developmental and relational trauma. While not ignoring a person's past, NARM emphasizes working in the present moment to focus on clients' strengths, resources, and resiliency in order to integrate the experience of connection that sustains our physiology, psychology, and capacity for relationship.

***

"Seasoned clinicians Larry Heller and Aline LaPierre weave a rich and coherent synthesis of childhood development in the pioneering tradition of Wilhelm Reich, Erik Erikson, and Alexander Lowen. They provide easy-to-understand tools for all of us who are seeking a better understanding of our fundamental conflicts. *Healing Developmental Trauma* is a vital and accessible map supporting emotional maturity and psycho-spiritual growth."

—Peter A. Levine, PhD, author of *In an Unspoken Voice: How the Body Releases Trauma and Restores Goodness* and *Waking the Tiger: Healing Trauma*

Index

A

abandonment,
  in case example, *271, 277*
  mother's sense of, with child's autonomy, *518*
  self-assertion and, *92*
abreaction, *401*
abuse,
  abused and hated child, *213, 215*
  splitting in response to, *238, 240*
  and Trust Survival Style, *56, 58*
acceptance,
  in Autonomy Survival Style, *92*
  of self, *385*
activation, versus coherency, *182*
addictions, *158*

ADHD, misdiagnosis of, *175*
adoption, *215, 217*
adrenal glands, *154*
affairs, in Love-Sexuality Survival Style, *105*
affect regulation,
  in Attunement Survival Style, *38*
  in Connection Survival Style, *25*
  disorders of, *158*
  see also self-regulation,
agency, *392, 394, 396, 399, 439, 534*
aggression,
  acting in and acting out, *240, 243, 245, 510, 522, 524*
  distortions of healthy, *243*
  healthy, *529, 531*

splitting off, *238, 240, 243, 510*
see also anger; rage,
aliveness,
  in case example, *273, 290*
  diminishment in, *117*
  increasing capacity for, *373*
  lack of, in Connection Survival Style, *29, 217, 220*
  rebound reaction and, *273*
  supporting, *366*
alliance, therapeutic, *25, 414*
ambivalence,
  of Autonomy Survival Style, *79, 83, 90*
  of Connection Survival Style, *17, 310, 311, 389, 392, 414, 416*
American Medical Association, *197*
amygdala, *145*
anger,
  acting in and acting out, *240, 243, 245*
  as default emotion, *315, 317, 522*
  exercise to explore, *510, 513*
  fear may mask, *407, 516*
  identifying, containing, and tracking, *524*
  implicit intention driving, *527*
  integrating, *524, 527*
  splitting off, *238, 240*
  survival energies inherent in, *396*
  of Trust Survival Style, *51*
  working through split-off, *394, 396*
  see also aggression; rage,
anorexia, *40*
anxiety,
  anger and, *522, 524*

chronic, in Connection Survival Style, *188*
spectrum disorders, *158*
armor(ing), 'as if' behavior, *52, 54, 58, 72*
attachment or Attachment Theory,
　building bonds of, *445, 448, 450, 452, 455, 458*
　circuit permanence fosters long-lasting, *149*
　earned secure, *362*
　exercise to discern capacity for, *437, 439*
　eyes and, *346, 348*
　failures, held in implicit memory, *163*
　failures lead to disorders, *158*
　perinatal trauma affects, *207, 209, 211*
　prenatal, *199, 201*
　protecting, via survival styles, *5, 516, 518, 520*
　secure, *211*
　self-regulation and, *147, 209, 211*
　windows of sensitivity for, *147*
attunement (core need),
　relational, *423, 425*
　somatic, *362*
　(see also somatic mindfulness),
　survival adaptation of, *5*
　synchrony of, in case example, *473*
　in adult, *38, 40*
　development of, *32, 36*
　goal in therapy, *115*
　key features of, *44, 47*
　love and sexuality in, *98*
　subtypes of, *40*

autonomic nervous system, *127, 128, 129, 330*
autonomy (core need),
   intimacy and, *531*
   survival adaptation of, *5*
   in adult, *79, 81, 83*
   development of, *75, 76, 79*
   goal in therapy, *115*
   growth strategies for, *83, 90*
   key features of, *85, 88*
   love as trap, *98*
   resolution of, *90, 92, 94*
awareness,
   dual, of past and present, *164, 317, 319, 332, 389, 392, 401*
   mindful, (see also somatic mindfulness),

B

basal ganglia, *133*
behavioral strategies, *92*
beliefs,
   identifying fixed and rigid, *379, 383*
   survival styles and, *7*
betrayal, and Trust Survival Style, *52, 72, 73*
bias, toward the past, *145*
biological completion, *503*
bipolar disorder, misdiagnosis of, *175*
birth trauma, *204*
body,
   -based resources, *326, 335, 337*
   communication and information networks of, *120, 124, 127, 128, 129, 133, 136, 139, 141, 142, 145, 147, 149, 151, 154, 156, 158, 160, 163, 164*
   Connection Survival Style,

disconnected from, *13, 229, 231, 233*
dissociation as bodily process, *231*
distorted identifications reflected in, *379*
as enemy, *243*
impact of stress response on, *246, 248*
innate intelligence of, *120*
mindful bottom-up experience of, *139, 420*
naming experiences of, in case example, *430, 432, 434, 497*
referencing, *354*
shame about, *100*
shift focus to, *412, 414*
survival styles and, *7*
touch restores embodiment, *482, 484*
Trust Survival Style, disconnected from, *67*
boomerang effect, *412*
borderline personality, and anger, *522*
boundary or ies,
   in Autonomy Survival Style, *75*
   energetic, *251, 253, 255, 439, 441, 443*
   felt sense for, *437*
   setting clearer, *527*
Bowlby, John, *207*
brain,
   evolution of, *129, 133*
   predictive process of, *326*
   see also separate entries for particular structures,
brainstem, *133*

breaker switch state, *235, 238*
bulimia, *40*

C

caretaker role, of Attunement Survival style, *32, 43*
catharsis,
   NARM view of, *354, 355*
central nervous system, *124, 127*
change, paradox of, *392, 394*
cognitions,
   distorted in Attunement Survival Style, *38*
   emotions can affect, *158*
   moving away from trauma-based, *324*
cognitive therapy, *430*
coherency, *180, 182, 229, 245, 300, 348*

coldness, in case example, *275, 277, 279*
collapse, *171, 180, 197, 213*
competitiveness, of Trust Survival Style, *52*
compulsions, *158*
conflict, internalized, in Autonomy Survival Style, *79*
confrontation, in Autonomy Survival Style, *81*
connection (core need),
   basic steps to reconnection, *322*
   compromised, *7, 9*
   as cornerstone of identity, *188*
   emotional health and,
   evoking positive experiences of, *311, 313, 315*
   key features of, *19, 21*

in love relationships, *98*
primary principle of, *305*
repairing lost, in case example, *458, 460*
survival adaptation of, *5*
techniques facilitating, *357*

(see also connection; disconnection; tracking),
in adult, *14, 17, 217, 220, 222, 224, 227, 229, 231, 233, 235, 238, 240, 243, 245, 246, 248, 251, 253, 255, 257, 258, 260*
development of, *13, 14*
goal in therapy, *115*
growth strategies for, *17*
key features of, *21, 23, 25, 27, 29*
Polyvagal Theory helps us understand, *136*
principles and techniques in working with, *418, 491, 493*
resolution of, *21, 23, 25, 27, 29*
subtypes of, *14, 17*
summary of issues on which to focus, *260*
symptoms of, see symptoms,
therapeutic themes in working with, *375*
trauma sources creating, *193*
consciousness, and qualia, *141*
contact or contact-interruption or rupture, cycle, *27*

in case example, *264, 279, 282*
hunger for contact, in case example, *452*
mindful of, *362, 363*
tolerance for, *360*
containment, *354, 355, 399, 401, 403, 489, 500*
contraction or withdrawal, *203, 204*
  in case example, *425*
  identifying with content of, *370*
  working with, in case example, *460, 462, 464, 466, 468, 471, 473*
control, issue of, *61, 63, 245*
coping patterns,
  of Connection Survival Style, *13, 14, 17*
  developmental trauma impairs, *151*
  rigidifying effects of, *5, 7*

core needs,
  attunement, see separate entry,
  autonomy, see separate entry,
  connection, see separate entry,
  consequences of unfulfilled, *32*
  difficulty attuning to, *32*
  fulfillment of, inability to express, *35*
  love-sexuality, see separate entry,
  need-satisfaction cycle,
  tolerating fulfillment of, *47, 49*
  trust, see separate entry,
corrective experience, *363, 379*

cortex, *133*
cortisol, *158, 164*
counter-identifications, pride-based, *7, 19, 40, 43, 44, 69, 85, 105, 107, 503, 531*
curiosity, *171, 300, 355, 383*

D

Damasio, Antonio, *497*
defensive-orienting response, *167, 168, 173, 197, 222, 297, 300*
denial, *67*
dependency, danger for Trust Survival Style, *51, 52*
depression, *158, 188*
deprivation, *32, 43*
designated issue, *224, 227, 384, 385*
   of Connection Survival Style, *13, 14, 211, 213*
   early sources of, *193*
   interplay with shock trauma, *211*
   interplay of top-down and bottom-up dynamics, *503*
   life force diminished by, see life force,
   of mothers of people with Attunement Survival Style, *36*
   sensory-motor functions affected by, *432*
   shock trauma versus, *173, 175, 501, 503, 506*
diaphragms, *246, 248, 257, 258, 282*
dimmer switch state, *235*
discharge,
   in case example, *269, 282, 284, 295*
   and grounding, *405*
disconnection,
   of abused and hated child, *213, 215*

of Attunement Survival Style, *36, 38*
grounding as antidote to, *403*
see also

disidentification, *326, 337, 379, 383, 384, 385, 388, 437*
dissociation,
　brain function of, *133, 136*
　in case examples, *267, 277, 286, 510, 522*
　of Connection Survival Style, *5, 229, 231, 233, 235, 238, 240, 243, 245, 300, 305, 337*
　continuum of, *235, 238, 240, 243, 245*
　diminished, *527*
　energetics of, *233*
　eye contact and, *264*
　of neglected child, *215*
　orienting decreases, *407*

　resolution of, *286, 305*
　stuck in, *180*
　touch as antidote to, in case example, *445, 482, 484*
　as universal human response, *231, 233*
　working with, *352, 354, 355*
dissociative identity disorder, *245*
distress,
　biological, *203*
　cycle, see distress cycle,
　in search of an explanation, *220, 222*
distress cycle,
　in Connection stage, *193*
doers, *105*
'drop the baby', *452, 464*
'dual unity', *207*
dysfunction,
　how patients maintain, *396, 399*

reinforcing, *326, 332*
dysregulation,
  emotions can lead to, *156, 158*
  sympathetically dominant, *197, 506* (see also symptoms, sympathetically dominant),
  systemic, *248, 251*

E

eating issues or disorders,
  in Attunement Survival Style, *35, 38, 40*
  emotional dysregulation can lead to, *158*
efforting traps, in Autonomy Survival Style, *90*
emotions,
  default, *315, 317*
  distrust of, *105*
  dysfunctions caused by, *158*

emotional brain, *133, 164*
  judgments or fears about, *341, 383, 384*
  and memory, trauma, *163, 164*
  overview of, *156, 158*
  primary, *315, 317*
  unavailability of, to baby, *36*
  words to describe, in case example, *432, 434, 489*
  working with fear of, *355*
empathy,
  central nervous system role in, *127*
  retrieving implicit memories requires, *160*
empowerment, *392, 394, 396, 399, 437, 527*
endocrine system, *149, 151, 154, 156*
energy, regulation and dysregulation of, *246, 248*

(see also dysregulation),
evolution, bottom-up, *129, 133*
executive prefrontal cortex, *133, 145*
expansion or contraction pendulation,
  in case example, *271*
  described, *409, 412, 414*
  dynamic of expansion, *366, 368, 370*
  tolerating, in case example, *455, 486, 489*
expectations,
  in Autonomy Survival Style, *81, 92*
  in Love-Sexuality Survival Style, *96*
  therapists cannot always live up to, *360*
explicit memory, *160*

exploratory-orienting response, *171, 300*
eyes or eye contact or gaze,
  attachment dynamics and, *346, 348*
  in case example, *263, 264, 269, 273, 275, 282, 284, 297*
  engaging, *341, 346, 348, 350*
  role in projection, *257, 258*
  therapists should modulate their own, *348*
  as windows to the nervous system, *257, 267*
  working clinically with, *348, 350*

F
failure,
  fear of, *63, 65*
  to thrive, *215*

false self, of Trust Survival Style, *52, 54, 56, 72*
family,
  impact on fetal development, *201, 203, 204*
fantasy, *258*
Feeling of What Happens, The, *497*
felt sense, *23, 163, 286, 288, 354, 437, 450, 477, 493, 495, 500, 524*
Field, Tiffany, *445*
fight-flight responses, *128, 145, 147, 154, 167, 168, 171, 213, 503*
figure-ground process of therapy, *308*
flashbacks, *164*
Focusing, *493*
'football father', *52*
foster home, consequences of placement in, *217*
fragmentation, *245, 339, 458*
  of abused and hated child, *213, 215*
  brain function of, *133, 136*
  in Connection Survival Style, *27, 217, 300*
  of infant, *193, 204*
  moving out of, in case example, *267*
  of neglected child, *215*
  in trauma response, *167, 168, 171, 177, 180*

G

gaze,
  see eyes,
General Adaptation Syndrome, *151*
Gendlin, Eugene, *493*
global high-intensity activation (GHIA), *204*
'good boy', *79, 81, 92*
'good-enough' mother, *464*

grandiosity, *63, 377, 379*
grasp reflex, *466*
grief, *49, 452, 473, 486, 529*
grounding, *335, 339, 403, 405*
guilt, *518*

H
Hartzell, Mary, *209*
hatred,
   of the child, *213*
   of self,
   see self-hatred,
   splitting off, *238, 240*
headaches, *257*
health issues, chronic, *248, 251* (see also symptoms),
heartbreak, *96, 105*
Hebb's law, *139*
hippocampus, *145, 193, 197*
homeostasis, *120, 154, 156, 350*
hormones, overview of, *149, 151*
HPA, axis (HPA), *151, 154*
hypothalamus, *154*
hypotonicity, *7, 346*
hypertonicity, *7, 346*
hypervigilance, *168, 197, 222, 253*

I
identifications,
   as good but powerless, *240*
   shame-based, *7, 19, 40, 43, 44, 69, 85, 105, 107, 188, 370, 373, 375, 377, 379, 503, 531*
identity,
   adolescent sense of, wounded, *100*
   of Attunement Survival Style, *43*
   beginning of, *188, 190, 193, 197*
   of Connection Survival Style, *17*

distortions in, *220, 222, 366, 368, 370, 373, 375, 377, 379, 383, 384, 385, 388, 503*
exploring, *366, 368, 370, 373, 375, 377, 379, 383, 384, 385, 388*
of Love-Sexuality Survival Style, *105*
survival styles and, *5, 7*
of Trust Survival Style, *61*
image,
and Love-Sexuality Survival Style, *105, 109*
and Trust Survival Style, *61*
immobilization,
in Autonomy Survival Style, *79, 83*
brain function of, *133, 136*
of infant, *193*
see also freeze,
implicit memory, *160*
neglect held in, *215*
trauma held in, *193, 197, 286*
implicit relational knowing, *163*
impotence, *111*
inauthenticity,
dangers of, *357, 360*
incubation experience, *207, 518*
infant,
freeze response of, *193*
surgical trauma of, *197, 211*
vulnerability of, *193*
inflammation, *248*
information,
self-reinforcing loops of, *450*
top-down and bottom-up flows of, *399*
inhibited subtype, *40*
inquiry,

distortions in identity uncovered via, *147, 383*
therapist's, *355*
insight, *373, 389, 513*
interdependency, and Trust Survival Style, *73*
interpretation, avoiding, *273*
intimacy, Autonomy Survival Style fear of, *79, 81*
introjection, therapeutic, *363*
isolation,
   in case examples, *423, 522*
   of Connection Survival Style, *17, 136, 253, 255*
in Trust Survival Style, *65*

J
Journal of Clinical Endocrinology and Metabolism, *203*

K
Klein, Melanie, *238*

L
language,
   common, *425, 434, 489*
   simple, *330*
laughter, *384*
learning,
   basic mechanism of, *139*
   brain function of, *133*
   state-dependent, *164*
Levine, Peter, *180*
life force,
   fear of, *370, 373, 475, 477, 480, 482, 534*
   healthy differentiation and integration of, *529, 531, 534*
   in NARM, *9, 180*
lifestyle, of dissociation, *233, 235*
limbic system,
   evolution of, *133*

less plasticity of, *149*
stress affects, *141*
loneliness, *458, 466, 468*
love (relationships),
  in Autonomy Survival Style, *76, 79*
  in Connection Survival Style, *98*
  sexuality split off from, *98, 111*
  surrendering to, *113*
love-sexuality (core need),
  survival adaptation of, *5*
  in adult, *100, 103, 105, 107, 109*
  development of, *96, 98, 100*
  goal in therapy, *115*
  growth strategies for, *109, 111*
  resolution in, *111, 113, 115*

M

Mahler, Margaret, *207*
Mandela, Nelson, *534*
manubrium, *471*
maturity, in case example, *286*
meaning,
  search for, *229*
  translating implicit information into, *495, 497*
memory,
  and emotions, trauma, *163, 164*
  impairments in, *164*
  limbic system impacts, *133*
  nature and kinds of, *158, 160, 163, 164*
  of positive life experiences, *322, 324*
  shift focus to resources, *412, 414*
mindfulness (traditional),

see also somatic mindfulness,
mirroring,
   in case example, *269, 290*
   positive capacities, *324*
   supporting reconnection, *352*
   see also reflecting,
misattunement, *32, 173, 357, 452*

N

narcissistic,
   gratification, *54, 56*
   personality disorder, and anger, *522*
NARM,
   core principles of, *308, 310, 311, 313, 315, 317, 319, 322, 324, 326, 328, 330, 332, 335, 337, 339, 341, 346, 348, 350, 352, 354, 355, 357, 360, 362, 363, 366, 501*
   goals of, *115*
   healing cycle, *305*

narrative, *23, 133, 182, 245, 288, 290, 317, 319, 489, 495*
neediness, in case examples, *484, 516*
needs,
   see core needs,
need-satisfaction cycle,
neglect,
   in case example, *430, 452*
   dissociation in response to, *215*
   splitting in response to, *238, 240*
nervous system,
   autonomic nervous system, *128, 129*
   building blocks of, *136, 139, 141, 142, 145, 147, 149*
   central nervous system, *124, 127*
   feedback loops strengthened, in case example, *450*
   'feeding' in case example, *480*

flooded with shock energy, *350*
increasing organization of, *23, 313, 315*
infant's, influenced by mother's communication, *428, 434*
need-satisfaction cycle disrupted, overview of function of, *120, 124, 127, 128, 129, 133, 136*
peripheral nervous system, *127*

NeuroAffective Relational Model®, see NARM,

NeuroAffective Touch®,
  as antidote to dissociation, in case example, *445, 482, 484*
  critical role of, in biology and psychology, *445*
  ethical considerations in, *497, 500*
  in relation to client's need, *445*
  restores embodiment, *482, 484*
  as specialized use of connection, in case example, *423, 437, 439, 441, 443*

neuroendocrine communication network, *120* (see also endocrine system),

'nice girl', *79, 81, 92*

non-goal orientation, working with Autonomy Survival Style, *90, 92*

working with Connection Survival Style, *337*
'not knowing', *355*
numbness or numbing, *35, 177, 229, 235, 238*
  (see also freeze; immobilization),

O

object,
  constancy, *455*
obsessions, *158, 370*
obsessive-compulsive disorder (OCD), *222*
OCD,
  see obsessive–compulsive disorder,
ocular block, *258*
'opening the heart', *113, 115*
opioids, stress and, *154*
organization,
  defined, *317*
  of nervous system, *23, 273, 275, 277*
  resources and safety reinforce, *401*
  supporting, in therapy, *308, 310, 311, 313, 315, 317, 319, 322, 324, 326, 328, 330, 332, 335, 337, 339, 341, 346, 348, 350, 352, 354, 355, 357, 360, 362, 363, 366*
  symptoms reveal, *220*
  tracking, *317, 319, 322*
orienting, *405, 407*
overpowering subtype, *58, 61*

P

pacing, *139, 147, 311, 319, 322, 363, 407, 409*
parasympathetic nervous system, *128, 129, 171, 180*
parent(s),

fulfilling ambitions of, by Trust Survival Style, *52, 54, 56*
undermining child's need for autonomy, in Autonomy Survival Style, *75, 76*
parentification, *54*
pattern-matching, *142, 145, 147*
pendulation, perception, *142*
peripheral nervous system, *127*
permanence, and plasticity, *149*
personal space, *251, 253, 255*
pituitary gland, *154*
'plasticity' of brain, *147, 149*
polyvagal system, *133, 136*
Polyvagal Theory, *128, 129, 133, 136, 267*

Porges, Stephen, *129, 133, 136, 248, 267*
posterior cortex, *156*
posttraumatic stress disorder (PTSD), *164, 175, 203*
power,
   sought by Connection Survival Style, *245*
   sought by Trust Survival Style, *51, 58, 61, 63, 67*
   see also empowerment,
powerlessness, *516*
premature birth, *207, 510*
present moment, NARM anchored in, *17, 147*
   (see also awareness, dual),
projection versus, *258, 260*
pressure, in Autonomy Survival Style, *81, 83*
projection,

in case example, *516*
eyes, role in, *257, 258*
physiology of, *257, 258*
present moment versus, *258, 260*
projective identification, *65, 67*
pruning, *139, 141*
psychoeducation, *409, 434, 437*
psychopathology, focus on, and limitations of, *23*
psychotherapy, conceptualized in NARM as, *147*
psychodynamic,
PTSD,
see posttraumatic stress disorder,

Q
qualia, *141, 142*
questions, *352, 354, 401*

R
rage,
integrating, *524, 527*
splitting off, *213, 215, 238, 240, 513*
see also aggression; anger,
reconnection,
basic steps to, *322*
challenges of, *350, 352, 428, 430*
supporting, *352, 354, 355*
reentry, *141, 142*
reflecting,
in case example, *277, 286*
see also mirroring,
regression, *164, 279*
regulation,
affect,
see affect regulation,
internalizing, in case example, *428*
self,
see self-regulation,

Reich, Wilhelm, *258, 341*
rejection,
  already happened, *534*
  of children by parents who do not want them, *213*
  of self, *388*
  during sexual awakening, *98, 100*
relationship and sex,
  in Love-Sexuality Survival Style, *105, 109, 111*
relationship, therapeutic, *355, 357, 360, 362, 363, 366*
relaxation, *313, 315, 322*
repair, *360, 452, 455, 458, 460*
resignation, *32, 43, 518*
resiliency,
  and organization, *317*
  range of, *180, 399, 401*

secure attachment
  fosters, *209*
  trauma affects, *168, 204*
resistance, *363, 366*
resolution,
  in Attunement Survival Style, *47, 49*
  in Autonomy Survival Style, *90, 92, 94*
  in Connection Survival Style, *21, 23, 25, 27, 29*
  in dissociation, *286, 305*
  experiences of, *366, 368, 370*
  in Love-Sexuality Survival Style, *111, 113, 115*
  in Trust Survival Style, *67, 69, 72, 73*
resonance,
  emotional, in case example, *290*

vibrational, in case example, *471*
resources,
  connection as fundamental, *311, 313*
  NARM focus on, *23, 141, 147, 184, 322, 324, 326, 328, 330, 332, 335*
  protocol for evoking, *328, 330, 332, 335*
  resourcing oneself, in case example, *468*
  secure attachment fosters, *209*
  sensory details of, *332, 335, 337, 339*
  therapeutic impact of, *324, 326*
  working with, *326, 328*
  see also strengths-based approach,
responsibility,
  versus agency, *394*

'right to be', *305*
romantic subtype, *100, 103*
ruminations, in Autonomy Survival Style, *83*
rupture, *360, 362, 363*

S

sabotage, in Autonomy Survival Style, *90, 92*
safety,
  dorsal vagal and, *136*
  exploratory-orienting response needs, *171*
  how to address issue with clients, *414, 416*
  NARM focus on, *23, 160*
  positive resources evoke feeling of, *326, 328*
  therapist offers, *363*
SAM,

secret self, *76*
seductive subtype, *58*
seductiveness, in Love-Sexuality Survival Style, *103*
self,
  'bad', *510*
  somatic formation of, *423, 495, 497*
self-acceptance, *385*
self-aggrandizement, *63*
self-destructive, *63*
self-esteem, low,
  in Connection Survival Style, *188, 227*
  logic does not affect, *263*
  in Love-Sexuality Survival Style, *96*
  separate from designated issue, *385, 388*
  splitting leads to, *25*
self-hatred, *227, 240, 243, 245, 363, 516, 520*
self-image,
  early trauma affects, *227, 293*
  grandiose, *63*
self-regulation,
  attachment shapes, *147*
  in case example, *455*
  and trauma narrative, *407*
  see also affect regulation,
self-soothing, *23, 133, 313, 322, 455*
selling out,
  in Autonomy Survival Style, *92*
  in Trust Survival Style, *52, 54, 56*
Selye, Hans, *151, 257, 341*
sensations, judgments or fears about, *341, 383, 384*

linking with feelings and thoughts, in case example, *450*
organize into coherent narrative, *288, 290*
sensitivity, environmental, in case example, *428, 437, 460*
compromised boundaries lead to, *255*
sex or sexuality, as conquest, *65*
consequences of rejection during sexual awakening, *98, 100*
disconnected from, *103*
sexual subtype, *103, 105*
shame, of abused and hated child, *215*

addressing top-down and bottom-up, *383, 384*
-based identifications, *7, 19, 40, 43, 44, 69, 85, 105, 107, 188, 370, 373, 375, 377, 379, 503, 531*
in case example, *263, 288*
of Connection Survival Style, *13, 14, 227, 229, 293*
rejection during sexual awakening leads to, *100*
about sexuality, *113, 115*
splitting leads to, *25*
bottom-up approach to treating, *503*
of Connection Survival Style, *13, 14, 227, 229, 293*
developmental trauma versus, *173, 175, 501, 503, 506*

early sources of, *193*
interplay with developmental trauma, *211*
'shoulds', *81*
Siegel, Daniel, *209*
Social Engagement System (SES), *133, 248, 267, 273, 510*
socialization, brain development and, *133*
social phobia, *233*
Somatic Experiencing®, *167, 180, 204*
somatic mindfulness,
　in Autonomy Survival Style, *92*
　as core NARM principle, *120, 184*
　facilitating, *335, 337, 339, 341*
　as non-regressive, *293, 295*
somatic nervous system, *127*
somatic psychotherapies, disconnect with Attachment Theory, *209*
spiritualizing subtype, *14, 17, 229, 233*
splitting,
　in abused and hated child, *213, 215*
　in case example, *513, 516, 518, 520*
　in Connection Survival Style, *25, 238, 240*
'stage mom', *52*
startle responses, *164, 167*
state-dependent memory, *164*
strengths-based approach, *23* (see also resources),
stress (response),
　HPA at core of, *151*

impact of, on body's energy flow, *246, 248*
limbic system affected by, *141*
Selye's concept of, *151, 257*
see also distress cycle,
structure and function, interaction of, *246, 248, 251, 253, 255, 257, 258*
subtypes,
  of Attunement Survival Style, *40*
  of Connection Survival Style, *13, 14, 17*
  of Love-Sexuality Survival Style, *100, 103, 105*
  of Trust Survival Style, *58, 61*
survival styles,
  'adapt or perish', characteristic patterns of arousal, *246*
  distortions of, *9*
  internalize environmental failures, *9, 188, 227, 293, 377, 389, 531, 534*
  mindful awareness of, *354*
  physiological and identity patterns of, *9, 11*
  protect attachment relationship, *5, 516, 518, 520*
sympathetic-adrenal-medullary (SAM) system, *154, 156*
sympathetic nervous system, *128, 129, 168, 171, 177, 180*
symptoms,
  compromised boundaries lead to, *253*
  of Connection Survival Style, *19, 188, 190, 220, 489, 491*

of early trauma, *199, 201, 203, 204, 207, 209, 211, 213, 215, 217*
need-satisfaction cycle and, organizing life principle of, *220*
parasympathetically dominant, *32, 151, 204, 267, 506, 510, 513*
persistence of survival styles creates, *7*
psychosomatic, in case example, *432*
root causes versus, *305, 308*
of survival styles, *9, 11*
sympathetically dominant, *197, 238, 506, 522, 524*
vagal system role in, *136*
'terrible twos', *75*

T

terror, *197*
thalidomide, *203*
therapeutic strategies,
  for Attunement Survival Style, *47, 49*
  for Autonomy Survival Style, *94*
  for Connection Survival Style, *27*
  for Love-Sexuality Survival Style, *113*
  for Trust Survival Style, *67, 69, 72, 73*
thinking,
  power of positive, *67*
  subtype, *14, 229, 233*
threat, *197, 211, 297*
time, distortions in, *389, 392*
titration,
  in case examples, *273, 455*
  in Connection Survival Style, *27, 350, 360*
  described, *407, 409*
  of painful memories, *160, 354*

tonic immobility, *171, 180*
touch, therapeutic, *277*
  (see also NeuroAffective Touch),
tracking,
  client's response to positive areas of life, *330, 332*

  present-moment experience, *23, 120, 147, 156, 184, 271, 311, 317, 319, 388, 389, 392, 394, 396, 399, 420*
  somatic connection, *335, 337, 339, 341*
  (see also somatic mindfulness),
  of therapist by client, in case example, *425, 428*
transference,

challenge of, *360, 362*
dynamics, *357*
as ocular block, *258, 260*
trauma,
  birth, *204, 207, 430*
  (see also separate entry),
  and emotions, memory, *163, 164*
  as failure of reentry system, *142*
  HPA's function in, *151, 154*
  impact on early development, *173, 175, 177, 180, 182, 199, 201, 203, 204, 207, 209, 211, 213, 215, 217*
  implicit memory holds, *193, 197*
  pattern-matching and, *147*
  perinatal, *207, 209*
  prenatal trauma, *199, 201*

(see also separate entry),
stress levels related to, *151*
surgical, of infants, *197*
symptoms of early, *190*
time distortions result from, *389, 392*
types of trauma responses, *167, 168, 171*
'traumatic symbiosis', *207*
trembling, *339*
triangulation, *54, 56*
trust (core need),
  can't push for, *414*
  establishing, in case example, *425, 428, 452*
  repairing, in case example, *452, 455*
  survival adaptation of, *5*
  in adult, *58, 61, 63, 65, 67*
development of, *51, 52, 54, 56*
goal in therapy, *115*
key features of, *69, 72*
love and sexuality in, *98*

U
unsatisfied subtype, *40*
'use it or lose it', *139*

V
vagus or vagal system, *127*
  dorsal branch of, *133, 136, 267*
  ventral, *133, 136, 510*
van der Kolk, Bessel, *175*
victim, *240, 394, 399*
viscera, and emotions, *156*
void, in case example, *428, 450, 452*
vulnerability,
  to illness, *151*
  of infant, *193*

in Love-Sexuality Survival Style, *105*
normalizing, *437*

W
Williamson, Marianne, *534*
windows of sensitivity, *147*
World Trade Center attack, *203*

Y
Yehuda, R., *203, 207*
'Yes—but...', *90*

www.ingramcontent.com/pod-product-compliance
Lightning Source LLC
Chambersburg PA
CBHW071215290426
44108CB00013B/1187